Praise for *Genius and Anxiety*

'Lebrecht's passion is persuasive, while the depth and variety of his reading and the sweep of his writing consistently engage.'
—*Times Literary Supplement*

'Claims to have "changed the world" tend to be exaggerations, but Lebrecht's subtitle . . . seems understated . . . Narrated not by a straight-faced professional historian, but by a sprightly raconteur, with anecdotes and jokes, digressions and embellishments. Lebrecht piles them high in a ziggurat of enthusiasm.'
—*The Times*

'Lebrecht is an exuberant storyteller who ably brings these personalities to life . . . Impressively wide-ranging in scope and unflaggingly fascinating in detail.'
—*Financial Times*

'Mr. Lebrecht has written a lament for a lost world and a celebration of human endurance and the religious imagination.'
—*Wall Street Journal*

'Norman Lebrecht has a rare ability to evoke the past with the immediacy of a good journalist, broadcaster, novelist or blogger.'
—*Jewish Chronicle*

'The book features dozens of remarkable scientists, artists and politicians of Jewish descent. Lebrecht's wide net captures the usual suspects – Marx, Freud, Kafka, Einstein – but also many lesser-known, and equally fascinating, individuals.'
—*New York Times*

Also by Norman Lebrecht

The Maestro Myth
The Song of Names
Why Mahler?
Genius and Anxiety

WHY BEETHOVEN

A PHENOMENON IN ONE HUNDRED PIECES

Norman Lebrecht

PEGASUS BOOKS

NEW YORK LONDON

WHY BEETHOVEN

Pegasus Books, Ltd.
148 West 37th Street, 13th Floor
New York, NY 10018

First Pegasus Books cloth edition May 2023

ISBN: 978-1-63936-411-4

10 9 8 7 6 5 4 3 2 1

Printed in the United States of America
Distributed by Simon & Schuster
www.pegasusbooks.com

For Beatrice
(1930–2022)
who just missed it

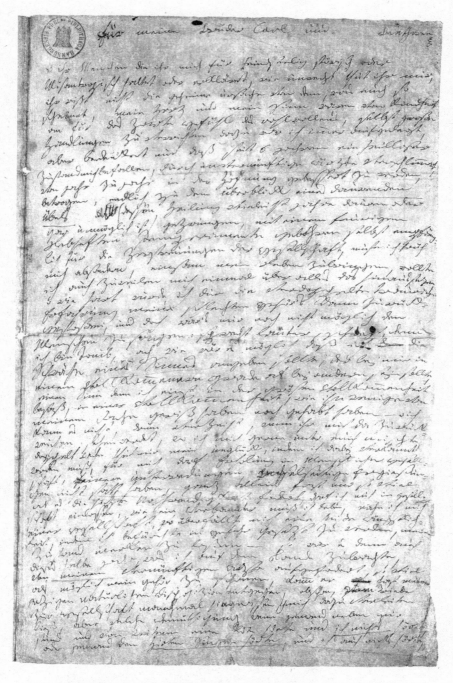

A manuscript page from the 'Heiligenstadt Testament', Beethoven's admission of deafness and declaration of renewed determination.

Contents

Prologue

I first met Till Janczukowicz one summer afternoon in the 1990s, at a bucolic festival in Schleswig-Holstein. We were attending the world premiere of an atonal string quartet in a cowshed amid the lowing of displaced Friesians in drizzling rain. Between a squeak and a moo, this round-faced young man shared with me his vision of making every classical recording available from a single source. 'The record labels will never go along with that,' I said with a shrug.

Quarter of a century on, I met Till again over dinner in a Kensington restaurant. He had just raised ten million dollars and was uploading the whole of recorded classical music, from Caruso to Yuja Wang, onto his website. Till had made his dream come true. Now he wanted to collaborate with my classical music news site and was pumping me for ideas.

'Beethoven,' I said.

'Why?'

'It's his 250th birthday coming up.'

'What do you have in mind?'

'A critical guide to the complete works,' I improvised.

'How many works?'

'250.'

'Recordings?'

'Around fifteen thousand.'

'How often?'

'Daily.'

'When can we start?' said Till.

On the bus home, my wife reminded me that I had two book tours coming up, was halfway through a new novel and was already working eleven-hour days. 'How will you fit this in?'

'I'll prioritise.'

'You're no good at that,' she objected.

'You'll help me.'

I reckoned it would take me four years, doing nothing else, to listen to fifteen thousand Beethoven records. That would mean this book would appear on his next anniversary in 2027, which seemed a long way off. On reflection, though, did I really need to spin-test every single disc? As a record omnivore I know the catalogue as Demetrius knew the library at Alexandria and Elias Canetti the book stacks in *Auto-da-fé*. Much in the vaults consists of duplicates and trivialities. By cutting out vanity fare, reissues and no-hopers I could whittle Beethoven on record down to a discussion of one thousand items. That began to look almost manageable. Even fun.

All the research was done, no further travel required. Beethoven's world was matchbox small. He lived in Bonn and Vienna, never saw the sea. He took his summer break in a spa. I had visited his homes, his resorts, his woods, his lakes, his grave. His life was sedentary, uneventful, with few highs and frequent lows. Near-autistic, he failed regularly in love and probably never had sex, at least within an identifiable relationship. From the age of thirty-one he was profoundly deaf, his social life reduced to jottings in conversation books. He lived in squalor, offending visitors with foul smells and filthy floors. Yet even as he drove people away, Beethoven reached deeper into the human condition than any musician before him. Mozart and Haydn beside him were mere crowd pleasers. Once his music surpassed mortal understanding, he just (to paraphrase Churchill) kept burrowing on. Delving deep, he was a self-made man on a self-made mission. By the last masterpieces it is no longer clear if he knows where he is going.

He was inhibited by the worst disability that could befall a musician, the inability to hear. That fact alone makes his triumph unique. That Beethoven composed at all is miraculous; that he wrote above and beyond any music that had been heard before almost defies understanding. Like a pope in a pandemic, he reached for the one above: yet Beethoven never attended church. What he believed is uncertain. How he kept composing without hearing what he produced is an act of stubbornness unparalleled in creation. It is also an inspiration for every human being with a creative spark never to give up making art so long as there is breath in the lungs and bread in the bin.

Why Beethoven? The question has nagged me all my life. How could he write the Emperor Concerto while cowering beneath Napoleon's cannon? What impelled him to shatter convention, adding singers to a symphony and seven movements to a string quartet? Why is 'Für Elise' the biggest piano hit in China? Does his music mean today what it once did, or does its shape shift through time? The only way to address that question was to approach Beethoven both through the music he wrote and through the ways it has been interpreted and reinterpreted on record by artists as disparate as the heavy-bearded Joseph Joachim and the micro-skirted Yuja Wang. Each generation and every artist finds a different Beethoven. As in Shakespeare and the Bible, interpretation counts at least as much as text.

I started, with a nod to Neil MacGregor's *A History of the World in 100 Objects*, by arranging Beethoven's works in a hundred chapters. It made no sense to follow the catalogue order of opus 1 to 138, both because the dating is unreliable and because with Beethoven there is no fixed order of invention. A theme for a royal cantata, knocked off when he is nineteen, might ultimately turn into the climax of his opera *Fidelio*. The fifth symphony's fateful knocks start life in a juvenile sketch for two pianos. Beethoven sometimes operates in blocks: half a dozen sonatas or string quartets, then a decade until the next. He will be stuck in a sheaf of Irish songs when, out of nowhere, up pops the Hammerklavier. Existing in self-made disorder, he leaves his chroniclers free to find their own connections. In doing so, one follows his hand down the manuscript pages, noting hesitations, interruptions, erasures, food stains, all of them part of the process of creation.

After much deliberation, I decided to examine the works from a midpoint and fan outward in both directions – the way pianists do when playing the 32 sonatas as a cycle over a week, never in order of publication but mixing works from different periods to uncover their coherence and consistency. Beethoven's stream of consciousness runs not from one score to the next, rather between a handful of overarching ideas that form the arteries of his creative corpus.

The place to meet Beethoven is in the music. Since each of us relates to music in a personal way – formed by place and time, learning and heritage, quirks and gifts – every approach to Beethoven is bound to be subjective and every study will expose as much of yourself as it does of the subject. In the course of this book I found myself confronted by long-buried childhood traumas, by insights into adult relationships and by various tramlines that Beethoven laid down in my life. By revisiting overgrown research paths, I have also stumbled on the shocking identity of the mysterious 'Für Elise', among other mysteries, and the very diverse roots of his original ethnicity. Beethoven exists, in life, on the page and on record, as a sub-awareness in all our lives, a splinter beneath a cuticle, a buried memory that bursts into flower at inconvenient moments. Seeking Beethoven through his music, across a span of two hundred and fifty years, is the purpose of this book.

As a person Beethoven is portrayed by most biographers as unruly, unkempt, bullying to underlings, rude to friends, unrewarding to know. After two years in his company I see him as an almost ideal human being. He is resilient to fate and awesomely independent, serving neither church nor state. He goes from one composition to the next, not knowing who will pay for it. He believes that each day, in most ways, he can do better. He treats critics and fans with equal disdain.

Amid the hierarchies of top-down Vienna, he refuses to bend the knee like Mozart to men in power and invents a recognisably modern form of arts sponsorship – a patron who pays for music in exchange for a name-check (who would ever have heard of Waldstein without his sonata?). When the rich and mighty order him about, he turns a deaf ear. He premieres the ninth symphony on a weekend when they are at their country homes and he can engage with real music lovers. His view of the world is self-limited. Ignorant of science, uninterested in philosophy, he mistrusts doctors, hates lawyers, despises landlords, owns no property. He speaks German, reads Latin, has a smattering of French, needs nothing more.

His habits are simple. He buys best-quality pencils and pens. He does not own a suit, or a dress jacket. His shoes are country-shod. He drinks coffee at breakfast and wine at night. He pees in a pot and shoves it under his chair, forgetting to empty it. When he cannot pee any more he dies, with grace. The more I follow his hand down the page, the more I revere his massive omniscience from so mundane a base. Where on earth did Beethoven get the idea that a mere musician could change the world?

ɞ

Before I put a word on screen, my world shut down. On 9 January 2020, days into Beethoven's 250th year, the Israeli pianist Ammiel Bushakevitz entered the Great Theatre in Wuhan, China, to perform Beethoven's Triple Concerto. The house, a red and gold swagger of post-Maoist prosperity, was sold out. Ammiel, who had played there before, sensed disquiet. 'There were definitely rumours of a coronavirus, it was mentioned by our guides and translators,' he e-mailed me. Seven days later, Wuhan locked down. None of us knew yet what was coming.

On honeymoon that week in the Galapagos Islands, a young mathematician saw tortoises that had been alive during Charles Darwin's visit in 1835. 'There were signs everywhere telling you to keep two metres from them,' said Professor Adam Kucharski. Back in London, a government official asked him what was the best distance to maintain between people during a pandemic. 'Two metres,' said Kucharski. That's how iron rules get made.

In March, Covid-19 came west. The first musician death to cross my screen, on 12 March, was that of Luca Targetti, a casting director at La Scala, Milan. Each morning brought more tragic news. Dmitri Smirnov, a Russian composer living in England, was suddenly unable to breathe. A Brazilian conductor, Naomi Munakata, was disturbed by a lack of masks in rehearsal. Both died. Vincent Lionti, a violist, left his colleagues in the Metropolitan Opera orchestra mute with grief. A music critic passed away in Madrid, a dramatist in Manhattan, a Beethoven string quartet lost its cellist, an Indian composer died on hospital steps.

As the skies emptied of aircraft, the streets of cars, I sat on a sunny patio listening to the birds. They sang softer, no longer competing with machines. On AbeBooks I bought a book titled *Was Beethoven a Birdwatcher?* He must have been, with a nightingale played by a flute in the Pastoral Symphony, a cuckoo by the clarinet and an oboe that gives a kind of quail-wail. In a disturbingly hot April, swallows flew in from Africa, mocking our confinement. At the first easing of travel I ran up the hill to the station, prepared to break all rules in order to smell the sea. Beethoven, landlocked all his life, stopped me from jumping a barrier.

A teenaged grandson moved in. He knew nothing of Beethoven. Supervising his schoolwork, screen time, exercise, sleep and nutrition, I imagined Beethoven caring for his orphaned nephew without the most elementary household skills. Beethoven drove himself half-mad in the process and his nephew to near-suicide. He was not a role model for practical parenting.

In life's crises I used to ask myself what Gustav Mahler would have done in similar circumstances. During Covid-19, I could not bring myself to listen to Mahler, not knowing when I might hear his music again in a concert hall. Beethoven, on the other hand, kept going. He had music for all media, all moods. Musicians in their bedrooms played Beethoven on Zoom to each other and posted the results on YouTube. A woman in her kitchen in the middle of England Zoom-conducted amateurs all over the country in the nine symphonies. Half a million Philadelphians tuned into the fifth. When vaccines arrived, Beethoven played to mile-long queues of bared arms, as the world queued to resume normality.

There were downsides, too. In the first Covid summer, voices within a Black Lives Matter insurgency called for aspects of Western culture to be 'cancelled'. The chief music critic of the *New York Times* advised orchestras to impose quotas on white composers. An op-ed in the *Chicago Tribune* argued that Beethoven should be 'eliminated' for a year. Nobody called for a ban on Bach, Mozart, Verdi, Rodgers and Hammerstein or the Rolling Stones. Beethoven exemplified a form of excellence and aspiration that soared above street rhetoric and protected the rest of Western civilisation. While I grew up the Beatles sang 'Roll Over Beethoven', declaring classical music defunct. Despite their appeal, Beethoven endures, indestructible.

There are many books which claim that spending a year with Proust, Kafka, Shakespeare, Picasso or Einstein will make you happier, healthier, sexier and stronger. I have a weakness for such books and part of me hoped that living with Beethoven through a pandemic would give me back a full head of black hair, the blood pressure of an Olympian and the capacity to write all night long in three languages. It didn't, but I learned a few things.

Beethoven teaches us that bodily impairment can yield spiritual compensations. A Beethoven with full hearing could not have conceived the late quartets, works in which he reaches beyond the grasp of his musicians, beyond the here and now. Unbothered by practicalities, he touched the ethereal. Not a spiritual man in any religious or moral sense, he sought godliness in nature. He had no interest in progress and technology, never rode a train or tinkered with a machine. He was not intellectual or good at conversation. He was a musician: he wrote music.

But when the world stops on its axis, as it did in Covid, there is no wiser, saner, safer guide than Beethoven to walk us through the valley of the shadow and safely out the other side. In dark nights, when we mourned the day's dead and dreaded tomorrow's toll, Beethoven, like Winston Churchill in 1940, had the ring of truth, of confidence, of hope. Churchill, slurring his words in drink, steered my parents through six years of war. In our two years of plague, I never doubted for a moment that Beethoven would see us through and would still be there when the skies reopened and we flew again across the world to hug and kiss all those we had so sorely missed. Beethoven was and is and will be. His music is a bond of our common humanity. Why Beethoven – *a statement not a question.* We need him now, as ever.

Norman Lebrecht
St John's Wood, London, June 2022

**To hear some of the unique performances discussed
in this book, hover your phone over this
QR code and you will be directed to an online playlist.**

Introduction

Beethoven: The life

There is not much to tell. He was born in Bonn in mid-December 1770 (possibly on the 16th; he was baptised the next day). His father, a tenor in the ruler's chapel and a violin teacher on the side, was a rustic wretch, prone to drink and violence. After the death of his mother, Maria Magdalena, Beethoven moved to Vienna. Hailed as the new Mozart, he asserted himself as his own man, a composer who wrote as he pleased, not to please.

Patronised by the rich, he fell in love lucklessly with their daughters. He was not unattractive. Portraits show a man of medium height (around 5 foot 5), strongly built, high-browed and with bushy dark hair that turned grey. Women feared his intensity. He never married.

At thirty-one, going deaf, he contemplated suicide. Three prime years were wasted on a custody battle for a nephew who brought him no joy. In growing isolation, he pushed music beyond known limits. Music, he said, 'is the mediator between the spiritual and the sensual life,' a bridge between heaven and earth. He died aged fifty-six, on the stormy afternoon of 26 March 1827. His funeral drew the largest crowd Vienna had ever seen.

Beethoven: The music

Beethoven lives in his works. On paper we find a creator who cracks bad jokes and breaks off when bored, deciding that seven minutes is long enough for a piano sonata. He takes a routine susurration of strings and turns it into the allegretto of the seventh symphony. A quarter of his substantive works are for solo piano, ranging from 'bagatelles' – literally, sweet nothings – to the shocking, lopsided rhythms of his final sonata. He is a master of surprise. The listener, no matter how familiar, is not ready for what comes next.

Rage flares up and down the staves. The violin concerto is a war of one voice against authority. The Hammerklavier breaks pianos. The 14th quartet, in seven movements, smashes Haydn's perfect symmetry. Every work reveals something of Beethoven's inner life, from the lofty Missa Solemnis to the flimsy ditty 'I Love You'. Score by score, we enter his unconscious. Beethoven is a *perpetuum mobile*, a restless propulsion that spears out in multiple directions. Be surprised, he says. Be unprepared.

In discussing the works I avoid the tools and terms of academic musicology with its clunky categories of early, middle and late Beethoven and its Italianate names for quick and slow. Wherever possible, I avoid insider terminology. Beyond the analysis of form and text, I turn to Freud and Jung, Hegel and Marx, Kafka and Mann, Einstein and Kahneman, for larger meaning. If Beethoven matters, he must be viewed through the world of ideas and the unending march of interpretation.

Beethoven: The masters

Until 1900, music lived at home, around the family piano with, maybe, a flute or violin and a sheaf of well-worn scores. Concert outings would be previewed four-handed on the piano and replayed on return. Music, until 1900, was hands-on. Radio and recordings removed the need to make music with one's own hands and lips. Music could be consumed passively, without the hard slog of picking note after note. A performance was accessed from an armchair, through speakers.

The Berlin Philharmonic Orchestra recorded the first complete symphony, Beethoven's fifth, with the Hungarian conductor Arthur Nikisch, in 1913. Charismatic conductors acquired cult status. Wilhelm Furtwängler performed the ninth symphony for Adolf Hitler's birthday. Leopold Stokowski filmed it for Walt Disney's *Fantasia*. Herbert von Karajan harnessed Beethoven in Cold War Berlin. Leonard Bernstein conducted the ninth symphony for the fall of the Berlin Wall.

Politicians used Beethoven as political capital. Stalin twinned the Soviet Union's tenth anniversary to the centenary of Beethoven's death. Communist China ended the Cultural Revolution with a televised Beethoven's fifth. A French agitator used the seventh symphony in the

2022 presidential election campaign. The European Union claimed the ninth as its anthem. Everyone wanted a bit of Beethoven.

Chinese pianists – Lang Lang, Yundi Li, Yuja Wang – broke his music online, where viewers increasingly turned to older interpreters. 'Ashtray Annie' Fischer recorded with a fag between her lips; Glenn Gould squatted on a sawn-off piano stool; Friedrich Gulda played with a naked girlfriend at his side. Four Russians – Emil Gilels, Sviatoslav Richter, Maria Yudina and Maria Grinberg – are so convincing and so different you can hardly believe they are playing the same notes. The lives of great interpreters reflect fragments of Beethoven's.

The day I submit this manuscript, I receive the last release in a long-gestated cycle. The Canadian pianist Angela Hewitt recorded the 32 sonatas over sixteen years, almost as long as Beethoven took to compose them. Coming from outside the elite US and European conservatoire network and rejecting corporate Steinway pianos for a boutique Italian Fazioli, Hewitt's approach is refreshing, questing and undogmatic. I am shaken to the point of tears by her reading of the concluding opus 111 sonata with its unnerving syncopations and eventual consolation. I must have listened to this sonata a hundred times and it still has more to say about my life and times than I ever suspected. Why Beethoven? I ask myself yet again. Because whenever I think I'm getting close to understanding the man and his music, he delivers one more shattering revelation. And then another.

BEETHOVEN HIMSELF

1

Not pathetic

Piano Sonata No. 8, 'Pathétique', Op. 13 (1797–8)

BEETHOVEN, WHO GENERALLY HATES TITLES, DOESN'T MIND this one. New to Vienna's ballrooms, he bangs out a *Grand Sonate Pathétique*, its pathos striking a pose that is at once arrogant, wistful and ironic. The adjective 'pathétique' in 1790s Vienna, like its English equivalent today, can convey anything from fatal tragedy to mild contempt. It's a banal word like 'nice', best applied to biscuits. Over time, in an edition made by one of Beethoven's students, this sonata becomes a fixture in school curricula. A Year 10 teaching aid explains that 'pathétique' 'means "moving" or "emotional".' More people learn to hate Beethoven from being taught this sonata than by any other cause.

The front page offers a dedication to Prince Karl Alois von Lichnowsky, chamberlain of the royal court. Lichnowsky is a music buff who gives young Ludwig free lodgings in exchange for premiere rights to his music. The prince holds Friday soirées with the best musicians, no refusals accepted. Musicians are warned that he can be capricious, critical and downright cruel.

Lichnowsky was Mozart's patron until, tiring of his dependency, he sued the composer for an alleged debt and won a court order for 1,415 gulden (around £40,000 today). Mozart died a month later. Lichnowsky never claimed the cash. 'A cynical degenerate and shameless coward,' in the words of a family friend, his sexual predilections were deemed peculiar even by Vienna's debauched elite. His noble wife, Princess Christiane, was obliged to take a room in a brothel to receive him on marital nights as this was the only place apparently where the prince could achieve orgasm. His personal portfolio of temporal power, domestic sadism and musical immersion was unexceptional among Vienna's rulers. In a crowded field of hereditary autocrats he was, in many ways, the most corrupt.

Lichnowsky, however, was generous to Beethoven at the outset, giving him 600 gulden a year (£15,000) in spending money as well as two fine violins, a Guarnerius and an Amati. The prince also afforded him discreet protection, stepping in swiftly if Beethoven got into trouble. When musicians called a strike over an 8 a.m. rehearsal call for the second symphony, a work dedicated to Lichnowsky, the prince laid on a lavish hot breakfast to assuage their dissent. Beethoven showed minimal gratitude, never asking for more; that much he had learned from the Mozart experience.

The inevitable breakup came one September night in 1806 at Lichnowsky's Czech castle at Hradec. After his orchestra played the second symphony, the prince asked Beethoven to play something new for his guests. Beethoven, not a man to take requests, went about 'hitting the keys with the flat of his hand, or running a single finger up and down the keyboard, in short, doing all manner of things to kill time and laughing heartily,' we are told.

The prince repeated his demand, this time with menaces. His guests were French army officers, rowdy and vainglorious. Beethoven resented the French and resisted their occupation. Getting up from the piano he picked up a chair and threw it at the French, then charged 'indiscreetly and suddenly' out into a stormy night. He walked to the nearest town where, soaking wet, he cadged a bed in a doctor's house. Next morning he got a ride to Vienna. Once home, he took Lichnowsky's bust off a shelf and hurled it to the ground. When Lichnowsky demanded an explanation, he replied: 'Prince, you are what you are by circumstance and birth; I am what I am through myself. There are, and always will be, thousands of princes. But there is only one Beethoven.'

That epigraph went viral. Beethoven had just reset the historic relationship between composer and power, tipping it in his favour. Where Haydn and Mozart could be treated as staff, Beethoven was Beethoven. He would never take the knee to men of wealth and might, least of all to the monster who ruined Mozart. His timing was fortunate; Napoleon had fragmented and weakened the aristocracy. There was always another palace where a composer could play.

Soon after, Beethoven was approached by Lichnowsky's estranged brother, Count Moritz, asking if he could be his new sponsor. Beethoven, handing over his 27th piano sonata, opus 90, told Moritz: 'Live happily, my esteemed friend, and always regard me as worthy of your friendship.' The subtext: 'unlike your rotten brother.'

Five years on, in September 1811, Prince Karl, fallen from power, turned up one morning at Beethoven's studio. Beethoven, hearing his voice, got up from his desk and locked the door. The prince persisted, returning day after day, sitting on the steps until the composer finally came out to say good morning. Their roles were reversed. Beethoven was the benefactor, the prince his supplicant.

The '*Pathétique*' that he wrote for Lichnowsky remained Beethoven's favourite sonata (an Italian word for 'something that sounds', as distinct from cantata: something which is sung). His aide Anton Schindler heard him playing it often: 'What the *Sonata Pathétique* was in Beethoven's hands (although he left much to be desired as regards clean playing) was something one had to hear, and hear again, in order to be quite certain that it was the same well-known work. Every single thing became, in his hands, a new creation.'

The opening movement is deadly serious, the central section deceptively simple, chipping in a clip of Mozart's K457 sonata; the finale is cheerful. Marcel Proust, hearing his grandmother play the '*Pathétique*', calls it 'the steak and potatoes' of Beethoven sonatas. It lasts twenty minutes.

There are around 150 recordings, going back to Frederic Lamond and Wilhelm Backhaus in 1926–7. Edwin Fischer and his pupil Alfred Brendel present austerity. Arthur Rubinstein is all winks and smiles. Glenn Gould is a Mountie on a murder hunt, tension alternating with existential anxiety. His '*Pathétique*' was issued on an album titled *Build Your Baby's Brain*. Friedrich Gulda plays slow and decadent, my preferred choice. Among modern releases, I admire the dreamy Argentine Ingrid Fliter and the poetic Frenchman Jean-Efflam Bavouzet. No one, though, goes deeper than the Russian Emil Gilels. Just wait until we get to Gilels.

2

Silence, please

Piano Concerto No. 4 in G major, Op. 58 (1805–6)

IN THE 1970S, WHILE MY FRIENDS WERE WATCHING FOOTBALL and chasing girls, I was pulling round objects out of oblong sleeves. Collecting classical recordings, like buying a British car, was a game for losers. One in three releases was scratched, warped or wobbly and the machines we played them on were perilously frail, yielding nothing like the full, warm sound of a good concert hall. Expecting disappointment, geeks like me collected records as a penance for past sins, storing them in knee-high racks along the living room wall.

At the British Federation of Recorded Music Societies I met doctors, lawyers and lorry drivers who bought a dozen LPs every month, spending more on music than on wine or clothes. We politely debated the merits of Herbert von Karajan's latest Beethoven set against his three previous boxes. A consensus held that Karajan, an ex-Nazi, was the greatest living Beethoven conductor. My dissent was received by doctors with compassion, like a cancer patient who refused chemo.

The opinions in these societies were moulded by *Gramophone*, a magazine which served in relation to the classical record industry as *The Times* did to the royal family. *Gramophone* was stuffed with glossy eight-page advertising supplements paid for by corporate record labels. In *Gramophone*, all was for the best in the best of all recorded worlds. 'You see, Norman, I never like to write anything bad about anyone,' its chief critic Edward Greenfield told me over a Salzburg Spritzer. A former Westminster correspondent and a friend of ex-prime minister Edward Heath, Ted also turned out the *Penguin Record Guide* with two fellow *Gramophone* reviewers, Robert Layton and Ivan March. Together they sold more records than any single artist. Classical records, I slowly came to realise, were a bit like new Beaujolais, a really dull French product with sensational promotion. Somehow, I would have to develop a palate to tell greatness from rank.

We bought records in the basement departments of high-street pop stores. Upstairs you saw girls in mini-skirts and young men who cross-dressed; down below, men in frayed sweaters shifted furtively, like MPs in a sex shop. No one smiled. The secondhand shops were worse, stuffed with the detritus of deceased professors. I once saw a rat scuttle between Brahms and Bruckner in a Notting Hill store. Not one browser blinked.

America was better. On a virgin trip to New York, I entered a Fifth Avenue record store with dark-wood panelling, dimmed lights and central heating. Classical records, I saw, did not have to be dingy. Guys would sidle over to my rack to chat about tempi. I once convinced a till assistant to swap an Isaac Stern concerto on the store system for a smarter choice by Ivry Gitlis or Camilla Wicks. Sam Goody's on West 49th was classical heaven, though it could take forever to settle up while counter staff ran through the entire catalogue for a superior alternative. New York, New York was record heaven with a culture all its own. A friend hung out with Leonard Bernstein, who would play new releases with young guys in what they called a 'circle-jerk'.

The LP was on its last grooves. In 1980, gleaming, sterile, immaculate, digital compact discs were hailed by Karajan, no less, as absolute perfection. 'All else is gaslight,' he declared. Superficially (as ever), he was right. Digital recording eliminated clicks and scratches. You could spread jam on a disc – they did this in a Decca demonstration – and it still belted out the 1812 overture louder and more ominously than Napoleon at the gates of Moscow.

But there was a downside to perfection. CDs took the uncertainty out of record buying, and what is life without risk? Predictability killed my craving. Record labels, flush on CD profits, churned out the same old symphonies over and over and over again. Karajan recorded his ninth Beethoven box. Telling one set from another required supersonic hearing, a voluminous knowledge of Beethoven and a critical distance that grew with age and frequent disappointment. Which is not to say that I was impervious to acts of genius.

Had you asked me over a stiff Manhattan about the fourth piano concerto, I would have mulled around some outlying contenders before issuing an opinion that the *best* performance on record, undeniably the all-time *best*, was Emil Gilels with the Philharmonia Orchestra, conductor Leopold Ludwig, on the British EMI label which, for reasons too legal to recount, was known in the US as Angel. What put this 1957 oblong clean top of my all-time pile? Accuracy, to be sure, clarity of articulation and the capacity to surprise me on fifth, or fiftieth hearing. Gilels was a Soviet export artist who never gave an interview or a smile, but who played with transcendent detachment and a wondrously calibrated sound. Ludwig was a workaday German Kapellmeister. The orchestra was good in parts, the strings a bit thin, not on peak form.

What enthralled me, then as now, was poetry and lack of pretension. Gilels plays as if, like the prophet Ezekiel, he's hearing a voice and seeing visions. Midway through the central movement, I am unable to breathe for the tension he conjures. The space between each note is separated like chess pieces on a world championship board. How Gilels achieves this illusion is a mystery unfathomable by science. Somehow in Abbey Road on the morning of 30 April 1957 Emil Gilels entered a zone no other musician had ever visited and made it his own. The next morning he recorded the fifth concerto, the Emperor, competently but without comparable inspiration. He made five more recordings of the fourth concerto, none of which catch fire. The Gilels-Ludwig G major concerto stands forever in a class of its own. Such greatness is random and unrepeatable (of the internal world of Emil Gilels I would discover more on a subsequent occasion).

Which is not to discard all other contenders. Artur Schnabel's waspish 1942 reading with Frederick Stock and the Chicago Symphony Orchestra gives a glimpse of eternal life. The Chilean Claudio Arrau achieves celestial grace. The 1950s British pianist known as 'Solomon' offers a masterclass in understatement. Arthur Rubinstein is effervescent, András Schiff a tad precious and Ivan Moravec wilfully elusive. Radu Lupu flickers to deceive. Krystian Zimerman is vivid with Leonard Bernstein; Glenn Gould with the same conductor is most peculiar.

On the debit side, Pierre-Laurent Aimard, with Nikolaus Harnoncourt and the Chamber Orchestra of Europe, is too damn thoughtful; this is music, for heaven's sake, not a doctoral thesis. Van Cliburn bumbles around the lower end of the cerebellum, rubbing elbows with Liberace. Lang Lang's

2017 concert with Christoph Eschenbach and the Orchestra de Paris is quite the ugliest thing on record, the pianist's opening touch as thick as dumplings and his dynamic never softer than *mezzo-forte*. There you are: this 1970s record buff just saved you from three seriously dud buys.

{

The day before rehearsal Artur Schnabel takes a walk with the conductor Otto Klemperer to discuss the G major concerto. 'The opening,' says Schnabel, 'must be so quiet, it is practically immaterial.'

'Show me,' says the conductor.

Schnabel moves his lips, miming the first notes.

'Too loud,' says Klemperer.

No music has a softer introduction, the piano barely heard and the respondent strings soft as silk. This is a new kind of musical conversation. Never before has a concerto begun with a solo; never has the orchestra been put in a different key from the soloist. Beethoven is making a statement of intent: he is out to disrupt order, to break things. The soloist's hush is an instruction to audiences to shut their chatter and listen up. Beethoven, himself, cannot hear anything below *triple-forte*. The opening amounts to a self-designed hearing test that is bound to fail.

In the middle movement, the pianist breaks the orchestra's flow with an ultra-slow solo. In the finale Beethoven changes key to C major to bring in trumpets and drums while the piano finds its way circuitously back to G. He is dancing on the edge of chaos, a composer showing he can do anything he likes.

The concerto was premiered in March 1807 at the palace of Prince Lobkowitz, Beethoven's second major sponsor; Lobkowitz, for 4,000 florins a year, would receive dedications of the third, fifth and sixth symphonies. A good musician who played violin and cello and sang in a deep bass voice, Lobkowitz had twelve children with a Schwarzenberg princess to whom he was, against the norm, monogamously devoted. He spent all his money on music, winding up destitute (as did Waldstein and Fries, two other Beethoven backers).

We have no reports on the private premiere. The public concert on 22 December 1808 was catastrophic, a four-hour Beethoven bash on a freezing night that featured, besides the concerto, the fifth and sixth symphonies and the Choral Fantasy. 'Too much can be no good thing,' muttered one guest. The concerto, with Beethoven as soloist, bombed. His pupil Louis Spohr recalled:

'Beethoven . . . forgot at the first tutti that he was a solo player, and springing up, began to direct in his usual way. At the first *sforzando* he threw out his arms so wide asunder that he knocked both the lights off the piano upon the ground. The audience laughed, and Beethoven was so incensed at this disturbance that he made the orchestra cease playing, and begin anew. [Conductor] Seyfried, fearing that a repetition of the accident would occur at the same passage, bade two boys of the chorus place themselves on either side of Beethoven, and hold the lights in their hands. One of the boys innocently approached nearer, and was reading also the notes of the piano-part. When therefore the fatal *sforzando* came, he received from Beethoven's outthrown right hand so smart a blow on the mouth, that the poor boy let fall the light from terror. The other boy, more cautious, had followed with anxious eyes every motion of Beethoven, and by stooping suddenly at the eventful moment he avoided the slap on the mouth. If the public were unable to restrain their laughter before, they could now much less, and broke out into a regular bacchanalian roar. Beethoven got into such a rage that at the first chords of the solo, half a dozen strings broke. Every endeavour of the real lovers of music to restore calm and attention were for the moment fruitless. The first Allegro of the Concerto was therefore lost to the public.'

Music is littered with first-night failures, and those that we know about are the ones that eventually recovered. The G major concerto lay untouched for a quarter of a century until, nine years after Beethoven's death, music director Felix Mendelssohn tried it out on a concert audience in Leipzig. The composer Robert Schumann wrote in a review that night: 'I sat in my place, holding my breath and afraid to move'. Exactly as I do when I hear the Emil Gilels recording.

3

Down the lane

Gassenhauer Trio, Op. 11 (1800); Variations on 'Ich bin der Schneider Kakadu', Op. 121a (1824)

GASSEN ARE THE ALLEYWAYS OF OLD VIENNA, DARK LANES with large cobblestones. Hauer is a stone-hewer. A Gassenhauer is a tune that is whistled down the alley by delivery boys. Beethoven's trio gets its name when the main tune becomes an earworm. That is not his intention. The composer is writing for his life.

There are two forms of composing at the turn of the nineteenth century, private and public. Beethoven writes at his desk for all eternity. When called on stage, he faces demands for instant improvisation – a riff of variations, often competing with slick wizards. Anton Reicha, Beethoven's friend from his Bonn days, could play fifty-seven variations over ninety minutes on a theme he plucked from thin air. Beethoven tried to avoid such tests of a dubious skill, not always successfully.

In 1800 word arrives from Prague that a showman called Daniel Steibelt is making ladies swoon with lascivious variations, while milking their husbands in side-bets on how long he can keep it up. When Steibelt reaches Vienna Beethoven's patrons tell him to stop the upstart, 'knock him on the head'. A showdown is set up in March at the palace of the banker Count Moritz Fries.

Beethoven is first into the ring, playing a theme from his unfinished trio opus 11 for piano, clarinet and cello. It's a work in progress, never heard before. Steibelt responds with a riff on his own new quintet, adding tremolos to his playing, a sneaky technique that is calculated to flutter hearts. He is declared the winner.

A rematch is arranged for the weekend. Bets are taken. Steibelt weighs in with an impertinent improvisation on Beethoven's trio, which he has only heard once. He rises from the piano seat, beaming and hand-kissing all round. Beethoven is half-pushed to the piano. Seeing the score of Steibelt's quintet, he turns it upside down on the stand, picks out a cello line and, with one finger, dazzles off a sheaf of variations. 'He improvised in such a manner that Steibelt left the room before he finished, would never again meet him and, indeed, made it a condition before accepting an offer that Beethoven should not be invited.' Nobody ever challenges Beethoven again to a piano duel. There is a scintillating 1969 record of his Gassenhauer trio by Daniel Barenboim, Gervase de Peyer and Jacqueline du Pré.

The Kakadu variations for piano, violin and cello are spun off from a hit song in a 1794 musical comedy, *The Sisters of Prague*. Last revised in 1824, the final score allows us to see the work of young Beethoven reworked by the Beethoven of the ninth symphony. 'Kakadu' is German for cockatoo, so it's featherlight.

The first recording, in 1926, is by the French violinist Jacques Thibaud with pianist Alfred Cortot and the Catalan cellist Pablo Casals, three hard hitters in search of an anvil. The trio breaks up when in 1945 Casals learns that both his French partners have collaborated with the Nazi occupation in France.

In the Beethoven catalogue the Kakadu's number, opus 121a, is split with opus 121b – a six-minute 'Opferlied' ('song of offering') for voice, chorus and orchestra. Messier still, the Opferlied has two versions. His next work, opus 122, is the vacuous 'Bundeslied' for soloists, chorus and wind ensemble, part rambling song, part drinking ditty. After that, opus 123 is the Missa Solemnis, the Mont Blanc of sacred music. Beethoven can go from worms to angels at the turn of a page.

4

Bon-Bonn

Piano Trios, Op. 1 (1791–5)

IT IS SEPTEMBER 2009 AND I AM IN BONN FOR A FESTIVAL OF modern music marking sixty years of the Federal German Republic. This 'small town in Germany' (© John Le Carré) was a world capital until in 1991 the Bundestag moved to Berlin, gutting Bonn of half of its citizens and all of its status.

Our festival takes place in former seats of power. A morning recital is played in the Bundestag chamber. I take the seat marked Bremen, my wife has half of Bavaria. We observe Dieter Schnebel's anarchic 'Bauernszene', which requires four musicians to smash dinner plates. György Ligeti's Poème Symphonique for 100 Metronomes is performed in the old Federal Chancellery, actually in Angela Merkel's living room, which is being kept in perfect order in case she might, some day, return. Ironic metronomes tick down to nothingness, signalling the evanescence of power, how randomly it is given, how easily taken away. Bonn became capital in 1949 only because Chancellor Konrad Adenauer lived nearby. 'You know what people say about Bonn,' sighs a Le Carré spy, 'either it's raining, or the railroad gates are down.' The Rhine rolls by and the skies hang low. The town wrangles over commissioning a good concert hall and, in the absence of power, still cannot make up its desultory mind.

Beethoven's roots in Bonn are shallow. Grandfather Lodewijk van Beethoven, from Louvain in what is now Belgium, sang in the Prince-Archbishop's chapel. Promoted to Kapellmeister, or conductor, he runs a wine business on the side. His wife, then his son, become alcoholics. The son Johann, also a singer at court, plays violin, zither and keyboards. He marries a nineteen-year-old widow, Maria. Ludwig is their second child, of seven. He and two brothers survive.

The house where Ludwig van Beethoven gave his first cry, a 1700 structure with baroque stone frontage, was bought by a citizens' group in 1893, expanded by the Nazis and revitalised in the 1990s as a parting federal gift. Its connection to Beethoven is vestigial; he left this house at four years old. Today, the Beethoven-Haus is a repository for the largest collection anywhere of Beethoven letters and memorabilia, of busts and portraits, of his death mask and a lock of hair. It is not a house of happiness, by any stretch.

'People who've had very unhappy childhoods are pretty good at inventing themselves,' writes Le Carré, of himself. The same is true of Beethoven. He is a child prodigy whose father dreams of making him into the next Mozart. Is he a victim of child abuse? In a 2021 television documentary the conductor Charles Hazlewood claims: 'There are many theories surrounding what could have caused his deafness, but it is my suspicion, as with many others, that it was a result of the immense and relentless abuse he suffered as a child. His father – a musician himself and a violent alcoholic – would pull young Ludwig from his bed at all hours, forcing him to practise and in-between times punching him around the head, a constant act that arguably played a role in the dislodging of the composer's tympanum and subsequent deafness.' This is, in my view, far-fetched. Most children were hit by parents and teachers in those times, especially in music lessons.

Wary of his father, Beethoven has a mother who shields him from Johann's fists and boosts his self-esteem. 'She was such a good, loving mother, my best friend,' he writes after her death. He does not talk much about her, still less about his father. If, as some argue, he develops an adult personality disorder, it is unlikely to be the result of an upbringing that was not, by prevailing standards, uncommonly brutal.

In his teens he played viola in the ruler's orchestra. At twenty-one he set out for Vienna to study with Joseph Haydn. A patron, Count Waldstein, tells him: 'Dear Beethoven, In leaving for Vienna today you are on the point of realising a long-cherished desire. The wandering genius of Mozart still grieves for his passing; with Haydn's unquenchable spirit it has found shelter but no home . . . Work hard, and the spirit of Haydn's genius will come to you from Haydn's hands.' So, no pressure.

Haydn, just turned sixty, is back from the triumph of his life in London, as well as his first love affair. After a lifetime of servitude on the Esterhazy country estate, he is known in Vienna as 'Papa Haydn', a genial soul. Haydn has only one request: that Beethoven, on his first published score, should declare himself 'a pupil of Joseph Haydn'. Beethoven refuses. Haydn, without rancour, sees his pupil's first three piano trios through the press, warning that the third of them will go way above audience heads. At the trios' premiere at Lichnowsky's, Haydn is first to his feet to applaud. He takes Beethoven out for hot chocolate and lends him money. Beethoven, ungrateful, tells friends he 'learned nothing' from Haydn.

It is a point he makes in the third bar of the first trio, flattening the E flat major key with a heretical D flat. A visiting Englishman, William Gardner, is so stirred by this surprise that he finds 'all other music tame and insipid'. Beethoven revises the second trio and snorts defiance in the third. With Lichnowsky's backing, he secures a contract with Carlo Artaria, Mozart's publisher. Artaria requires payment in advance. Lichnowsky's circle subscribe around a hundred sets. In all, the trios sell just 241 copies, but Beethoven is up and away, publishing with Artaria for a decade until 1803, when they sue each other.

On record the Beaux Arts Trio give a riveting account of these disobedient pieces; the third trio is simply exhilarating. Daniel Barenboim, Pinchas Zukerman and Jacqueline du Pré indulge in too many in-jokes. The 2020 Van Baerle Trio of Maria Milstein (violin), Gideon den Herder (cello) and Hannes Minnaar (piano) on a small Dutch label, are youthful and exuberant, like a young composer who is smashing musical windows.

5

Third Man

Piano Sonata No. 4, Op. 7 (1796)

VIENNA HAS A MUSEUM FOR EVERYTHING. THERE ARE MUSEUMS of clocks, chimney-sweeping, mental illness and Sigmund Freud. There is art history, motor transport and music, not to mention the houses where Mozart, Beethoven and Schubert lived. No city has more museums per square mile, or more varied. There is even a museum of death. My favourite is the sewer museum.

The Museum of *The Third Man*, located beside an impressive tunnel, is the private passion of Gerhard Strassgschwandtner and Karin Höfler, a pair of collectors fixated on the indelible Carol Reed film of 1949. The script, by Graham Greene, explores a post-war Vienna infested with unregenerate Nazis and black marketeers. Few films have a more memorable ambience. Anton Karas' zither trembles through the opening credits. Bedecked with awards, *The Third Man* ran just six weeks in Vienna and vanished altogether from local memory until Gerhard and Karin opened their archive – complete with a live zither player and an in-person sewer tour (do not wear sandals, they advise).

Once you get down to ordure, Vienna has no secrets. The tunnels are a Freudian unconscious of human evacuation. Ardour is not far away either, a short walk to the concert halls and opera houses, where Vienna experienced post-war revival. The opera, without a roof or walls, incubated silvery new voices – Elisabeth Schwarzkopf, Sena Jurinac, Irmgard Seefried, Hans Hotter, Christa Ludwig, Julius Patzak – while the windowless Conservatory thrust forth a razzle of Beethoven pianists.

Friedrich Gulda won competitions and played Carnegie Hall at twenty. The quiet Paul Badura-Skoda scoured junk piles for Beethoven manuscripts. Jörg Demus raided antique shops for fortepianos. Between them they turned the clock back and forward on Beethoven, turning the key to a new kind of pianism.

Gulda could play anything, anywhere. The conductor Franz Welser-Möst speaks of his 'crispy sound and the carefree, youthful approach in the early sonatas . . . an immediate understanding of Beethoven's world'. In opus 7, Beethoven's first standalone sonata, Gulda arrests the attention like Orson Welles in *The Third Man*. He makes us laugh in Beethoven, makes us cry, makes us wish we'd heard him live. In 1999 he announced his death, followed by a comeback concert; Gulda died months later in January 2000.

Badura-Skoda is gritty and ominous in this sonata, laced with laconic caprice. His fortepiano sounds unusually grand. Demus never recorded this sonata, which may be a mercy since some of his fortepianos sound like cardboard. But listen to him play 'Für Elise', and you'll hear an interpretation that is ten IQ points above the field, at once analytical and entertaining, an exquisite legacy.

There is a fourth character in this *Third Man* scenario. Alfred Brendel, born in a Czech village and raised in Croatia, cuts his record debut in 1951 Vienna with a *Christmas Tree Suite* by Franz Liszt. Vox Turnabout, an American label that hires the Vienna Philharmonic under fake names, employs him to record the complete Beethoven piano music. Brendel, with goofy teeth, a receding chin and spymaster spectacles, is no one else's idea of a cover star.

He recalls 'winter mornings in dilapidated baroque mansions . . . where the logs in the fireplace cracked so loudly they had to be thrown into the snow before recording could begin'. He plays the complete concertos, sonatas and variations on Vox, to little immediate effect. 'When I was young my overall career wasn't sensational at all, it rather progressed step by step,' he writes. 'But then, one day [in 1970] I was performing a Beethoven programme in the Queen Elizabeth Hall in London. It was quite an unpopular programme, I didn't even like it much myself and the next day I got three offers from big record companies. It seemed really rather grotesque, like a slow, hardly noticeable rise on a thermometer or a kettle warming water suddenly beginning to boil and to bubble and the steam comes out.'

Brendel signs up to re-record Beethoven for the Dutch label Philips, part of an electrical conglomerate that issues recordings in the colour of an ironmonger's overalls. Brendel arrives in house colours, brown suit and tie. He makes few mistakes, needs no retakes and gets on outstandingly well with conductors who feel that he, somehow, brings the best out of them. He moves to London, where he records another Beethoven set every decade or so. No pianist matches his work rate and none, writes the *New York Times* critic Bernard Holland, 'so wilfully avoided the ordinary channels to success and formulas for stardom and still arrived at the top of his profession.' The piano maker Steinway labels him 'the thinking man's pianist'. He is first-choice purchase for the ordinary bloke in a raincoat in the Saturday morning record shop.

Brendel writes essays on music and several volumes of poetry. The *Guardian* editor Alan Rusbridger calls him 'a formidable musical and intellectual presence.' His retirement concert, at the Vienna Musikverein in December 2008, is a gathering of the great and the good with an atmosphere that, like a papal funeral, mingles formal lament with quiet relief.

Brendel's Beethoven is thoughtful, accurate, immersive and self-questioning. He is not an artist who takes music lightly or sleeps well at night. He is torn by conflicts: 'The profession of a performer is full of paradoxes, and he has to learn to live with them. He has to forget himself and control himself; he has to observe the composer's wishes to the letter and create the music on the spot; he has to be part of the music market and yet retain his integrity.' Listening to Brendel can make you forget that music is meant to be enjoyed. Like a footballer who has passed his prime, he makes fans suffer with every touch of the ball.

Brendel's prime, for me, is in *Third Man* Vienna. His Vox Beethoven sonatas, raw and rushed, maintain an unfading authenticity. His variations are astonishingly varied, a shock of amazement with each track. Each concerto sounds like a debut. That spontaneity is absent from many of his Philips releases. Where his Schubert is profound, his Mozart witty, his Brahms dark, Brendel's Beethoven runs too smooth. In the fourth piano sonata, where Friedrich Gulda is all flashing lights and emergency ambulance, Brendel is predictably reassuring.

The Brendel paradox is best captured by the moral philosopher Ronald Dworkin, husband of Brendel's ex-wife, Irene. 'Why does he think what he's playing is better than other interpretations?' wonders Dworkin in a 2011 interview. 'He must think it's better and the question is why. It's not because what he plays is more beautiful than what he might otherwise play. Because if he was aiming at beauty, he could depart from what the composer had written. But he is faithful to the composition. And yet, he's not just playing the composer's music, he's interpreting it.'

That fierce contradiction might fascinate a therapist, but to seekers of Beethoven, it feels like intrusion. Others will be awed by Brendel's energy, his persistence and his intellect. Myself, I prefer artists who buck the trend; Brendel, all too often, is the trend, a prisoner of his brand.

Late in life, he reproaches himself in an essay for an 'indefensible' lapse in two bars in the middle movement of his final recording of the opus 28 sonata. Why indefensible? And why bother to confess? Music is an ephemeral thing. When it's done, it's done. Brendel's regret over two lost notes is his problem, not ours. He is trying to convince us that on his records, in every session over half a century, every note was correct. That sounds like hubris. The other three men of Vienna, no less meticulous than Brendel, deliver the beating heart of Beethoven and don't berate us with late-onset conscience.

6

I hate music

Notturno, Op. 42 (1793/1804)

IN THE BONN ORCHESTRA A VIOLINIST, FRANZ GEORG Rovantini, teaches technique to the violist Beethoven. Friar Koch sits him at the organ. The conductor Christian Gottlob Neefe gives career advice. 'If I ever become somebody,' Ludwig tells Neefe, 'I shall owe it to you.' The viola, deeper than the violin, is the ruler's personal instrument. It gives Ludwig status. His instrument survives at the Beethoven-Haus, still playable. He has taken good care of his viola.

So here's the conundrum: in the complete works of Beethoven, he writes nothing at all for viola. There is plenty for cello, reams for violin but zero for viola – except, early on, a notturno for viola and piano that he lets a publisher carve out of his string trio serenade, opus 8 – and this only to feed his brother Carl Caspar's cupidity. Beethoven's irritation with the piece is evident: 'The transcriptions are not mine, but they have been reviewed by me and have been completely improved in places, so don't come to me writing that I've transcribed them, because you'd be lying. I would never have the time and patience to do it.' There is a zesty recording on the Hyperion label by Paul Coletti and Leslie Howard and another on Naxos by François René Duchâble and Gérard Caussé.

If Beethoven is dissimulating bad Bonn memories in the notturno, he does not let on. When his mother dies he obtains a court order to secure half of his father's wages for his brothers' upkeep. Johann gets fired in 1789, dies in 1792. Beethoven is done with Bonn.

But no one fully shakes off a dysfunctional childhood. In *Adult Children of Alcoholics* (1983), the psychiatrist Janet G. Woititz lists thirteen aberrant behaviours, among them impulsiveness, over-reaction, harsh self-judgement and an inability to relax. All apply to Beethoven, some to an extreme degree. He has been maimed by his father's addiction and harsh music training. Children of disciplinarians are prone to rebel. Many born in vicarages emerge anti-religious. String players' sons play heavy metal. The question we must ask is: does Beethoven hate music?

He has good reason to do so. Music made his father a failure, his mother a martyr. Music is a rich man's pleasure. To be a musician in Beethoven's time is one rung above ruin. He chooses the life because it is all he knows, and he knows he is good at it. But does he love music, or hate it?

His attitude to composing is that of a carpenter towards wood, calculating and practical. He shuns crowds and fears stability, changing lodgings every few months. He cossets himself with expensive breakfast coffee and evening wine. He neglects his appearance and avoids emotional commitment. These are signs of a personality disorder, obsessive-compulsive though not self-hating. He saves his venom for music.

From the third bar of his first published work, he breaks the rules his father drummed into him and shames his second 'Papa', Haydn. He attacks music every morning, not milking its sweetness as Mozart does but stress-testing the art in every way to see if it will break. No composer ever sounded or acted so angry. He rips scores to shreds. In the fifth symphony he stabs and stabs right through the page. Music is his father, his foe. Killing music may bring him maternal comfort.

In 1943 Leonard Bernstein, fed up with a flatmate who gave voice lessons, writes a song cycle, titled 'I Hate Music'. To drive the hate home, he gives the premiere in the public library of Lenox, Massachusetts, where his surrogate father Serge Koussevitzky presides over the Tanglewood Festival. Bernstein, like Beethoven, stores up vengeance in this cycle. Hating music is a precondition to loving it.

7

Take that, teacher

String Trio, Op. 3, Serenade, Op. 8, String Trios, Op. 9 (1796–9)

THE STRING TRIO IS A THREE-LEGGED TABLE, A QUARTET MINUS one violin. Of baroque invention, the string trio is perfected by Boccherini and Dittersdorf. In Vienna, Mozart and Haydn compose one each, Albrechtsberger a dozen. Johann Georg Albrechtsberger is master of music at St Stephen's Cathedral. You cannot be a composer in Vienna without his stamp of approval. Beethoven sees him for lessons three times a week for fifteen months.

Albrechtsberger calls him 'headstrong'. Beethoven dismisses the organist as 'a pedant' and decides to defeat him at his own game, the string trio. He writes opus 3 in six movements, defying the rule of four. It runs 40 minutes, tripping tune after tune and changing speeds like a Formula One car on the Monte Carlo circuit. A second set of string trios, opus 9, tempers propulsion with Italian lyricism. The second movement of opus 9/1, richly dramatic, mocks pedants in power, of whom there are plenty in musical life. Next time you meet one, whistle the opening bars.

My go-to version is played on Philips by the Italian String Trio (1970) – Franco Gulli, Bruno Giuranna and Giacinto Caramia – all sunshine and white wine. Something stronger? Rudolf Barshai, Leonid Kogan and Mstislav Rostropovich, three Soviets in 1956 Moscow concrete. In a 1957 Hollywood studio you will find Jascha Heifetz, William Primrose and Gregor Piatigorsky, stars aligned for a lovely sound.

After opus 9, Beethoven never writes another string trio. He is done with teachers.

8

Four times six

String Quartets, Op. 18/1–6 (1798–1800)

THE STRING QUARTET ARISES FROM HAYDN'S PERCEPTION THAT
two violins, a viola and cello balance each other in a living room as a full
orchestra does on a stage. Haydn realises this when he is just eighteen.
Mozart adds melody and mischief. Beethoven and Schubert take the quartet public, in grand salons.

Beethoven begins with six quartets for the violinist Carl Amenda,
concertmaster of Prince Lobkowitz's orchestra. He takes three years to
deliver and then calls them back. 'Don't let [it] be played any longer as it is,'
he tells Amenda in June 1800, 'I have altered it a great deal because I have
now learned how to write quartets properly – you'll see when you get it.' His
revisions raise the level of difficulty. He is Beethoven. He demands better.

'Great accuracy is necessary in the first movement,' advises the early-
twentieth-century Anglo-American composer Rebecca Clarke, herself a
professional quartet player. 'The abrupt and pithy subject is continually
tossed from one player to another, so that the joints must dovetail very
neatly; and they must be played with the same tone-colour, in order to
prevent the whole from sounding disjointed.'

The first quartet (in F) presents all four instruments in unison, without
harmony. Beethoven is saying 'listen up'. He is writing for attention, not
relaxation. Each instrument then plays a riff on the opening statement.
This is parliamentary debate, new to Vienna. Beethoven sets his music on
the side of free speech. He troubles the princes. Amenda, who gives up
music to become a pastor, says: 'I would have liked to dedicate my whole
life to this person.'

In the second movement we hear for the first time the existential,
must-it-be? question that returns in his final works. The third quartet is

subtle, the fourth rather weak and the sixth decisive. Its finale is called 'Malinconia,' which is Italian for a mood that can veer from mild despair to clinical depression, a scale with which Beethoven is closely familiar. He writes on the score in Italian: 'This movement must be played with the greatest delicacy'. There are hints here of the unwritten Eroica symphony.

The reception is mixed. A Leipzig critic calls Beethoven 'a broody old hen scratching away in the dust of pedantry,' adding that the quartets are 'difficult to grasp and not at all popular'. 'Ignore Beethoven,' growls Albrechstberger. 'He has learned nothing, and he'll never amount to anything.'

Picking a single recording is close to impossible. Opus 18/1 in the 1933 Abbey Road set by Adolf Busch and his quartet is remarkable for its vigour and novelty. Opus 18/6 gets an epochal reading in 1953 from the Vienna Philharmonic concertmaster Walter Barylli and three orchestral colleagues. Violinist Peter Oundjian and the Tokyo Quartet (1993) are life-savers in the heart-stopping 'Malinconia'. The Guarneri (1969) and the Emersons (1997) are the pick of American string quartets. The Alban Berg Quartet (1989) are so slick you forget how hard these quartets are to play. The French Ébène Quartet (2020) deliver subtlety with panache and the Spanish Cuarteto Casals (2017) are consolatory in the depths of 'Malinconia'.

9

Watch the birdie

Symphony No. 2, Op. 36 (1802)

IF A SECOND NOVEL SELDOM OUTSHINES THE FIRST, THE SAME is true of symphonies. Beethoven's effervescent first symphony is acclaimed on premiere in 1800, the second flops. He is fiddling with the form, dumping a dance movement and replacing it with nothing livelier. The second symphony lacks nutrients, a tune to whistle all the way home. Ask experienced orchestral musicians for the opening theme and you'll find that very few can play it from memory.

Written in an outlying village amid a roaring in his ears, its flaws are visible on the opening page, where a big band of drums and winds dissolves to a rish-rash of strings. There are caresses but no conquest. He is marking time, not mastering it. A Viennese musician describes the symphony as 'a loathsomely writhing, wounded dragon that refuses to die but bleeds to death in the finale'. A French conductor calls it a symphony 'of doves and crocodiles', an arresting metaphor of disconnected environments. So enigmatic is the work that Viennese wags say it echoes the composer's well-known digestive troubles (some Wikipedia musicologists repeat this jibe as reasoned analysis).

Beethoven shoves the symphony in a drawer for three years. When he tries again, there is no warmth in the reception. What are his listeners missing? In his chirpy study *Was Beethoven a Birdwatcher?*, the British journalist David Turner hears, at the opening of the finale, the call of a woodland bird known to ornithologists as Cetti's Warbler. I have checked and rechecked Turner's theory on field recordings and I find it, at once, valid and immensely valuable.

The warbler, named by an Italian Jesuit, Francesco Cetti, is small, brown and hard to pin down, a skulking bird. 'A reddish tint to its brownish plumage pushes it over the boundary from dullness into subtle beauty, but you will be lucky to appreciate this: the warbler hides itself in dense vegetation and . . . is more often heard than seen,' writes Turner. Breeding in central and south Europe, the warbler has a loud, sudden, not very pretty song. One heavy note, three light, one heavy, one light. Turner taps it out as: 'What? So why are You here?' Cetti's Warbler is a mocking bird. 'It is immensely fond of teasing birdwatchers, by quickly rattling off its machinegun-like song, scampering off somewhere else while birders try to locate the sound and then repeating the same discombobulating trick from a discreet distance.' In some ways, just like the second Beethoven symphony: fluttering to deceive.

Beethoven does not insert birdsong by chance. He lives in what Germans call the Age of Goethe, a time of romantic speculation about natural phenomena. Johann Wolfgang von Goethe floats theories about the metamorphosis of plants and the taxonomy of animals in a search for 'what sustains the world at its inmost point'. Goethe proposes 'a natural law' to explain life on earth. He rejects Isaac Newton's theory of colours, claiming that artists understand the universe better than scientists. 'Sciences as a whole,' argues Goethe, 'remove themselves more and more from life and return to it only via detours.' Goethe is a science sceptic.

Beethoven is monumentally aware of Goethe's writings: he owns the complete works and keeps them close to hand. His warbler in the second symphony signals that he knows what Goethe's up to and is prepared to take issue with wilful denials of empirical fact. 'Goethe should not write any more,' he protests at one point. 'It is the same with him as with singers' – in other words, Goethe does not know when to quit. The second symphony is part of this conversation. Beethoven is living in the heart of nature, capturing tweets while he still has the hearing to do so. He is also, page by page, breaking expectations with the longest introductory passage ever heard.

Recordings of the second symphony betray multiple confusions. Herbert von Karajan gives a vastly proficient account with the Berlin Philharmonic in 1977, horns and winds gleaming in the artificial sunlight of an urban hall. Bernard Haitink manages more warmth but no greater resolution in London's subterranean Barbican Centre, where no bird ever hovers, bar pigeons. Paavo Järvi, with a smaller German ensemble (2011), achieves a fleeting serenity.

It takes an off-message maestro to bring the work to life. The English pharmaceutical heir Sir Thomas Beecham liked to disparage Beethoven, calling the seventh symphony 'a lot of yaks jumping about' and advocating that the late quartets 'should only be listened to by a deaf man'. In the second symphony, however, recorded with the Royal Philharmonic Orchestra in 1957, Beecham infuses Mozart levity into a featherlight, fun-packed grouse hunt through the Vienna Woods. Untroubled by theory, Beecham is a messenger of pleasure. If you find Beethoven solemn or deterrent, this is his smiley face.

I know only one recording of comparable élan. It is by Roger Norrington with the London Classical Players, recorded in 1986. The son of an Oxford vice-chancellor, Norrington was pushing thirty before he quit academia to enrol at music college. Mingling with 'people who knew a huge amount about early instruments' he tried to produce Beethoven's music at a pitch and speed the composer might recognise. In the second symphony, he pins wings to the wall like a small boy with a lepidoptery manual, alternating like Goethe and Beethoven between transgression and transcendence. Some of the detail may be contentious but the whole is magically cohesive. On the periphery of professional recording I also like a dappled, richly detailed 2014 Philadelphia disc by Ignat Solzhenitsyn, son of the *Cancer Ward* novelist.

10

Holy fool

Symphony No. 8, Op. 93 (1812)

OF THE NINE BEETHOVEN SYMPHONIES, THE SECOND AND THE eighth are least performed. The second bewilders while the eighth regresses. Beethoven is looking back in a flush of indulgence, perhaps nostalgia.

So why am I drawn to the eighth? Because it's deceptive. This is not symphony-lite or Barbra Streisand in *The Way We Were*. Beethoven calls the eighth 'my little symphony in F', a nod to the Pastoral Symphony which is in the same key. He is still pushing out symphonic form, just not quite as far as usual.

Beethoven is having a bad time, a summer of pain, shortages, loneliness and heartbreak. Napoleon is charging into Russia, inflation has made the currency worthless and the rich have fled to their country estates where a composer cannot tap them for commissions. Beethoven fears a French victory. His music is the product of German civilisation and he's not about to change tune. Each day brings renewed fear and discomfort.

July 1812 is insufferably hot. The doctor recommends a spa cure. He books in at Teplice, in the Bohemian woods, fashionable and beyond his budget. He arrives on 5 July and writes three anguished letters to an Immortal Beloved. These are the only love letters where Beethoven uses the intimate pronoun 'du', so it must be serious. Many books claim to identify his Beloved. The likeliest candidates are Antonie Brentano, who is married, and Josefine Brunsvik, who is separated from her husband. We will meet them in a while. They play no part in the genesis of this symphony.

After twelve days in Teplice Beethoven is miserable and bored. 'I live alone! Alone! Alone!' he cries. On 17 July, Goethe arrives. He and Beethoven have long talked of getting together. Beethoven has composed

Goethe poems. Goethe is keen to discuss an opera. Both men are fighting to save German culture from French imperialism. If ever there is a meeting of minds, this ought to be it.

Goethe comes knocking on Beethoven's door and they go for a walk in the woods in pouring rain. Next day, they take a trip to a spa in Bilin. Two days on they dine together and Beethoven plays the piano, 'delightfully'. They see each other every day for ten days, after which Beethoven leaves for Karlsbad. Goethe follows, aiming to persuade the composer to make an opera out of *Faust*.

But nothing happens: there are too many differences. Goethe is the perfect civil servant, dressed in silks and velvet, powdered and perfumed. Beethoven is dressed like a tramp and has holes in his shoes. 'His talent amazed me,' writes Goethe. 'Unfortunately, he's an utterly untamed personality who while not altogether wrong in finding the world detestable, does not make it more enjoyable for himself or others. He is . . . much to be pitied as his hearing is leaving him.'

They meet twice more in Karlsbad. Beethoven softens, deciding Goethe is not clapped-out after all. 'What patience the great man had with me!' he recalls. 'How happy it all made me at the time. I would have died for him ten times over! . . . Since that summer . . . I read Goethe every day.'

But nothing comes of their creative flirtation and tongues start wagging. Spa-goers foment rumours of a furious row. Before long, this rift is taught as fact. Here's the legend, still widely believed:

Beethoven and Goethe, out walking one day, see the Emperor Francis and his entourage coming towards them. Goethe doffs his hat and bows. Beethoven, head high, strides ahead. When the Emperor is out of earshot, he scolds Goethe for his obsequiousness, telling him an artist must never defer to power. Goethe walks off without another word. This mythical encounter is so pervasive that a painting of it by Carl Röhling hangs in many German sitting-rooms as a mark of household culture; thousands are retrieved by Allied soldiers from 1945 rubble. Soon, fresh reprints go up on family walls. The Beethoven-Goethe axis is rooted too deep in German identity to be destabilised by historical fact. Germans need to believe that art will surmount might, even when modern history demonstrates the opposite. They yearn for Goethe to be more like Beethoven, better than he really was.

Beethoven's only reward from the summer of 1812 is the eighth symphony, its mood and rhythms taken from Czech dances seen in Teplice squares and bars. The opening movement is more like a finale, boisterous and bombastic. The second section makes tick-tock mockery of new-fangled metronomes, maybe also a wind-up of Haydn's Clock Symphony. The third movement dances a courtly minuet; the finale toys with five optional endings. Beethoven is being a tease. Yet his heartache gets worse each day as the postman brings no letters. He has lost again in love. At the symphony's premiere in February 1814 his conducting is so wayward the concertmaster has to take over the beat.

The symphony remains forever a misfit, too long for the first half of a concert and too short for the second. Conductors often play it as curtain-raiser to the ninth symphony. The earliest recording by Otto Klemperer (Berlin, 1924) trundles along for a lugubrious twenty-six minutes. 'Historically-informed' conductors John Eliot Gardiner and Frans Brüggen clip that to twenty-three. Wilhelm Furtwängler pursues a Haydn-like tiptoe airiness; a Vienna Philharmonic concert at the 1954 Salzburg Festival, months before he died, is a twinkle-eyed invitation to the dance. Other superb accounts include Toscanini (1939), Erich Leinsdorf (1969), Bruno Walter, Andris Nelsons and Simon Rattle. Myself, I cherish Klaus Tennstedt.

Rings no bells? Tennstedt rose from nowhere in 1975 and was finished by 1990. A teenaged concertmaster in Halle after the war, his playing was terminated by a growth on his hand. The Communists sent him to conduct in seaside towns along the Baltic coast, but he kept riling the regime until Party chief Erich Honecker was persuaded by his pet conductor Kurt Masur to let Tennstedt leave. In West Germany, he carried on conducting along the seaboard until a Canadian manager heard him in Kiel and booked him for Toronto. After a Boston concert of Bruckner's eighth symphony, the *Globe*'s headline read: 'Tennstedt – BSO – Once in a Lifetime'. In Philadelphia, he reduced musicians to tears with the pathos of his Beethoven. Chicago, Minnesota, New York all fell to his spell. His 1983 *Fidelio* is one of the Metropolitan Opera's historic triumphs.

Unable to believe his reception by America's greatest orchestras, Tennstedt suffered a mental breakdown. Back home in Kiel, he found empathy in Gustav Mahler's symphonies, which he began performing with the London Philharmonic to an ecstatic response. But he was always on the brink of calamity. Managers watched him walk onto the stage, terrified that he would trip on a shoelace and break his neck. His capacity for self-harm was ever-present. He drank, smoked and pursued women. 'If I cannot make love, I cannot conduct,' he told one lover. Cancer struck. He laid down his baton at sixty-seven and died, in 1998, aged seventy-two.

His Beethoven Eighth of 1975 with the Boston Symphony Orchestra is an act of inexplicable elucidation by a non-analytical interpreter – bombastic at first, light-footed on the dance floor and peppered throughout with questions, fears and inspirations. It is Beethoven to the life: a look back without rancour and forward, full of curiosity. Tennstedt, whom I knew quite well, was what the Russians call a 'holy fool' – wild in gesture, eruptive in his frustrations, loveable in his naked vulnerability. I know of no truer guide to this symphony.

11

Berlin calling

Cello Sonatas Nos. 1 and 2, Op. 5 (1795)

BEETHOVEN'S ONLY CONCERT TOUR RUNS FROM FEBRUARY TO July 1796, visiting Prague, Dresden, Leipzig and Berlin. Not yet committed to Vienna, he wants to test other waters. In Berlin he is brought before King Friedrich Wilhelm II, a keen cellist with two virtuosos at his court, the French brothers Jean-Pierre and Jean-Louis Duport. The younger Duport has been praised by the philosopher Voltaire: 'Sir, you will make me believe in miracles, for I see that you can turn an ox into a nightingale.' Napoleon, trying his hand at Louis' Stradivarius cello, leaves an irreparable dent in the woodwork.

Beethoven writes two sonatas for Louis, with himself at the piano. He takes three long minutes to get the measure of the cello and the temperature of the room, but his first melody is so rich it spins off almost twenty variations. The second sonata throws Louis a slow theme, so slow it makes his shoulder ache. The Prussian King gives Beethoven a gold snuffbox filled with coins – 'no ordinary snuffbox, the kind of thing he might give to an ambassador' – but Berlin is a garrison town with a militant court and Beethoven is not tempted. He leaves with a new skill, knowing how to write for cello.

Pablo Casals sets the bar high on record. A Catalan exile from Spanish fascism, he acquires unequalled authority in Bach. He is less comfortable with Beethoven. His 1939 set with Mieczyslaw Horszowski is full of energy and yearning. In 1951 with Rudolf Serkin, Casals emits grunts of satisfaction at his own angelic geniality. A decade on with the German Wilhelm Kempff, he's mischievous. The glory of Casals is that he is so many cellists in one.

Mstislav Rostropovich performs on the same instrument that Louis Duport played with Beethoven. In a filmed YouTube recording with

Sviatoslav Richter as partner, the risks they take alarm the poor page-turner so badly he hardly knows when to turn. Jacqueline du Pré and Daniel Barenboim lack spark in these works. A 1990 Brussels recording by the Russian exile Mischa Maisky with the Argentine wanderer Martha Argerich sounds like a morning-after hotel breakfast, desultory but deeply affectionate.

12

God's beloved

**Variations in F major on Mozart's 'Se vuol ballare'
for Violin and Piano, WoO40; Variations in C
major on 'Là ci darem la mano' by W. A. Mozart
for 2 Oboes and Cor anglais, WoO28 (1792–3)**

THE STORY GOES THAT BEETHOVEN, SIXTEEN YEARS OLD ON HIS
first Vienna trip, knocks at Mozart's door, sits at the piano and plays his C
minor concerto from memory. Mozart tells his wife, 'watch out for that
boy, one day he'll give the world something to talk about.'

This story is told by the composer Johann Nepomuk Hummel, Mozart's
pupil:

> All of a sudden, the master turns directly to me whom Beethoven had
> completely overlooked. 'Nepomukl, wouldn't you like to play the young
> gentleman from Bonn a few variations extempore? I want to show Ludwig
> how singing and rounded piano playing can be . . . You will immediately
> hear the difference . . . You know my 'Figaro'. How about 'Se vuol ballare'?
> And Master Mozart seats himself on the piano bench, pushes Ludwig to
> the side and quietly plays the Se vuol ballare theme. In F major, with pedal,
> delicately staccato, like a pizzicato, almost like a harp.

Sadly, this is fiction. Letters show that Mozart is out of town in February
1787 when Beethoven comes calling. Still, one remark rings true:

> Mozart advises the departing Ludwig to adopt the variation . . . and to
> practise it constantly, improvising on the piano: 'The variatio sets all our
> imagination free; the simpler the material, the better. The variatio leaves
> us much freedom and at the same time constrains us within a tight cage.

Remember that! I think he'll sometime achieve in the world great things in the variation.'

Beethoven, we know, is squeamish about variations. But in November 1792 in Vienna's eleventh month of mourning for Mozart, he riffs off two sets on famous arias. 'Se vuol ballare' from *Marriage of Figaro* uses the violin as a plucked instrument; there is a jolly recording by Yehudi Menuhin and Wilhelm Kempff (1970). 'La ci darem' from *Don Giovanni* is set for various instruments. Among many recordings, Sabine Meyer, her brother and a friend play a version for two clarinets and a basset horn. François Leleux prefers oboe, clarinet and bassoon. Both are colourful and amusing.

Beethoven pays a few more dues to the man he never met. His first piano sonata harks back to Mozart's 14th (K457). The Eroica symphony opens with a snatch of Mozart's opera *Bastien et Bastienne*. The third movement of the fifth symphony starts with the same eight notes as Mozart's finale for the 40th symphony. Beethoven references Mozart without resentment or homage. He has no need to erase Mozart from his system.

The cerebral American pianist Charles Rosen makes a provocative case that Mozart is actually the more advanced composer of the two, more relevant to our times. 'Mozart's chromaticism is greater than Beethoven's,' Rosen argues. 'What Beethoven takes from Mozart is what I call chromatic saturation, where you play all the notes of the chromatic scale in some way or another (in the same phrase). You get it in Mozart's G minor symphony and in Beethoven's opus 111. This runs through the nineteenth century and reaches its peak in Arnold Schoenberg.'

Schoenberg's signature twelve-note row is heard first in the statue scene of *Don Giovanni*. That makes Mozart, in Rosen's eyes, a midwife to modernism and therefore more far-sighted than Beethoven. Rosen is, of course, completely wrong-headed. Mozart writes within the conventions of his time, where Beethoven has one foot way outside of them. Mozart is concerned with the here-and-now, Beethoven with the great beyond. Mozart's fantasy is limitless. With Beethoven the fascination is not so much what he does as where he is going. For a brief young moment, Mozart is possibly the composer Beethoven wants to be. The moment passes.

13

Master pieces

**Variations in F major on 'Ein Mädchen oder Weibchen'
from Mozart's *Die Zauberflöte*, Op. 66; Variations
in E flat major on 'Bei Männern, welche Liebe
fühlen' from *Die Zauberflöte*, WoO46; Variations in
G major on 'See the conqu'ring hero comes' from
Handel's *Judas Maccabaeus*, WoO45 (1796–8)**

'OF ALL COMPOSERS, BEETHOVEN THOUGHT MOST HIGHLY OF
Mozart and Handel, and then Seb. Bach,' writes his student Ferdinand
Ries. 'If I found him with music in his hand or if anything lay open on his
desk it was sure to be a composition by one of these heroes.'

Still riding a Mozart wave, Beethoven leaves the King of Prussia a pair
of *Magic Flute* variations. This is top-class hackery, delightfully recorded
by Casals and Serkin (1951) and Maisky and Argerich (1993).

The Handel riffs run deeper. In Berlin, Beethoven is exposed to
Handel's 1746 oratorio, *Judas Maccabaeus*, a celebration of the Hanoverian-
German dynasty's victory over the Scottish Stuarts for possession of the
English throne. Beethoven is overwhelmed. 'He is the greatest composer
that ever lived,' he cries. 'I would uncover my head and kneel before his
tomb.' Elsewhere he advises: 'Go and learn from [Handel] how to achieve
vast effects with simple means.' Handel, an unruly bachelor with manic-
depressive tendencies, is the predecessor who arouses the closest
empathy.

He draws twelve sumptuous variations for cello and piano from the
signature aria in *Judas Maccabaeus*. The eleventh is by some stretch the
longest of the set, as if Beethoven cannot bear to draw a double line. He
revisits Handel while preparing Missa Solemnis and the ninth symphony,
telling an English visitor, Edward Schultz: 'Handel is the greatest, the

ablest composer that ever lived'. Dying, Beethoven reads a new Handel edition, saying, 'I can still learn from him'.

There are many recordings of the Judas variations – playful from Gregor Piatigorsky and Lukas Foss, affectionate from cellist Adrian Brendel's saunter with his father Alfred, cross-cultural from the Frenchman Pierre Fournier and Austrian Friedrich Gulda. For me, Maisky and Argerich nail it.

14

With chips

Variations in C major on 'God save the King' for Piano, WoO78; Variations in D major on 'Rule Britannia' for Piano, WoO79 (1803); Variations in B flat major on 'La stessa, la stessissima' by Antonio Salieri, WoO73 (1800); Variations on themes by Giovanni Paisiello, WoO69–70 (1795)

MUCH AS HE SCORNS VARIATIONS, ONCE STARTED HE CANNOT stop. The English anthem comes somehow to his attention. Is Beethoven a secret Anglophile? Does he drown his schnitzel in brown sauce and drink his beer warm? Is he a cricket fan, a racing man, a rubber of church brasses? Not so far as we know. Shown these variations late in life he gives a deep sigh and says 'Oh, Beethoven, what an ass you were in those days.' But they are neither asinine nor isolated.

'God Save the King' is already a composer magnet. Johann Christian Bach has inserted it in a 1763 harpsichord concerto; Bach's biographer Johann Nikolaus Forkel writes variations in 1791. Hummel, Rossini, Paganini, Liszt, Reger, Charles Ives and Jimi Hendrix will all have a go. Even the Frenchman Claude Debussy is tempted. Beethoven, having twirled seven variations, sends his set to an Edinburgh publisher, George Thomson, and licenses a London edition to the composer-publisher Muzio Clementi, who promptly composes a set of his own.

On record, Alfred Brendel, an Austrian in London, courts irony. The Canadian Angela Hewitt is respectfully reticent. Two French pianists, Cécile Ousset and Anne Quéffelec, dip a royal curtsey. The Englishman John Ogdon finds exquisite tenderness in the third and fourth variations.

Rule Britannia yields less than five minutes of Beethoven variations, but he reuses the tune in the second movement of his 24th piano sonata, opus 78. In the fourth variation, the Dutch fortepianist Ronald Brautigam discovers anticipations of a future Chopin march.

Beethoven is in the zone. Everyone knows what the court composer Antonio Salieri did to poor Mozart. To be safe, Beethoven pays him homage with variations on a theme from his opera *Falstaff*, for which Salieri is effusively grateful. Brendel, Ogdon and Brautigam play these baubles well; the Bulgarian Plamena Mangova knocks them out of the park. Another Italian composer, Giovanni Paisiello, has two or three new operas on the Vienna stage every year, ninety-four altogether. Beethoven duly delivers. He can't stop writing variations. He's like a millennial kid playing spaced-out computer games, losing his way back to base.

≀

The condition known as obsessive-compulsive disorder is identified in the late nineteenth century by Pierre Janet and Sigmund Freud. OCD takes many forms. The most recognisable is repetitive activity, such as hand-washing, checking door locks and performing complex actions in unvarying order. People with OCD scrub their skin raw, whisper prayer words under their breath and get up several times a night to make sure the cooker is off. Beethoven exhibits some symptoms of OCD in his variations phase. An English music critic, Ernest Newman, remarks upon an 'obsession bordering on the insane'. Newman is not alone in guessing a mental health issue, but is this the right one? There are counter-indications. OCD usually shows by the age of twenty and its most prominent symptoms are a fear of dirt and a love of order. Beethoven, in his twenties, is unwashed and chaotic. He is not obsessive-compulsive.

Others suggest Beethoven is autistic. The term 'autism' is first used in 1911 for a form of schizophrenia. In 1943 Leo Kanner in Baltimore isolates 'autistic disturbances' in children; the following year Hans Asperger in Vienna finds a correlation between high intellectual achievement and poor social interaction in school. A British psychiatrist, Michael Rutter, writes that 'the autistic child has a deficiency of fantasy'. The 1990s sees the acceptance of an autistic 'spectrum'.

Beethoven, atypical as he may be, does not fit a mainstream autistic diagnosis. His view of the world is never binary and, while his behaviour can be extreme, he always seems master of his situation and able to stand outside of it. Nevertheless, contemporaries consider him abnormal and the twentieth-century profession of psychiatry devotes many papers to his neuroses.

Carl Jung is constrained from composer analysis by a vow of faith: 'I believe in God, Mozart and Beethoven'. Jung exempts creative geniuses from general responsibility for their conduct: 'The biographies of great artists make it abundantly clear that the creative urge is often so imperious that it battens onto their humanity and yokes everything to the service of the work, even at the cost of ordinary health and human happiness. The unborn work in the psyche of the artist is a force of nature that achieves its end either with tyrannical might or with the subtle cunning of nature herself, quite regardless of the personal fate of the man who is its vehicle.'

Freudians concur with this license for artists to be irresponsible. The Austrian Kurt Eissler attributes the creative urge to an 'asocial element' in an artist's personality. Eissler, curator of the Sigmund Freud Archives, writes: 'What appeared as dissociality, rudeness, brutality, in Beethoven's everyday life was the cornerstone of his creativity. A mastered emotion would never have led to those musical compositions which we admire.' Eissler is telling us to look at what is odd in Beethoven in order to understand what makes him great. This direction has been seized upon by some Beethoven biographers to run riot with fantastical speculation about his imagined sexual predilections. Floodgates opened in the 1970s by Maynard Solomon have, however, long run dry. Beethoven and sex is a short story with an unsatisfying outcome.

Might he be bipolar? An American authority on manic depressive conditions, Kay Redfield Jamison, finds a high incidence of manic depression in composers and includes Beethoven in her studies. She is not the first. An 1884 study of genius and madness by a German clinician, Paul Radestock, identifies extreme mood swings in Beethoven as a symptom of mental imbalance. Like Handel, he goes from sunshine to storm, and back. He lacks, however, other defining symptoms. He eats heartily and sleeps well. He never spends a day in bed. His work rate is unaffected by setbacks. He contemplates suicide only once. Bipolarity has no effect on his music. 'Personal causes,' argues Jung, 'have as much or as little to do with a work of art as the soil with the plant that springs from it.' Whatever his internal fluctuations, Beethoven will always write as Beethoven.

The most perceptive assessment of his mental state can be found in an early Freudian study of his peripheral variations. Theodor Reik examines Beethoven's little piano piece 'Rage over a Lost Penny'. In this comic rondo a man is driven to uncontrollable fury by losing a small coin under a piece of furniture; he ends up, after much fuss and bother, helplessly laughing at himself. Reik writes: 'It emerges from violent impatience and expresses itself in the numerous variations of the initial theme, making fun of the composer's unreasonableness.' The subject and object of this rondo are, in Reik's view, Beethoven himself.

Reik, author of an important study of Mahler's second symphony, characterises Beethoven as 'one of the clumsiest human beings . . . That master of rhythm could never learn to dance . . . how he ever learned to shave himself was hard to understand, even if one takes no account of the frequent cuts on his cheeks . . . Beethoven rarely took anything into his hands without letting it fall or breaking it. No piece of furniture was safe in his presence. He often dropped the ink bottle into the piano. He washed his hands in such a way that the whole floor was awash with water that leaked through the ceiling to the apartment below'.

Beethoven, says Reik, could not manage his temper: 'as a matter of fact, one cannot even say he lost control because he had almost none.' Reik breaks down the 'Rage over a Lost Penny' into two parts, one being the outburst itself and the other being Beethoven standing outside of it, mocking his own actions with a detachment that is not only certifiably sane but which shows an unusually high degree of self-awareness. Normal or not, he is certifiably stable.

I am not looking for a definitive diagnosis. Dr Amir Mandel, Tel Aviv psychiatrist and chief music critic of *Haaretz*, warns me that 'history-based, document-based, diagnoses are always surrounded by a significant cloud of doubt.' Mandel finds that Beethoven suffers from 'trust issues and poor social adjustment', arising from a miserable childhood. It may be – and this is my take – that the pattern-making activity of composing variations offers a defence against abuse by the external world during a time of personal fragility.

Beethoven's variations fix fades as suddenly as it started. From 1806, he writes no variations until, near the end of life, he produces out of nowhere the Diabelli Variations, the most cerebral and challenging exemplar of the form since Bach's unsurpassable Goldberg Variations. That's Beethoven: always unexpected.

15

Basket of deplorables

'Rage over a Lost Penny', Op. 129 (1795)

NOT EVERY BEETHOVEN WORK IS IMMORTAL. WHAT BECOMES of the rest? Record labels like to box up all of Beethoven in coffin-like sets. Artists take a different view. Here is Alfred Brendel introducing his Vox-Turnabout 'complete' edition:

> This first recording of Beethoven's piano works, which I made for Vox-Turnabout between 1958 and 1964, is not entirely complete. There seemed to me little virtue in rescuing from oblivion works that are totally devoid of any touch of Beethoven's mastery and originality. It was without regret, therefore, that I omitted pieces like the deplorable Haibel Variations, which could have been written by any of Beethoven's contemporaries, as well as certain student exercises, Albumblätter, studies, sketches and curiosities, most of which were never intended for publication – pieces, that is, which are merely of interest to the historian. These include the total output of the Bonn period (among which are the Variations on a March by Dressler by the twelve-year-old Beethoven and the two preludes through all the major keys, curiously published later on as opus 39), the Easy Sonata in C major WoO51, the Variations on the 'Menuet à la Vigano' by Haibel which I have already mentioned, the pieces WoO52, 53, 55 (the Prelude in the style of Bach), 56, 61 and 61a, as well as the little dance movements WoO81–86, of which I retained only the Six Écossaises, WoO83, although in all likelihood these are transcriptions of an orchestral score, and the single extant copy, passed down by Nottebohm, may well be dubious in some of its detail . . .

But, as Reik shows, even marginal Beethoven can be monumental. 'Rage over a Lost Penny' turns up as a scrap in a sale of Beethoven's house effects in November 1827. The publisher Anton Diabelli, dating it to the 1790s, gives it a colourful title and nets a fortune.

The manuscript is headed by the words '*Alla ingharese, quasi un capriccio*' – a kind of capriccio in Hungarian style. The composer Robert Schumann describes 'an agreeable, harmless anger, like when one pulls a shoe off one foot and sweats and stamps about while the shoe stares phlegmatically back'.

Pianists who record it include Schnabel, Kempff and the fastidious Brendel. The US-Chinese pianist Yuja Wang videoed her performance at ten years old. Alice Sara Ott is leisurely and elegant. Evgeny Kissin speeds up. Sir Clifford Curzon is serene and decorous. Eugen D'Albert, a crusty German composer, tosses it off in a 1918 studio as if it's something really nasty that got stuck to his shoe.

16

Slava

Cello Sonata No. 3 in A major, Op. 69 (1808)

THE THIRD SONATA IS PURE PLEASURE. WE CANNOT ALWAYS BE sure if Beethoven loves the cello, but here he is besotted. The music is warm, hummable and evenly shared between cello and piano. A major is Beethoven's happy mood and the glorious melody tells us he is in peak form, writing in the year of his fifth and sixth symphonies. The work is top heavy, almost half the material jammed into the opening movement. It is premiered by Nikolaus Kraft, a Duport pupil, together with one of Beethoven's piano students, Dorothea von Ertmann.

Four recordings predominate. Pierre Fournier, a French general's son who switched from piano to cello after suffering polio, recorded this sonata with Artur Schnabel. Fournier was a German collaborator, Schnabel a Nazi exile; the tension is palpable. The American Lynn Harrell has a bearish half-hour in 1987 with the Russian Vladimir Ashkenazy; and the Maisky–Argerich pairing (1994) is peerless. But the transcendent duo, filmed at the 1964 Edinburgh Festival, are the Soviet emissaries Mstislav ('Slava') Rostropovich and Sviatoslav Richter.

The liberties they take are limitless, the fantasy unbounded. At one point, around eight minutes, they wink at 'Baa, baa, black sheep'. Richter gives Rostropovich a smirk, knowing that Slava (meaning 'glory') is all too easily bored. Both musicians are larger than life and neither shrinks from risk.

Raised in Azerbaijan, Rostropovich's Polish and Jewish lineage gave him a multifarious exoticism. He won an all-Soviet competition in his teens, playing piano as well as cello. Meeting Prokofiev and Shostakovich gave him a hunger for new music. Short and stout, he wooed and wed the Bolshoi's prime soprano Galina Ustvolskaya. To secure limited freedoms and luxuries, he bribed commissars with branded whisky from his tours abroad. Blessed with an irresistible giggle, Slava was a happy hedonist in the Soviet bunker. 'For us,' he said, 'music was the only window onto the sun, oxygen and life. For that reason, we loved music even more than anyone in the West.'

In 1974 he got thrown out of the country for giving shelter to the banned novelist Aleksandr Solzhenitsyn. His passport confiscated, his identity compromised, he was given shelter in their London home by impresarios Victor and Lilian Hochhauser until Washington, DC hired him as music director. Although conducting was the least of his talents and his English was non-existent, he got by on force of personality, enthusiasm and an abundant generosity. Incurably insecure, he bought homes in Paris, London, everywhere. After a London concert he would go home to Maida Vale, drop to his knees and scrub the kitchen floor – staying grounded, he called it. The first time we met for a formal interview in a windowless cell at London's Barbican Centre, Slava plonked a magnum of Veuve Clicquot on the table and cried, 'Nobody leaves room until bottle is empty.' At his sixtieth birthday in Washington, Nancy Reagan jumped up to conduct the orchestra in 'Happy Birthday'. During the 1991 coup attempt against Mikhail Gorbachev, he was pictured holding his bodyguard's rifle while the beardless lad grabbed a few minutes' sleep on his shoulder. His concern for others was awe inspiring.

Where Slava radiated bonhomie, Richter was severity incarnate, immersed in the act of performance. Beneath that outer shell, he was impulsive, improvisatory, unpredictable, a challenge to all who had dealings with him. One summer's night after a recital in Paris, he vanished. His KGB minders turned ashen, anticipating disciplinary action in the Lubyanka cells. Victor Hochhauser, fearing his artist might come to harm, went searching for him in the boy bars of Pigalle, without success. Walking down a boulevard at two in the morning, he heard the sound of four hands at a piano through a fourth-floor window. After puffing his way up the stairs, he knocked at the door. It was opened by Julius Katchen, an American pianist. Richter had heard Katchen playing from the street below and just walked in, happy to while away the night with a like-minded artist, and to hell with the consequences.

Rostropovich and Richter playing Beethoven together are ice and fire, black and white, not a shade of compromise, nothing like it on record.

17

Fat man

Violin Sonatas Nos. 1–3, Op. 12 (1798–9); 'Schuppanzigh ist ein Lump', WoO100 (1801), Falstafferl, WoO184 (1816)

ART IS CRUEL TO THE OVERWEIGHT. SHAKESPEARE AND VERDI mock Sir John Falstaff for his gluttony, Richard Strauss depicts Baron Ochs as a corpulent bum. Walter Scott uses Friar Tuck as a butt of *Ivanhoe* jokes, while the Fat Controller in *Thomas the Tank Engine* inculcates in infants an image of anti-obesity. Put a fat man on stage and the public will laugh, put one on a football pitch and they will roar.

Beethoven is mean to outsized men. He fat-shames a close friend in two caustic canons, needling him persistently, cuttingly, needlessly. Ignaz Schuppanzigh is the busiest violinist in Vienna, arguably the best. Six years younger than Beethoven, he was his first teacher on arrival from Bonn. Beethoven continues to consult him when composing violin sonatas and string quartets. At the premiere of his ninth symphony, Schuppanzigh is his concertmaster, 'a natural born and really energetic leader of the orchestra'. No musician makes himself more useful to Beethoven, is more willing and less complaining. None of which stops Beethoven from calling him 'a *Lump*, a fat sour-belly, the biggest donkey'. Why?

Envy, most likely. Schuppanzigh earns a secure living as Prince Lichnowsky's house violinist, later Prince Razumovsky's. He finds a nice girl to marry, a goldworker's daughter named Barbara Killitschky, and seems generally contented. Barbara's sister Josephine sings in *Fidelio*. The family are kind to Beethoven and he spits in their soup. (Details of the relationship are sketchy. The only study of Schuppanzigh is an unpublished doctoral thesis by a past chairman of the Vienna Philharmonic Orchestra.)

Schuppanzigh moves to St Petersburg when the French occupy Vienna.

Returning in 1823, he finds Beethoven writing his last string quartets and talks loosely of them 'writing a new string quartet together'. Beethoven hires him for a premiere, dumps him, books him again. Schuppanzigh outlives Beethoven by three years and is written out of music history. The *New Grove Dictionary of Music and Musicians* gives a wrong date of birth. There is no Schuppanzighstrasse in Vienna. Yet his practical influence on Beethoven is undisputed. He is present in every violin score from opus 12 on, and all we know of him, thanks to Beethoven, is that he was fat.

In these first sonatas Beethoven treats the violin and piano as equals. A quasi-martial opening leads to a maypole dance. The second sonata has a skippy jollity, the third a blaze of confidence. The *Allgemeine Musikalische Zeitung* of Leipzig berates it for 'contrariness and artificiality'.

Yehudi Menuhin, aged thirteen with sister Hephzibah at the piano, is too cute by half. With his brother-in-law Louis Kentner in 1955 he sounds detached. His 1970 recording with an ex-Nazi, Wilhelm Kempff, wears distaste like a yellow star. Three Menuhin recordings, and none quite works.

Joseph Szigeti, with Claudio Arrau in 1944, is slick and quick, keen to get home to hear news of the D-Day landings. Jascha Heifetz crushes his pianists; a 1947 release with Emmanuel Bay shows him flawless, cold, metronomic. Itzhak Perlman (1977), with Vladimir Ashkenazy, is Heifetz with central heating. Gidon Kremer and Martha Argerich (1984) are gin and tonic, chilled at 6 p.m. Anne-Sophie Mutter (1998) dominates Lambert Orkis. The Soviets get it right – David Oistrakh with Richter and Leonid Kogan with Emil Gilels. Look no further.

18

Meet his maker

Piano Sonatas Nos. 1–3, Op. 2 (1795)

A VAST APARTMENT IN BUDAPEST IS FILLED WITH PIANOS, EACH gifted to Franz Liszt with a significant mechanical improvement by the manufacturers: Bösendorfer, Steinway, Erard, Pleyel and more. In Beethoven's life, there is no such rush to make a better mechanism. Beethoven calls the piano 'an unsatisfactory instrument'. By opus 10 he has outrun the capacity of all extant keyboards.

In Vienna he finds one that works. It is a copy by Gabriel Anton Walter of a prototype by Johann Andreas Stein of Augsburg, a craftsman and musician whom Beethoven met in Bonn. Stein was a master, Walter was not. Mozart swore by Walter pianos. Beethoven swore at them. In 1802 he ordered an Erard from Paris with an extra half-octave. Beethoven claims it is a gift from Sébastien Érard; in fact, he pays for it, in instalments. The Erard is furnished with an extra pedal, giving him improved volume and colour control. At the start of the Moonlight Sonata he writes 'always with pedal'.

His next piano, in 1811, is a Fritz, made in Vienna and not very good. So he orders another from Nannette Streicher, daughter of the Augsburg Stein. Nannette, a year older than Beethoven, is married to Andreas Streicher, a composer and dreamer, a friend of the poet Schiller. Streicher stays in the workshop while Nannette runs the business. When Beethoven buys her piano, Nannette becomes an intimate friend, the subject of much gossip. She is seen going in and out of his house at all hours, unbefitting for a married woman. She advises him on domestic affairs. If his house-keeper quits, she hires another. 'The day before yesterday,' he informs her, 'my splendid servants took three hours, from seven until ten in the evening, to get a fire going in the stove. The bitter cold . . . gave me a bad chill and I could hardly move a limb all day . . . If by chance you are back home today do come to me quickly.'

In January 1818 he sends Nannette his accounts for checking. 'The book alone will not give a satisfactory account of all things,' he writes, 'you should pop in unexpectedly now and then during mealtimes to see how we are getting along . . . Miss Nany [a maid] is much changed since I threw a few books at her head. Maybe something penetrated her brain, or her evil heart, the full-bosomed swindler.'

Around sixty letters survive. Nannette, touched by his loneliness, is proud to be of value to so historic and helpless a man. Acquaintances comment on her strength and capability. 'Everyone who laid eyes on this cheerfully open woman was impressed by her somewhat harsh, sharply angular but expressive features, her intelligent yet well-meaning demeanour and her lively, almost manly way of being and speaking,' writes a family friend. A portrait, by Ludwig Krones, shows her in profile, a white bonnet over her dark hair, thin lips pressed close together, giving nothing away. She is wife, mother, craftswoman and successful businesswoman. Hers is the hard head that Beethoven needs.

'Nannette Streicher, née Stein', is listed as sole owner of the piano business. The composer J. F. Reichardt remarks that 'Streicher has abandoned the softness, light action and repercussive rolling of other Viennese instruments and, following Beethoven's advice and wishes, gives his instruments greater resistance and elasticity so that the virtuoso . . . is more able to control the instrument, halting and carrying phrases, and in the finest of touches and deductions . . . To every virtuoso who seeks more than just the light and bright way of playing, his instruments are the most satisfying. All of his work is of rare quality, elegance and longevity.' King George IV of England plays a Streicher piano.

The Streicher factory at Ungargasse 375 contains a 300-seat recital hall. It is here that the *Gesellschaft der Musikfreunde*, the city's concert organisation, is brought into being. Nannette plays Sunday-morning recitals with her daughter, Sophie. A bust of Beethoven dominates the entrance. The workshop and concert hall remain in existence until 1959, when developers tear down the building.

If Beethoven is good for her business, Nannette is his life support. 'In the past night I often thought of my death,' he tells her in 1818, 'but these thoughts are no less common in daytime . . . You won't forget to talk to me about the linen, will you?' He acts with her like a motherless child. If there is physical contact between them her hands, calloused from carpentry, are uninviting. There is no talk of love in their letters, nor would sex be possible in servant-filled houses. Nannette is Beethoven's chamberlain, his voice of reason and crisis resolver. There is no equivalent relationship in the whole of music between creator and maker, artist and artisan. Nannette Streicher, a daily visitor, is among the last to see him alive.

Beethoven, however, has eyes for other pianos. Although he 'always specially favours' a Streicher, he accepts a gift in 1817 from Thomas Broadwood of an English piano with six extra bass keys that he works into his Hammerklavier Sonata. Hearing that Nannette has been studying the Hammerklavier for three months and is still stuck on the beginning, he makes a caustic remark. Months before his death he solicits a last piano on loan from the Viennese maker, Conrad Graf.

His first batch of sonatas is dedicated, finally, to Haydn. The first two follow the Haydn-Mozart trail. The third, twenty-five minutes long, is Beethoven himself.

On record the Canadian Glenn Gould is brittle in the first sonata, with variable speeds and a bizarre atmosphere. Sviatoslav Richter is self-contained. The Hungarian Annie Fischer finds compassion in the slow movement and macabre humour in the finale. Mikhail Pletnev is determinedly different in the second sonata, awkward and offputting. Claudio Arrau, in a 1964 Amsterdam recital, takes the pace of a lame snail. Lev Oborin, locked away by Stalin after winning the 1927 Chopin Competition, gets to record this sonata when he is fifty, achieving an existential solitude of stunning beauty.

Two Italians grab the third sonata. Arturo Benedetti Michelangeli, a stale-air fiend who cancels concerts at the sight of an open window, teases, taunts and tangles themes to a point where, at the end of the first movement, they are irresoluble. Then, by magic, he unravels the knot. There are ten Michelangeli recordings; take the one dated 1965. Maurizio Pollini, his sometime pupil, goes the opposite way, seeking simplicity at superhuman speeds. Pollini can be overly serious in Beethoven. In this sonata in 2007, he is borderline frivolous.

19

Irish eyes

Piano Sonatas Nos. 5–7, Op. 10 (1795–8); 3 Marches, Op. 48 (1802); Variations on a Russian Dance, WoO71 (1797)

THE PERSON PAYING FOR THIS SET IS COUNTESS ANNA Margarete von Browne, wife of an Irish brigadier in the Russian army (yes, you read that right). Mrs Browne, known as Annette, is descended from Catherine the Great's conqueror of two Baltic states, titled the King of Livonia. Serf labour on her family estates buys her all she could possibly want in Vienna.

Her Irish husband, Count Johann Georg von Browne-Camus, is head of intelligence at the Russian Embassy, a superspy. A man of 'dissipation and depravity', he orders music from Beethoven – the trios opus 9, followed by opus 22, 45 and 48. Browne is so thrilled to see his name on a music sheet that he sends Beethoven the gift of a horse, an accessory the composer fails to notice until he receives a bill for stabling, at which point he sells the beast. Annette Browne follows up with an order for three piano sonatas on her own account and some variations on Russian dances, which she plays quite well.

The family comes to a sad end. Annette dies mysteriously at thirty-four. The Count goes mad and is locked in an asylum. Their son dies on army duty. Beethoven is their sole legacy.

Annette's first sonata is written in the 'heroic' C minor key. The second, in F major, changes key several times. The third, in D, has a melting *largo e mesto* and a jokey finale. The Swiss pianist Edwin Fischer tells Daniel Barenboim that this is the acme of humour in music. Claudio Arrau calls it the depth of tragedy. 'For me,' concludes Barenboim, 'this remains the perfect example of the danger of choosing adjectives to explain the music. Music can only be explained through sound.'

Really? I run this thought past a number of people who make their living writing about music. Alex Ross of the *New Yorker* responds: 'A world in which we are obliged to remain utterly mute in the presence of music would be an impoverished one. Artful commentary can lead us toward music, and it can take us deeper into music. In the end, music and language exist in a state of eternal interdependence.' Professor Tim Page writes: 'The thought that music has no actual human meaning beside itself strikes me as over-simplified. As far as I'm concerned, Beethoven is full of humour and he is full of tragedy – and the Opus 10 sonatas contain much of both. Of course, we are still allowed to laugh at something other people find tragic (if we do it quietly).' Fiona Maddocks of the *Observer* says: 'Our response to music is entirely personal, no shoulds or oughts. But words are our tool. We are messengers, describing in as informed a way as we can muster, what we hear, what it was like to be there, why it matters.'

Anne Midgette, formerly of the *Washington Post*:

> Words can intensify our relationship to music and our reactions to it, and allow us to prolong the experience that we had when hearing it, and compare it to someone else's experience. Words are also able to open up various pathways into the music for those who are unfamiliar or uncertain or not used to trusting their own reactions (a not uncommon mindset among classical music audiences who have had it drummed into them over the years that they must sit in passive silence during a performance and that as laypeople they are not really qualified to 'understand' it). I would also argue that the fact that two people hear opposite things in the same piece of music is not a demonstration, as Barenboim seems to believe, of the inadequacy of words, but rather of the richness of experience.

Against these validations, many musicians persist in believing that they alone own the right to interpret the meaning of music. The American composer Virgil Thomson says: 'Verbal communication about music is impossible except among musicians.' Aaron Copland quips: 'If a literary man puts together two words about music, one of them will be wrong.' The Scottish analyst Donald Tovey takes against music criticism as 'one of the unlovelier forms of parasitism.' The violinist Patricia Kopatchinskaja's response to reviews is: 'the dog barks, the caravan moves on.' The pianist Igor Levit has likened critics to eunuchs. If any of these authorities is even halfway right, you should stop reading this text right now and listen to Levit or Kopatchinskaja play Beethoven (provided some writer has told you where to find it).

The need for objective commentary ought to be self-evident. Musicians are too close to the mechanics of music to see the whole machine. To leave analysis in their hands would be like giving priests a monopoly on the meaning of God. Musicians, in any case, cannot agree about the notes they play – Fischer and Arrau, two of the wisest, fall out over a fairly elementary sonata.

Music, like sport, requires a dimension of distance. Concertgoers see better what's going on than players on a stage. A critic's job is to convey the big picture. The composer writes the music, the performer plays it and the critic interprets that performance within the context and the moment that it is given, for the benefit of those who were and were not present. Each element is integral to the making of music. Without the third, the first two might pass unnoticed. 'Someone has to bring the news from Ghent to Aix,' says Maddocks.

The critic has more to add by way of humour, rancour and reproach. The English critic Neville Cardus, who spent his days watching cricket and his evenings at music, often took conductors to task for taking Beethoven too slow. When Sir Hamilton Harty objected to being reviewed by a stopwatch, Cardus replied: 'I must warn you, man to man, that if you conduct the Ninth Symphony again in the future, I shall bring with me – not for critical purposes, but for personal convenience – not a stopwatch but an alarm clock.'

Those who devote their lives to writing about music do so in order to shed light on the art, to extol its glories and expose abuses. From time to time, they raise the experience of listening to music above passive reception to a higher level of understanding, an ecstatic penetration that Arabs call 'tarab'. Most cultures accept that music cannot be transmitted without textual commentary. Even Daniel Barenboim has been known to write a book or two.

Criticism offers a definition of human difference. Neville Cardus, reviewing Vladimir Horowitz, explains what makes a great pianist:

What are the attributes of perfect piano-playing? (I use the word 'perfect' only as a convenient way of suggesting the finest qualities that a cultured mind can visualise.) A warm musical touch; melody that sings freely but does not weaken rhythm and harmony; rhythm that is spontaneous, and a source of delight in itself; harmony that is rich and attractively shaded, with the central note, or notes, illuminated. The whole interpretation balanced, and governed by sensibility: by the poet's power to ravish music, while leaving it proud and free.

You may agree or disagree, but criticism is the only means by which we can decide which, of thousands of Beethoven recordings, might reward an hour of our time and which are of lesser interest. In the opus 10 sonatas, I strongly advocate Annie Fischer's fury in opus 10/1, Boris Giltburg's restraint in opus 10/2, Barenboim's practicality in opus 10/3. In Countess Annette's Russian dances, Vladimir Ashkenazy has just the right nonchalance for the occasion.

20

Simple, isn't it?

Piano Sonatas Nos. 9 and 10, Op. 14 (1798–1800)

LACK OF PROGRESS IS SO RARE IN BEETHOVEN THAT IT'S A relief to find him, for once, marking time. The opus 14 sonatas are written for Baroness Josefine von Braun, wife of the Theater an der Wien manager whom Beethoven needs to impress if he ever wants to stage an opera. The sonatas are so uncomplicated you wonder if they weren't written for children. The ninth sonata opening calls to mind the Scottish dirge 'My Bonnie lies over the ocean', most expressively in the Sviatoslav Richter performance on YouTube.

Other pianists vary in their approach. Maurizio Pollini (2013) is a brain surgeon cracking a walnut. András Schiff (2006) starts playful but turns solemn. Murray Perahia (2008) is blood and thunder. Angela Hewitt helpfully points out that 'small hands will have difficulty with bars 17–20 and breaking the chords is musically not very satisfying . . . The notes aren't complicated, but their characterization is.' Hewitt has a way of suspending animation to allow reflection. She started out as a church choirmaster and knows how to breathe in a long span of notes, always an asset.

The tenth sonata harks back to halcyon Haydn: it's a sunny afternoon and there's a girl in a dirndl bringing a two-foot foaming glass of beer to a gasping composer. Richter (on YouTube) dissents: for him, it's more like a midnight flit from Siberia.

In the Holy Land, Barenboim protégé Saleem Abboud Ashkar, a Christian from Nazareth, outshines his mentor in the colours of his fantasy. Einav Yarden of Tel Aviv, a Leon Fleisher student, is persuasive but forgets to smile. The Lebanese Abdel Rahman El Bacha, who recorded all 32 sonatas on the Mirare label, is so fast he could licence this sonata to Peloton as a workout track.

On YouTube, Trudelies Leonhardt, sister of a Dutch early-music pioneer, delivers the most compelling Beethoven I ever heard on a period keyboard, deep-voiced and at once authoritative and amusing. The film is dated 2015. Trudelies Leonhardt, still alive in her nineties, is unkissed by fame.

21

Washed out

Piano Sonata No. 11 in B flat major, Op. 22 (1800)

HALF OF BEETHOVEN'S PRE-1800 WORKS ARE PIANO SONATAS, designed for home play. After supper, or in a Sunday afternoon glow, father or mother, bored son or daughter, sits at the parlour piano and fingers the latest Beethoven. He keeps it fairly simple, although this score shares a key and half an opening theme with his future Hammerklavier.

Beethoven is prouder of this sonata than anything he has done so far, adding that the work has 'washed itself', meaning that it has sold well and wipes off any residual Haydn influence. Instead, it looks forward to an age of thicker chords and romantic narratives. The second movement has strong anticipations of Chopin. In terms of academic categorisation, this sonata closes Beethoven's early period. He is washed out of amateur productions.

On record, my choices are the Austrian Badura-Skoda, the Hungarian Annie Fischer and the aggressively enigmatic Russian, Maria Grinberg.

22

The cyclist

Piano Sonata No. 31 in A flat major, Op. 110 (1821)

ON THE MORNING OF 21 JANUARY 1932 A TUBBY LITTLE MAN bustles into EMI's newly opened recording centre at number 3 Abbey Road and demands that the brand-new house piano in Studio 3 be replaced by a Bechstein, his brand. Once the fuss dies down and a suitable instrument is located, transported, installed and tuned, Artur Schnabel sits down and plays four minutes of Beethoven's penultimate sonata. It marks the start of a seven-year odyssey that will go where recording has never gone before.

Schnabel has long been dissatisfied with the way Beethoven sounds. His scores (now in the Library of Congress) are disfigured with page by page changes and annotations, a profusion of graffiti that he collates into a two-volume Schnabel edition of the Beethoven sonatas, published in 1935. He claims no absolute truth. Schnabel's Beethoven is exactly what it says, a personal approach. He searches for something above and beyond the composer's inscriptions. 'It is a mistake to imagine that all notes should be played with equal intensity or even be clearly audible,' he says. 'In order to clarify the *music* it is often necessary to make certain *notes* obscure.' In time, he will be memorialised in the *New York Times* by the critical pianist Harold Schonberg as 'the man who invented Beethoven'.

His odyssey begins in 1927 with a cycle of the 32 sonatas performed for the centenary of Beethoven's death to uncomprehending ovations in Berlin, London and New York. 'The public applaud,' he complains, 'even when it's good.' He is a master of acerbic put-downs. 'I know two types of audience,' he says. 'One coughs, the other doesn't.'

A prodigy from an eastern province, he is brought to Vienna aged six to study with Theodor Leschetizky, whose teacher was Carl Czerny,

Beethoven's pupil. 'You'll never be a pianist,' declares Leschetizky, 'you're a musician.' Johannes Brahms takes him for walks in the woods. Schnabel moves to Berlin and marries a contralto, Therese Behr.

Despite his diminutive stature – Therese is a foot taller – Schnabel is an arresting presence in a fashionable three-piece suit, with a cigar between his fingers or his jaws. His luxuriant moustache twitches humour and disdain. His speaking voice is deep and melodious. Musicians live in awe of his forceful intellect. 'I am no better than anyone else at playing the notes,' says Schnabel, 'but the pauses in between . . . ah, that's where the art resides.'

The EMI producer Fred Gaisberg sets out to lure him into his new studio: 'It was given out that Schnabel would never stoop to recording, as he considered it impossible for a mere machine to reproduce the dynamics of his playing faithfully. Therefore, when I interviewed him he was coy but, all the same, prepared to put his theory to the test, though he would need a lot of convincing. At long last I was able to overcome all his prejudices. Tempted by a nice fat guarantee he eventually agreed that it was possible to reconcile his ideals with machinery . . . on the sole condition that we must record all the piano sonatas and the five concertos of Beethoven complete.'

This is a massive undertaking for an industry in the grip of the Great Depression. Schnabel agrees to let EMI offer advance subscriptions to his project, unsure that he will complete it. Gaisberg is inundated with money orders and Schnabel turns up to record opus 110, the penultimate sonata in the set. 'I am attracted only to music which I consider to be better than it can be performed,' he tells a journalist.

He turns fifty and everything changes. Hitler comes to power and Schnabel, who is Jewish, decides to leave Berlin, knowing he is on a Nazi hit-list. His mother, who stays behind, is murdered. Schnabel will never set foot again in Austria or Germany. After a spell in Italy, he migrates to Britain and America, remoulding the English-speaking world's perception of what it means to be an artist.

The Beethoven cycle becomes his portable home. In studio he has good days and bad. He might waste half an hour insisting that his piano is moved half an inch to the right or left or blow up at someone who moves behind the glass wall. To Therese, he complains of tyranny:

One can only play for four minutes. In these four minutes sometimes 2,000 or more keys are hit. If two of them are unsatisfactory you have to repeat all of the 2,000. In the repeat the first faulty notes are corrected but two others are not satisfactory, so you must play all 2,000 once again. You do it ten times, always with a sword of Damocles over your head. Finally you give up and 20 bad notes are left in it. I am physically and mentally too weak for this process and was close to a breakdown. I began to cry when I was alone in the street. Never before had I felt deeper loneliness. My conscience tortured me. Succumbing to evil, the betrayal of life, the marriage by death. It is perfect nonsense, totally unnatural.

He demands that all his wrong notes are left in. He wants the record to resemble a concert as closely as possible. Each morning he decides which work he will play, informing the producer on arrival. Gaisberg writes:

Schnabel is both a trial and a joy . . . I supervised every one of our 20 sessions per annum [!] over the next ten years and rate the experience of hearing his performances and listening to his inevitable impromptu lectures as a most liberal allowance of instruction combined with enter-tainment . . . He is a born pedagogue and never so happy as when he is seated at the piano, with his legs crossed, his left hand caressing the keyboard and his right gripping a choice cigar, and surrounded by a bevy of students, chiefly girls, who hang on to his every word.

The girls are his weakness. Correspondence that comes to light long after his death in 1951 reveals an intense affair with an American student, Mary Virginia Foreman. There are others. Like Beethoven, he lives in hope of perfect love. Schnabel, at least, experiences the physical rewards of love.

Beethoven is of a similar age and frame of mind to Schnabel when he composes opus 110. His assistant Schindler recounts: 'This music sprang in the first place from a profound personality and is only fully intelligible and useful to profound personalities.' The finale is titled '*Klagende Gesang*', a mournful song, but the colouring is neither dark nor deathly. The sonata ends with an abrupt A flat major chord, as if to say: that's it. The American pianist Charles Rosen intuits a terrible grief, perhaps for the recent death of a distant beloved, Josefine Brunsvik. Others hear intimations of the death of Jesus in Bach's *St John Passion*.

Schnabel slows down and grows quiet in the final pages; in this end is his beginning. His cycle is unforgettable and inimitable. Sviatoslav Richter, whose performance of opus 111 is morose, mordant, verging on violent, denounces Schnabel as 'totally unacceptable, absolutely impossible to listen to'. Emil Gilels hears woodland sounds. Solomon, Gulda, Gould, Brendel, offer different truths. Schnabel, wrong notes and all, remains the benchmark.

The British pianist Stephen Hough tells me:

> In the car last summer, with no wifi or 4G, we had only Schnabel's sonatas downloaded on my phone. We drove through Yellowstone with them on shuffle and I was astonished again and again at how utterly fresh they were – the pieces and the performances. And never mind the musical insights (bar after bar), he was a dazzling virtuoso, with his reedy Bechstein a perfect compromise between historical instruments and the modern Steinway. So often I thought, 'this has never been bettered'.

Schnabel never ceases to regret recording the sonatas: 'I did not like the idea of having no control over the behaviour of the people who listened to music which I performed – not knowing how they would be dressed, what else they would be doing at the same time, how much they would listen.' Above all, he hates the realisation that he has fomented an illusion that the art of music, free-flowing as a mountain brook, can be trapped, bottled, commodified and compared by listeners who neither give it full attention nor are even properly dressed.

There is no artifice to his grief. He wears an air of defeat in photographs, his eyelids drooping. You want to put an arm around his shoulders and assure him that no harm has been done, that by leaving in the wrong notes he has left room for others to take a different angle, for the brook to continue to flow, for the work to be renewed in other times and circumstances. It takes a while for anyone to match him until, in the 1960s, Brendel records night and day in Vienna, Barenboim plays cycles on London's South Bank and Wilhelm Kempff drives straight down the middle of Deutsche Grammophon's Autobahn.

Others pile in. Rudolf Buchbinder on the C Major label and Paul Badura-Skoda adds Viennese pastels on the aptly named Arcana. A thick-set Englishman, Bernard Roberts, thunders in a Welsh castle on Nimbus. Claudio Arrau underplays on Philips, Claude Frank is the acme of refinement on Elvis Presley's American label, RCA.

More? Annie Fischer on Hungaraton, John Lill on ASV, the wild-haired Yudina and Grinberg on Soviet vinyl, deft Vladimir Ashkenazy on Decca, Stephen Kovacevich on EMI. Richard Goode is very good on Nonesuch, Paul Lewis is on Harmonia Mundi, Jenő Jandó on Naxos. Maurizio Pollini, starting in 1975, completes his DG set in 2014. There are twenty-first-century cycles by Bavouzet on Chandos, Hewitt on Hyperion, HJ Lim on EMI, Jonathan Biss on Orchid, Andrea Lucchesini on Stradivarius and Igor Levit on Sony. Who needs so much Beethoven, and will it ever 'wash itself'? If you want to know why classical labels shrank and sank, look no further. Producers, addicted to completism, flooded the world with Beethoven boxes.

If I could only have one it would be Schnabel. His tone, like Laurence Olivier's in *Hamlet*, is conversational. Schnabel is no more Beethoven than Olivier is Shakespeare. Neither lives like the great masters; neither could tolerate their privations. But if the job of an artist is to make a work come alive, and stay alive for all time, that is what Schnabel does.

Cardus, a sworn admirer, writes: 'There must reside in his being some stuff which has kith and kin with Beethoven's own immortal mortality; in other and even more reckless language, Schnabel is spiritually related to Beethoven.'

One sunny day, Cardus takes Schnabel across Abbey Road to watch a game of cricket at Lord's. Cricket is a pastime of English-speaking nations. As much ritual as sport, its celebrants clad in virgin white, it is certifiably impenetrable to a first-time spectator. Its progress is slow to static and ever dependent on uncertain English weather. A match can last up to five days, often ending without result. Cardus must have known that a German speaker like Schnabel would struggle. He settles them in seats in the hallowed pavilion and Schnabel puts his great mind to the proceedings, gazing out over the green swards of Lord's turf. After a while, he offers a clear interpretation of the English game. 'When the batsman is "in",' decides Schnabel, 'he goes out; when he's "out" he comes in. Then, it rains.'

23

Late review

Symphony No. 1, Op. 21 (1800)

IN BEETHOVEN'S VIENNA, A NEW SYMPHONY IS NO BIG DEAL. Mozart wrote thirty and Haydn sixty before anyone started counting. Italians churn out symphonies in six-packs. Beethoven's first, performed in an 'Akademie' concert at the Burgtheater on 2 April 1800, is no head-liner. To attract an audience, he adds a symphony by Mozart and two arias from Haydn's *The Creation*, topping off with his own piano concerto and a septet for wind instruments. Tickets are sold from his lodgings at Tiefen Graben no. 42. There is no impresario, no manufactured hype.

The reception is hard to gauge since no review appears for six months and, when one does, it is from an insignificant writer in faraway Leipzig. 'This was truly the most interesting concert in a long time', remarks the critic, meaning interesting for all the wrong reasons. He reports chaos in the orchestra, with two players refusing to follow Beethoven's beat. 'In the second part of the symphony they became so lax that despite all efforts on the part of the conductor no fire whatsoever could be gotten out of them, particularly from the wind instruments.' That's as much as we know about the concert. We're not even sure which piano concerto Beethoven plays, presumably his first. The closing wind septet, however, is an instant success. It gets to a point, writes Czerny, that Beethoven cannot 'endure his Septet and grew quite angry because of the universal applause it attracted'. From which we can adduce that his first symphony is a write-off.

There is, to be fair, not much new in it. Beethoven takes the C major key from Mozart's 'Jupiter' symphony and the duration, twenty-five minutes, from Haydn. The first twelve bars consist of a 'musical joke', a tease between winds and strings. The second movement is a slow dance, the third fizzes and the finale eventually yields a big bang. Years later, some around him reckon that his first symphony is a settling of accounts with Haydn, Mozart and C. P. E. Bach.

On record Arturo Toscanini is hectic and exhilarating. George Szell in Cleveland adds clarity to propulsion. Among period-instrument bands Christopher Hogwood is full of bluff and bluster, Roger Norrington is supple, elegant, ultimately superficial. David Zinman with Zurich's Tonhalle Orchestra blends period style with maestro micro-detail. Riccardo Chailly brings Milanese bravura and gelato flavours to the Leipzig Gewandhaus. We are usefully reminded that the symphony, or sinfonia, is, like most concert forms, an Italian invention.

Two recordings by Herbert von Karajan raise the bar to Olympian heights. Karajan, an Austrian who joined the Nazi Party in early 1933, never recanted his affiliations. After the war he seized musical summits, heading the Berlin Philharmonic, Salzburg Festival and Vienna State Opera, an unprecedented aggregation of power. No maestro ever made so many records, 900 in all. While many are repetitive to the point of narcissism, some early efforts confirm the range of his abilities. Two Karajan takes on Beethoven's first symphony – with the Philharmonia in 1953 and the Berlin Philharmonic a decade later – are thrilling. Karajan adds the impatience of a young Beethoven to the finesse of an expert chocolatier, polishing each morsel to shine in shop-window light. His London session is combative, fast and a trifle raw. By 1963 in Berlin he has perfected a product, gleaming in every part and ever so slightly impersonal, a shade bored. He will enjoy a quarter of a century of world dominance.

24

Magic seven

Septet, Op. 20/Trio, Op. 38 (1800)

SCHUBERT WRITES THE BEST QUINTET, BRAHMS THE SEXTET, Mendelssohn the octet, each attracting numerous imitators. Nobody attempts to match Beethoven at the septet. Using clarinet, bassoon, horn, violin, viola, cello and double bass, he caricatures the ever-expanding orchestra as a fox mocks fowl from behind a fence. His septet yields a totally novel sound, a shock to the ear. Where else do we encounter such a thing? In Mozart's twelve-note row in *Don Giovanni*, in Wagner's *Rheingold* prelude, Stravinsky's *Rite of Spring*, the start of Berg's *Wozzeck*, Ravel's *Bolero*, maybe in 'Moon Dreams' on the Miles Davis album *Birth of the Cool*. Not often.

Beethoven tells the Leipzig publisher Franz Anton Hoffmeister that his septet is 'very popular', meanwhile offering it to Johann Peter Salomon, Haydn's London impresario. Friends in Vienna make copies for personal use. He is soon begging Hoffmeister to issue a piano reduction before all sales are lost; he also produces a three-instrument version, opus 38.

His septet is made up of folk tunes, street cries, a boatman's song from Bonn and a snatch of a future piano sonata, opus 49/2. It's a kaleidoscope of possibilities. The public demands more. Beethoven shrugs, never writing another septet.

Income from opus 20 enables him to move out of grace-and-favour rooms in rich men's mansions to rent a place for himself. The problem is, he has no idea where to look, or how to look after himself. Every place he rents, thirty over three decades, descends into noisome squalor. Neighbours complain. He moves in with his brother. As a man of no fixed address, he gets arrested one night as a vagrant. Homelessness is his natural state.

The need for a home is an important concept in psychoanalysis. Freud's assertion that 'the ego is not master in its own house' is a foundational statement, the start of the process by which the individual explores the unconscious. Jung sees the house as a metaphor for the psyche, protector of one's sanity. Beethoven has no need for physical stability. Homelessness means he is free to get up and go. Dirt is a deterrent against time-wasters. Living in abysmal conditions means there is no place he can bring a wife and start a family, even if he wants to. Not having a home sets him apart from other men. He rejects security, solidity and the consolations of intimacy.

Among many enticing recordings of the septet, players of the Vienna (1977) and Berlin Philharmonic (1979) offer stark alternatives in texture and timbre. In November 2020, locked-down musicians in an Amsterdam Concertgebouw video produce what is improbably the happiest finale on record.

25

Publishers be damned

Sextet for 2 Clarinets, 2 Horns and 2 Bassoons, Op. 71; Sextet for 2 Horns, 2 Violins, Viola and Double Bass, Op. 81b; Wind Octet, Op. 103 'Parthia' (all in E flat major) (1792–6)

MUSIC PUBLISHING IS NOT A FIRST-CHOICE CAREER. EARLY publishers are failed or fed-up musicians who exploit their former colleagues. Publishing relationships in Beethoven's time are neither fixed nor trusting. He shops around for the best deal; publishers play on his insecurities and try to beat him down. In the absence of copyright protection, neither side has absolute rights.

Publishers have stores where they sell sheet music, as well as violins, strings, reeds, pencils, paper and whatever else the customer might require. One such shop, Musikhaus Doblinger, remains open in Vienna to this day. For a lonely composer, hunched over scores, these places are essential social amenities. The music store is where Beethoven goes to trade gossip, drink coffee, pick fights and buy things he doesn't need.

In 1802 he sues Artaria for issuing a string quintet that he has previously sold to Breitkopf & Härtel. Beethoven wants Artaria to melt the plates. Artaria refuses and countersues for libel. Lawyers rub their hands. During two years of litigation, Beethoven drops in frequently to Artaria's store on the Kohlmarkt in search of pencils, paper and company. One day, he is approached in store by a commercial artist, Sebastian Höfel, who wants to take his portrait. The result is the best likeness ever made of him. Artaria publishes the engraving and makes a fortune. Beethoven gets nothing. Years later, when short of cash, he accepts an interest-free loan from Artaria. Beethoven repays the publisher with the Hammerklavier Sonata. There is no rancour involved. As they say in *The Godfather*, it's just business. Beethoven says: 'There ought to be in the world a market for art, where the artist would only have to bring his works and take as much money as he needs. But, as it is, an artist has to be to a certain extent a businessman as well.'

Beethoven's first symphony earns him 100 florins, enough to pay six months' rent. He demands 250 for the next, but publishers haggle, pay him late, falsify sales figures and fill his printed scores with so many errors that he threatens to take an axe to their premises.

The hub of music publishing is Leipzig, where Bernhard Breitkopf set up shop in 1719 shortly before J. S. Bach arrived. Peters (1800) and Hoffmeister (1807) set up in competition. Schott is founded in Mainz in the year of Beethoven's birth. Vienna has Artaria (1778). Beethoven is the first composer with a wide choice of imprints. He seems quite fond of Hoffmeister, whom he addresses as 'dearest brother and friend', but not for long. After selling him a job-lot of the septet, first symphony, second piano concerto and a piano sonata, he offers him nothing more for nineteen years.

Breitkopf & Härtel becomes his mainstay once he sells them, for 250 florins, a package of *Fidelio, Christ on the Mount of Olives* and the Mass in C. The contract states he is to be paid in silver pieces; the publisher cheats him with devalued Banco-Zettel currency. Months later, he turns up again at Breitkopf with a sheaf of scores, opus 74 to 86. Once again he wants 250. The publisher sticks at 200. Beethoven responds with an appeal to the publisher's sense of fairness, while demanding in the same breath that they keep the deal secret so as not to damage his rates with other firms. Here's part of the letter:

> It is not my aim, as you suppose, to become a usurer in art, one who only composes to become rich, heaven forbid. However, I like to lead an independent life and I cannot do so without a small fortune – so the composer's reward must reflect honour on the artist and all he undertakes. I will not tell anyone that Breitkopf & Härtel gave me just 200 ducats for these compositions. You, more humane and educated than other publishers, should also try not to pay the artist as little as you can, but rather to make it possible for him to achieve all that he has in him, and all that can be expected from him.

He assures Breitkopf that he prefers him to other imprints, 'even those in Leipzig who keep approaching me and will pay me as much as I want'. He is well aware that Breitkopf also publishes the *Allgemeine Musikalische Zeitung*, a journal of music criticism. Beethoven does not want bad reviews. He is caught between hot metal and a hard place. Breitkopf & Härtel, on its 2021 website, lays claim to be the firm that 'reinvented Beethoven'.

These three works are from a batch sale to Breitkopf. The sextet opus 71 aims for a Mozart effect, clarinets and bassoons up front. The wind ensemble of the 1950 Vienna Philharmonic are unbeatable. Opus 81b gets a civilised play from the UK's Melos Ensemble (1972). The opus 103 wind octet is a reworking of the string quintet, opus 4. Once again, it's a shootout on record between Vienna and Berlin. This time, Karajan's Berlin all-stars have the best of it.

BEETHOVEN IN LOVE

I'm yours, or your sister's

Andante favori, WoO57 (1803–4); 'Ich denke dein', WoO74/136; 'An die Hoffnung', Opp. 32 and 94 (1799–1803)

IN HIS PHYSICAL PRIME, BETWEEN HIS ARRIVAL IN VIENNA AND accepting deafness, Beethoven is often in love. The women have one thing in common: they are unattainable. Most are upper-class, some are already married, others are otherwise taboo. Their families will never let them marry a musician and they will not defy the rules to live in poverty. He knows his love is doomed, knows it from the first flush of desire. That knowledge gives him the freedom to express fierce emotion without the slightest taint of risk. Beethoven in love is protected by his choices.

The young women, some of them half his age, soon come to their senses and break his heart. Each time he is stirred to a richer outpouring of emotion. Beethoven, in his inner psyche, does not want fulfilment in love. His ideal is a Distant Beloved, eternally untouchable. The film industry will have a field day with ridiculous romances. Beethoven has been acted on film by Fritz Kortner (1927), Harry Baur (1936), Albert Bassermann (1941), Erich von Stroheim (1955), Karlheinz Böhm (1962), Donatas Banionis (1976), Gary Oldman (1994), Ian Hart (2003), Ed Harris (2006), Tobias Moretti (2020), among others, none particularly illuminating.

In twenty years of seeking love, Beethoven never has sex. The evidence of his chastity and prudishness is overwhelming, only slightly clouded by one anecdote suggesting that Schuppanzigh once took him drunk to a brothel. If this ever happened Beethoven will have been revolted. When sex comes up in conversation he scowls like a maiden aunt. He reviles the sexual depravity that has surrounded him all his life. In Bonn, everyone knew that Archduke Maximilian fathered illegitimate children with an abbess whom he shared with his finance minister. Vienna is worse. Haydn's patron, Esterházy, bought pre-teen girls from their parents. Haydn's copyist Elssler and his concertmaster Tomasini were rumoured (perhaps unfairly) to have sold their young daughters to Prince Kaunitz, a predator who was eventually ordered to leave Vienna after being caught pimping girls from the Children's Ballet. Kaunitz's portrait still hangs in a place of pride in the Czech National Gallery.

Beethoven warns his brothers against 'unchaste women', managing only to inflame their curiosity. He boycotts a Mozart pupil, Magdalena Hofdemel, on hearing that she had sex with her teacher. Magdalena's husband Franz had assaulted Mozart a few days before his death. He then attacked Magdalena with a razor, leaving her in a pool of blood while killing himself in the next room. Magdalena, scarred for life, never performed again.

Beethoven abhors Mozart's licentiousness, refusing to watch a performance of *Don Giovanni* on the grounds that: 'Art, which is sacred, should never be degraded to serve as a pretext for so scandalous a subject.' He jots in a notebook: 'Sensual gratification without a spiritual union is, and remains, bestial; afterwards one has no trace of noble feeling but rather remorse.' This may indicate that he once experienced some kind of sexual contact, but he never pays a return visit.

He tells Ferdinand Ries about 'a certain beautiful lady [who] had captivated him more intensely and longer than any other – seven whole months'. But when Ries asks if he made a move on her, Beethoven issues a withering put-down: 'If I had wished to give my vital powers to that life, what would have remained for the nobler, the better?' Like many in his time, he believes that seminal emission can deplete a man's creative force. Ries describes how, one moonlit night, he and Beethoven tracked a fine lady to her chateau, only to find that she was otherwise engaged as a prince's mistress. Beethoven does not seem disappointed. 'He loved to look at women, especially beautiful, young faces,' writes Ries. 'If we passed a charming young woman, he would turn and squint at her through his glasses, laughing if he saw I was watching. He was often in love, but only for a short duration.'

He began by idealising his mother. In his earliest known letter, dated 17 July 1787, he writes: 'She was such a good, kind mother to me, and indeed my best friend. Oh! Who was happier than I, when I could still utter the sweet name of mother and it was heard and answered; and to whom can I say it now?'

A Bonn matron, Helene von Breuning, offers comfort after his mother's death, nudging her daughter Eleonore towards Ludwig. Something goes wrong: a 'wretched quarrel'. He tells Eleonore: 'My conduct presents itself as most despicable, but it was too late; oh what would I not give to obliterate from my life those actions so degrading to myself and so contrary to my character.' One is tempted to suspect he took her hand or gave her a kiss, but let's not guess. The quarrel cannot have been serious since Eleonora's brother Stephane becomes one of Beethoven's closest associates in Vienna, dedicatee of his violin concerto, and Eleonore's husband Franz Wegeler assists Ries in writing the first Beethoven memoir. The Breunings are his most trusted friends.

Between the ages of twenty and forty he dallies with society girls without much thought of marriage. Then, over three spa summers, 1810 to 1812, he proposes serially to several women. The first, Therese Malfatti von Rohrenbach zu Dezza, is a relative of his doctor's, an Italianate beauty in black curls. Beethoven also fancies her kid sister, Anna. Both are around twenty. Therese is soon married off to an imperial courtier, Anna to a baron. No hope there for Beethoven, as he knows all along.

He pursues a Berlin singer, Amalie Sebald, in Teplice in the summer of 1811, but she goes home and marries a court official. He then spends time with Countess Josefine von Brunsvik, who has lost her husband while pregnant with his fourth child. Beethoven has been teaching her piano for years. Love flares one summer's night but Josefine lets him know she needs a man of means. In her early thirties, she lands a more suitable suitor and lets Beethoven know she is spoken for: 'I would have to violate sacred bonds if I yielded to your request – believe me – that I, by doing what is my duty, suffer the most.' Beethoven, saddened, writes the pensive Andante favori piano piece, which has a repeated Jo-se-fin-e motif. When he sees her again next summer she is with a new husband, an Estonian baron.

Josefine's older sister, Thérèse, is next in line. Thérèse is a woman of striking looks and strong personality who goes on to found a chain of Pestalozzi pre-schools in Hungary and Austria. Some suspect that she was always the object of his attention and recipient of his letters, though this seems far-fetched. Thérèse receives the dedication of Beethoven's 24th piano sonata. She never marries.

Another candidate that summer is the Brunsviks' cousin, countess Giulietta 'Julie' Giucciardi, dedicatee of the Moonlight Sonata. Beethoven tells Schindler he truly loved Julie, 'but she was of a different class'. Back in Vienna, he pays frequent visits to Antonie Brentano, who is married to his friend Franz Brentano and heavily pregnant. This does not stop scholars from speculating that she might be the 'Immortal Beloved', a title attached to three heart-breaking letters from the composer that summer. These letters constitute his absolute farewell to love.

> Though still in bed, my thoughts go out to you, my Immortal Beloved, now and then joyfully, then sadly, waiting to learn whether or not fate will hear us – I can live only wholly with you or not at all – Yes, I am resolved to wander so long away from you until I can fly to your arms and say that I am really at home with you, and can send my soul enwrapped in you into the land of spirits – Yes, unhappily it must be so – You will be the more contained since you know my fidelity to you. No one else can ever possess my heart – never – never – Oh God, why must one be parted from one whom one so loves . . . Be calm – love me – today – yesterday – what tearful longings for you – you – you – my life – my all – farewell. Oh continue to love me – never misjudge the most faithful heart of your beloved.

He has danced (as Leonard Cohen will put it) to the end of love. Who, then, is the Immortal Beloved? The seminal letter tells us it is someone he has known for a long time, and that's about all. If it is Josefine or Antonie, both are married to someone else and one is pregnant at the time.

After the summer of 1812, he gives up on love. He is not the only composer to accept bachelorhood. Others include Handel, Brahms, Bruckner, Mussorgsky, Ravel, Schubert and Chopin. Of them all, Beethoven is the one who says most often that he wants to be married, while probably not meaning it.

There is one loose end. Nine months after Beethoven wrote the Immortal Beloved letter, Josefine von Brunsvik gives birth. It is her fifth child – her first by the Estonian husband, who accuses her of infidelity, claiming to have been away in the week the child is conceived. This is a ruinous charge. The Estonian, whose name is Christoph von Stackelberg, fathers two more daughters with Josefine and, one day, kidnaps all three. Josephine falls in love with her sons' mathematics tutor and is soon pregnant again. In the summer of 1816 she may have met Beethoven one last time in a spa. In March 1821, she dies of tuberculosis, aged forty-two.

Beethoven, when he hears of her death, is composing his last piano sonata, opus 111. He inserts a phrase of the Andante favori, Josefine's theme, into the sonata as a remembrance.

Josefine names a daughter Theresa Carolina, known in the family as 'Minona', an anagram of 'Anonim', or no-name. Only her sister Thérèse attends the birth. Might Beethoven be the father? Given his abhorrence of immorality he would have been hard to seduce, but Josephine is lonely and Beethoven is madly in love with her. It's unlikely that he slept with her, but not altogether impossible.

What becomes of Minona? After Stackelberg's death, she and her sister Maria Laura live with their aunt Charlotte on her Romanian estate. Both Maria Laura and Charlotte die in 1843, prompting Minona to return to Vienna, living as a lady's companion to Countess Bánffy, a distant relative. In 1858 she meets Franz Liszt. She has two small pieces of music, Écossaises, published by F. H. Kuhnel in Leipzig. Two alleged photographs of her, young and old, bear a faint resemblance to Beethoven, though doubts have been raised concerning their authenticity. In 1865, Minona takes a spinster apartment at Habsburgergasse 5. Never married, she dies on 21 February 1897, aged eighty-three. At no time does she make any claim about her paternity, perhaps in an effort to preserve Josefine's somewhat tarnished good name.

Josefine's Andante favori is one of Beethoven's most infectious inspirations. Concert pianists use it as their last encore: go home now. Richter and Brendel frown at us. Anne Quéffelec, the French pianist, gives a gentle wave.

'Ich denke dein' is a little piece that Beethoven wrote for Josefine to play four-hand with Thérèse. The words, from a Goethe poem, say 'I think I'm yours', wishful thinking without commitment. Another song, *'An die Hoffnung'* ('to hope') voices hopeless yearning.

27

Love you

'Ich liebe dich' (1795 or 1798), woO123; 'Adelaide',
Op. 46 (1796); 'Der Küss', Op. 128 (1822)

AWKWARD IN LOVE, THIS EARLY SONG BETRAYS NAIVETY AND detachment. The words are from a poem by a German pastor, Karl Friedrich Wilhelm Herrosee.

I love you as you love me,
In evening and in morning,
There is no day when you and I
Fail to share our worries.

And thus they are, for me and you,
Once shared, a whole lot lighter;
Your comfort eases my concerns,
I weep amid your sorrows.

May you be blessed by God's kind hands,
You, my life's rejoicing.
God protect you just for me,
Protect us both together.

This is so chaste it might be intended for a maiden aunt. There is no daring, no heat or dust. Beethoven's tune, like a hiking chant, lilts along a humdrum trail. So artless is the song that the Italian crooner Andrea Bocelli makes a YouTube sensation of it in 2020 with his eight-year-old daughter at the piano, attracting two and a half million viewers (I prefer Fischer-Dieskau on record with Demus).

'Adelaide' is a proper love song, written for tenor or soprano. She wanders lonely as a Wordsworth cloud, crying 'Adela-ide'. If this were by Schubert, it would end in tears. With Beethoven, it plods. The author of the poem, Friedrich von Matthisson, denounces Beethoven for the least sensitive musical setting of any of his work (he is not remembered for any other). But the Vienna critic Eduard Hanslick calls it 'the only Beethoven song whose loss would leave a gap in our nation's emotional life'. You decide. A 1939 recording by the Swedish tenor Jussi Björling floats a top note out of this world. Tenor Fritz Wunderlich and baritone Matthias Goerne offer contrasting rescue missions. All are worth hearing.

Do they tell us more about Beethoven in love? The American writer Maynard Solomon, in a 1988 psychobiography, declares against most evidence that the young Beethoven goes on brothel crawls, citing 'lightly disguised references to prostitutes' in Beethoven letters to the cellist Nikolaus Zmeskall. Solomon also claims that a member of the Lobkowitz household offers to fix Beethoven up with his own wife. These speculations are quashed by a 2020 biographer, Jan Caeyers, a Dutchman who attacks Solomon for going 'out on the longest speculative limb'. Viennese experts claim that Solomon misread or mistranslated documents. In one letter Beethoven tells Zmeskall: 'I thought you had the idea that I did not wish to stop in swampy places.' Solomon interprets this as an invitation to low pleasures when it is, in fact, the very opposite. In December 1817 Beethoven spends thirty-four kreutzer at a 'Lusthaus', which Solomon renders as a house of lust or desire. This Lusthaus, however, is a perfectly respectable outdoors café on Praterstrasse packed with young families; and what Beethoven forks out is the price of one coffee and cake. Several books claim that Beethoven caught syphilis. 'There is little clinical or autopsy evidence that Beethoven suffered from syphilis,' says the latest academic consensus.

There is still, however, room for slight doubt. In 1819, Beethoven buys a book titled 'The art of identifying, protecting against and curing all types of venereal disease'. Why would he do this unless he has VD anxiety? Around the same time, while composing Missa Solemnis, he knocks off a wicked little ditty called 'The Kiss'. The words are by Christian Felix Weisse, a poet favoured by Mozart (the translations are mine):

I was with Chloe all alone,
And really longed to kiss her:
But she said she would give a shriek,
And nothing would come of it.
But I got brave and kissed her,
Overcoming her resistance.
And did she shriek? Oh yes, she shrieked.
But that was a long time after.

Beethoven, deaf and decrepit, admits to having violent sexual urges, to the point of forcing himself on an unwilling Chloe. The German tenor Fritz Wunderlich sings this song with breathtaking wonderment.

28

A Jew in love

'An die ferne Geliebte' ('To the distant beloved'), Op. 98 (1816)

BEETHOVEN IS NOT A NATURAL SONG WRITER. HIS MELODIES struggle to match words. He repeats lines in 'The Kiss' to make the music fit. He is not lyrical as Mozart is, let alone Schubert. Beethoven writes songs when he has nothing bigger to do.

Quite by accident, he invents a new musical form, the song cycle. World leaders are gathering at the Congress of Vienna to carve up postwar Europe and restore the divine right of princelings. In a sour mood, Beethoven is introduced to a medical student from the Czech town of Brno (Brünn). Alois Isidor Jeitteles is a bright young man, founder of a Jewish newspaper, *Siona*. Descended from rabbis and doctors, he learns Spanish and Italian in order to translate baroque plays for the German theatre. At the Burgtheater he meets the playwright Grillparzer and the composer Salieri. Through them he obtains access to Beethoven.

He asks to show Beethoven some love poems. Beethoven mutters away about his Immortal Beloved, the '*only one*, whom I shall doubtless never possess'. Jeitteles writes about a man sitting on a hill contemplating a girl beyond his reach. They share the same mood. Beethoven takes a liking to Jeitteles, twenty-four years younger, not least because the medical student is someone who will listen to his litany of bodily ailments. Jeitteles is his Jewish friend. They stay in touch until Jeitteles qualifies in 1821 and returns home to enter general practice. Under Habsburg law only 134 Jews are allowed to live in Brno and Alois requires a special permit to allow him to treat Christian patients. He is a hero in two cholera epidemics, saving countless lives; he also sets up a free clinic at two charities, one of which is the Institute for the Deaf and Dumb, attracted perhaps by a fond memory of Beethoven. Alois lives until sixty-three and is buried in the Jewish cemetery at Brno. His family flourishes in public life. One cousin produces one hundred published novels, another compiles a fifty-volume concordance to the Talmud. (Most of the Jeitteles line perishes in Hitler's Holocaust, although the Talmudist is removed from a train bound for Auschwitz when a German officer decides that the day's quota has been exceeded by ten.)

The six songs in the cycle are dedicated to Prince Lobkowitz, who is mourning his wife, Karolina. The German singer Dietrich Fischer-Dieskau had tragic experience of losing his first wife, the cellist Irmgard Poppen, shortly after giving birth to their third son. I asked him in a late interview if an event like this coloured his interpretation of the 'ferne Geliebte'. 'Absolutely not,' snapped the singer. 'The act of making art must transcend one's personal history.'

Fischer-Dieskau is the most ubiquitous Lieder singer on record. Equipped with exquisite diction and filigree subtleties, he covers every vocal range from low baritone to mid-tenor, and every songwriter from Bach to Bartók. To describe him as dominant is an understatement. 'I did too much,' he told me two years before his death in 2012, confiding that he told his sons to change their names because of the burden of his ubiquity.

Fischer-Dieskau's 1957 'Distant Beloved', with his English partner Gerald Moore, is stainless steel, every note and syllable banged into a perfect product. Fischer-Dieskau, to whom singing came easy, missed the point about Beethoven, who can never get the one thing that he wants in a song: everlasting love.

The antidote to Fischer-Dieskau is the young German tenor Fritz Wunderlich. With Heinrich Schmidt as his partner, Wunderlich flies effortlessly high, close to the sun. He is a happy-go-lucky performer, something of a playboy. His singing pierces the heart, stab, stab, stab. He is not a natural Beethoven interpreter, but by heavens he is beautiful. Not long after this record was released, and weeks away from his Metropolitan Opera debut, Fritz Wunderlich fell down a flight of stairs at a hunting lodge and died of head injuries, aged thirty-five. The coroner's verdict was accidental death, a trip over an untied shoelace.

Baritones are a safer bet. Olaf Bär (1993) gets dark introspection. Christian Gerhaher (2012) channels Fischer-Dieskau in pitch and diction.

Matthias Goerne in a 2019 DG recording with the Canadian Jan Lisiecki at the piano is rich in timbre, pastel in colour. He's a man in mid-life, quietly lamenting all that he can never recover from the pain of long-lost, unrequited love. It's a timeless reading, pitch perfect.

29

B-sides

**Songs, Opp. 52 (1793), 75 (1803), 82 and 83
(1809–10); 'An die Geliebte', WoO140 (1811)**

BEETHOVEN'S SONGS DO NOT IMPROVE WITH EXPERIENCE. Monochrome and methodical, he is a b-side writer. He uses lots of Goethe. 'Maigesang' (May Song), from opus 52, has all the joy of a Lutheran Lent. 'Marmotte', from the same set, is a chant for country ramblers in bare knees and burnt shoulders.

'Mignon', the lead song in opus 75, is a kidnapped girl pining for her Italian home: 'D'you know the land where lemons bloom . . .?' Schubert takes that line and snaps our hearts in two. Beethoven delivers pathos on pizza. Opus 75/5, 'An den fernen geliebten', a dry run for his Distant Beloved song, never gets past courtesy. 'Sehnsucht' from opus 83, is wistful where it should be chilling. The opus 82 'Arietten' are vegan gelato, lacking the milk of empathy.

Which leaves the intriguingly uncatalogued miniature 'An die Geliebte'. A tripsy piano opening betrays a certain lack of seriousness and a punch-line of 'Well, do [tears] on your cheeks / betoken your fidelity?' hardly wrenches the heart. What we hear is that Beethoven is no longer quite so keen on the unnamed Geliebte. His opus 83 set is addressed 'to my excellent friend Toni Brentano', certainly not a lover's declaration. If he once loved her, he's over it.

Fischer-Dieskau finds psychological insights. Fritz Wunderlich lets 'Mailied' flow like a summer brook. The American soprano Rachel Willis-Sørensen is surprisingly good as Mignon, as is the Italian mezzo-soprano Cecilia Bartoli in the 'Arietten'.

30

Both ways

Piano Sonata No. 24, 'A Thérèse', Op. 78; No. 25, 'The Cuckoo', Op. 79 (1809); Écossaises, WoO83, 86 (1803)

THE TWENTY-FOURTH SONATA, FINISHED AROUND THE TIME that Haydn dies in May 1809, is dedicated to his memory. But it is also named for Thérèse von Brunsvik, for whom Beethoven has a different kind of feeling. So which is it – late teacher or resistant lover? The music lasts eight minutes, too short to tell. Another enigma: what's 'Rule, Britannia!' doing at the start of the second movement? Beethoven is toying with multiple meanings, leaving future artists with enigmas.

Ferruccio Busoni, one of the piano's great minds, declares that it is the duty of interpreters to rescue composers when they fall from 'sublime heights'. Beethoven, writes Busoni, 'is a master of psychological tragedy', his internal drama. If Haydn and Thérèse appear on the same page, they must shed light on the recesses of his mind; likewise 'Rule, Britannia'. 'In the most tragic situation, Beethoven is ready with a joke,' says Busoni, 'in the most hilarious, he manages a learned frown.' Busoni, who has a huge skull and brooding air, is mistaken for Beethoven in the street. Like Beethoven he reads Goethe, writing a Faust opera. Unlike him, he is immensely practical, fluent in several languages and at home in two identities, Italian and German. Busoni, says Alfred Brendel, 'signifies the victory of reflection over *bravura*', intellect over sleight of hand. He is the only travelling soloist whom Gustav Mahler respects as an intellectual equal. A YouTube track contains a rare recording of Busoni, in 1922, playing his own arrangement of a Beethoven Écossaise, a Scottish dance; listening to it is like eavesdropping on a composers' summit meeting in the smoking room of Valhalla.

The Canadian Glenn Gould is best known for playing Bach. In Beethoven he revels in unsolved mysteries, at times with an affinity that verges on symbiosis. As a boy, Gould fell off a boat on an Ontario lake and suffered a back injury that left him, like Beethoven, in frequent pain. Concerts gave him contempt for 'hedonist' soloists who pretend music is for pleasure and a public that is too easily pleased. At thirty-two, he retired from concerts to make records and radio shows. A documentary series, 'The Idea of the North', finds Gould wandering with the indigenous people of northern Canada, cut off like himself from an over-crowded world. He emotes with Beethoven's isolation.

Gould's Beethoven playing is often at odds with received opinion, not least for his habit of singing along as he plays, but once the listener overcomes these irritants, Gould offers unique insights. Beethoven, he says in a 1967 talk,

> is a kind of living metaphor for the creative condition. In part he is the man who respects the past, who honours the traditions [from] which art develops, and while never other than intense and constantly gesticulating with those rather violent gestures which are so peculiarly his own, this side of his character leads him to smooth off the edges of his structure sometimes, to be watchful and even painstaking on occasion about the grammar of his musical syntax.
>
> And then there's this other side, the fantastical romantic side of Beethoven, which draws from him those unapologetically wrongheaded gestures, those proud, nose-thumbing anti-grammatical moments which, in the context of tradition [and] against the smooth and polished edges of classical architecture, make him unique among composers for the sheer devil-may-careness of his manner. But in the end this sort of amalgam exists for every artist, really; within every creative person there is an inventor at odds with a museum-curator.

That crucial dichotomy is exposed in Gould's 1975 recording of the 24th sonata. A minute faster than anyone else, he plays the first movement like a harp in a Beatles song and the second like crazy paving in a suburban garden. No child learning to play Beethoven should be allowed to hear this; no adult should miss it.

Gould apart, the one pianist you must hear is Heinrich Neuhaus. The most influential piano teacher in Moscow, Neuhaus numbered Richter and Gilels, Zak and Khrennikov among his pupils. As a young man he cut his wrists in despair after hearing the brilliant Arthur Rubinstein. Under Stalin, his life was one private hell after another. His wife Zinaida left him for the poet Boris Pasternak, his son caught tuberculosis, his friend Osip Mandelstam was murdered and Neuhaus himself was sent to Siberia, where he lost all his teeth. Through these torments, he taught each morning with benign calm. Although he had firm views on Beethoven, Neuhaus was open to persuasion by pupils that there could be another way. Gilels and Richter, his star pupils, could hardly be more different in temperament and interpretation. The 1950 Neuhaus recording of the 24th sonata is whimsical and lighthearted; perhaps he is not taking Beethoven as seriously as he should.

Having given short measure in the 24th sonata, Beethoven writes a 25th that publishers name 'the Cuckoo'. It is nine minutes long, and dull. However, the playwright George Bernard Shaw, writing in March 1927, takes a view that nothing in Beethoven is without interest. Beethoven, says Shaw,

> could take the driest sticks of themes and work them up so interestingly that you find something new in them at the hundredth hearing . . . his diagnostic, the thing that marks him out from all the others, is his disturbing quality, his power of unsettling us and imposing his giant moods on us. Berlioz was very angry with an old French composer who expressed the discomfort Beethoven gave him by saying '*J'aime la musique qui me berce*,' 'I like music that lulls me.' Beethoven's is music that wakes you up.

The Cuckoo's first section ends in mid-phrase, the second in a deserted ballroom. Not many modern pianists crack the riddle. Igor Levit is faster than light. Jonathan Biss (2015) is deadly *serioso*, Maurizio Pollini (1989) too agitated. Schnabel in 1935, quippy and ironic, opens a portal to hidden depths that others will, for all time, explore.

31

China doll

'Für Elise', WoO59 (1810)

PARENTAL WARNING: THE FOLLOWING CHAPTER CONTAINS theft, fraud, sex, Nazis, wilful deception and corrupt detection. It is an everyday story of evidential musicology with a sting that may harm star egos and their commercial myths. Much of what you are about to read has not been revealed before.

The story begins one Friday in July 1865, a generation after Beethoven's death, when a young music professor, Ludwig Nohl, pays a call on a retired teacher, Babette Bredl, at her central Munich apartment on Salvatorstrasse 15. Nohl, editor of the Beethoven letters, has heard that Miss Bredl might have some autographs in her possession. Over (let's assume) afternoon coffee and cake, the elderly spinster fishes into a drawer and produces what she calls a 'bagatelle' by Beethoven. Nohl recognises the spidery notation instantly but the music is unfamiliar. The inscription at the top of the sheet reads, according to Miss Bredl: 'For Elise, in remembrance of L. v. Bthvn, April 27.'

Quivering with excitement, Nohl goes to the parlour piano and plays 'Für Elise'. Miss Bredl, a trusting soul, lets him take the sheet home. He gets her to sign a paper: 'I gave the above piano piece to Prof. Dr. Nohl to copy the original manuscript from Beethoven's own hand and allowed him to use and publish it in any way. Munich July 14, 1865. Babeth [sic] Bredl'.

The manuscript is never seen again. That need not immediately concern us; music sheets are forever getting lost and found. This one, however, acquires an afterlife so powerful that it affects Beethoven appreciation for ever more.

'Für Elise' is first published in Nohl's 'New Beethoven Letters' in 1867. It gets amateurs and teachers very excited. It looks so easy to play and it has a romantic tease: who is Elise? Its appeal just grows and grows. 'Für Elise' will be heard in two dozen movies, from Roman Polanski's *Rosemary's Baby* (1968) to Lars von Trier's *Nymphomaniac* (2013). It is a pop song by Caterina Valente ('Red Roses Will Bloom') and it is jazzed up for orchestra by Chick Corea. There is scarcely a space on earth that it does not invade – from airport lounges to phone ringtones to headsets in a dentist's chair. It is certifiably the most popular piece of Western classical music in twenty-first-century China.

However, in an era when all information is supposed to be retrievable online, tracking down the real Elise has proved frustrating. Experts warn me that the trail is littered with ruined reputations and there is underlying pressure from the classical music industry not to tamper with one of its most profitable legends.

Two facts can be easily confirmed: the music is by Beethoven, and the year of composition is 1810. The Beethoven museum in Bonn owns a near-identical sketch from the spring of that year. Beethoven also airs the theme elsewhere, in the finale of his Tempest sonata (opus 31/2). The music is prime Beethoven, no doubt about that. But who is Elise? And why have we not met her anywhere among his immortal beloveds? Could this be a darker secret?

In the notebooks where Beethoven conducted everyday conversations, there are six women called Elise or Elisabeth. Unfortunately, only two appear in or before 1810. One, Elise Barensfeld, is a soprano from Regensburg, thirteen years old, a lodger with the metronome inventor Johann Nepomuk Maelzel. Beethoven is not interested in underage girls. Maelzel, on the other hand, monstrously is. He gets questioned by police in 1813 about having sexual relations with a minor and Elise leaves his premises soon after, joining the Archduke of Baden's household. No more is heard of her until 2012 when Canadian academic Rita Steblin, styling herself 'the Miss Marple of musicology', flourishes a sheaf of police records purporting to show that Elise Barenfeld from Regensburg is 'most likely' Beethoven's one and only Elise. Headlines ensue the world over.

Dr Steblin basks in a full fifteen minutes of fame before her claim falls into the hands of Michael Lorenz, a Mozartian at the University of Vienna. Dr Lorenz is a renowned expert at finding and deciphering records of musicians' births, baptisms, deaths and wills. The phrase 'most likely' to

Dr Lorenz is like a mouse to a mongoose. He pounces on Miss Marple with claws unsheathed. 'None of the scans . . . and charred police documents presented by Steblin in her article has anything at all to do with Beethoven's "Elise",' he declares. 'They simply serve the obvious purpose of distracting the reader from the fact that the article does not deal with the identification of the latter at all. Steblin provides absolutely no proof that Elise Barensfeld was Beethoven's "Elise." ' So there.

Musicology, you may not be aware, is a pagan god that requires regular human sacrifice. Lorenz, normally a polite and amiable colleague, is roused to fury by this fake Elise. He follows up: 'Steblin is widely known for presenting a mere hypothesis as a solution of a mystery . . . Such a sensationalistic procedure is not only embarrassing but damages the reputation of historical musicology in general'. Steblin, offering no defence, dies in 2019. Her one achievement is to convince the ancient town of Regensburg to name a street after Elise Barenfeld, just in case she's the one in Beethoven's score.

Another candidate Elise is Elisabeth Röckel, a Mozart soprano of seventeen. Röckel, while singing Donna Anna in Bamberg in 1810, meets the young composer Johann Nepomuk Hummel and, in 1813, marries him. The Hummels are friends of Beethoven and stay that way all the way to his deathbed, where Elisabeth snips a lock of his hair and steals the pen from his dying fingers. Later, she claims he once pinched her arm in affection. In June 2009, a German composer called Klaus Martin Kopitz names Frau Hummel as the real Elise, splashing his 'discovery' in *Der Spiegel* magazine and the London *Daily Telegraph*. Kopitz claims that Beethoven, yearning for Elisabeth Röckel while she is singing in Bamberg, writes 'Für Elise' in an anguish of love.

Before Kopitz manages so much as fifteen minutes, Michael Lorenz douses him with an ice-bucket of factual refutation. 'There is not a single document where Frau Hummel called herself "Elise",' he states. 'She called herself Betty or Maria Eva. Elise is a name used by her mother.' As if that's not bad enough, he points out that the souvenir hunter Elisabeth Hummel would never have relinquished a Beethoven manuscript that he gave to her when she clung to his pen and his curl unto her dying breath and bequeathed it to her descendants (one of whom, Mike Hummel, gave them to the University of San Jose, California). Betty Hummel is definitely not the delightful Elise. So who is?

An older hypothesis comes back into play. In 1925, a crotchety Beethoven-Haus scholar, Max Unger, attacks the credentials of Ludwig Nohl, claiming that he, 'by no means one of the most dependable expositors of the composer's handwriting, probably deciphered the inscription [of 'Für Elise'] incorrectly.' What should it really read? Not Elise, apparently, but Therese. 'Therese, written in German characters on a long-lost manuscript, might easily be mistaken for Elise,' argues the combative Max Unger.

Unger's expertise is unquestioned. It is underwritten not just by the Beethoven-Haus but by Nazi leaders who, plundering manuscripts in occupied territories, need to know which ones are worth stealing. From his new Swiss home, Unger acts as music adviser to Reichsleiter Alfred Rosenberg, one of the nastiest Nazi ideologues, and advises him directly on looting the Paris apartment of the venerable Polish-Jewish harpsichordist Wanda Landowska. Rosenberg ends up in Nuremberg on the end of a rope. Unger is still cited to this day on the Beethoven-Haus website as 'one of the most important Beethoven scholars of the first half of the twentieth century'.

Just because he is a racist and a lousy human being does not mean Unger is wrong about Elise. His argument that the piece was written for Therese von Malfatti, Beethoven's summer love of 1810, is supported by a farewell note to her that ends: 'You receive, herewith, respected Therese, what I promised.' Could that promise be the 'Für Elise' sheet? Nohl seems to think it is: 'this quite charming little piano piece comes from the estate of Therese von Drosdick, *née* Malfatti.' He adds that she 'had given it to Miss Babette Bredl of Munich'. But what is their connection, and why does she give it away? Nohl compounds my frustration by stating that the piece 'was <u>not</u> composed for Therese [Malfatti]'. So who's Elise?

Let's persist with Therese. After Beethoven, she marries Johann Wilhelm Freiherr von Drosdick, councillor of the war chambers to the Austrian Emperor. They have no children and lead separate lives. Therese holds court at her Kärntner Strasse apartment, regaling friends with tales of her glory days with Beethoven and Schubert. She plays Beethoven sonatas with 'incomparable virtuosity' and gives rooms in her apartment to the virtuoso pianist Adolf von Henselt as 'a household friend'. When Henselt goes on tour, Therese replaces him with another pianist, Rudolf Schachner, who is twenty years old, good looking and lower class. Tongues wag. Therese, at her death in April 1851, leaves everything to her husband – everything, except 'her piano and all the music in her possession' which go to a 'dear friend, the composer and pianist Josef Rudolf Schachner' (I am indebted to Dr Lorenz for the wording of the will).

Whatever Schachner means to her, Therese wanted her Beethoven relics to remain in musical hands. Finding that Schachner comes from Munich, Dr Lorenz dives into Bavarian state archives. There, in the last will and testament of Babette Bredl, he finds that she leaves everything to 'my illegitimate son Josef Rudolph Schachner'.

We're almost there. The unmarried Babette, it turns out, had a child in 1815 with a Viennese craftsman, Jacob Schachner. Raising her son in Munich as a single mother, she had him tutored by the court organist and, in 1835, sent him to Vienna. So long as Therese is alive he remains her devoted 'household friend'. A year after she dies he marries Elisabeth Wendling, granddaughter of a soprano for whom Mozart wrote a role in *Idomeneo*. Schachner's wife is known to her family as Elise. The couple are then blessed with a daughter, who is christened Elise.

Babette is thrilled to have a grandchild, and devastated when the young family decides to move to London in search of musical employment. When Ludwig Nohl comes by on his fishing mission in July 1865, Babette has her loved ones in mind. She reads out the title of the manuscript as 'Für Elise', either as a slip of her tongue because she is thinking of her granddaughter or deliberately, to ensure that her little Elise in London should enjoy this scrap of posterity. There is further evidence, unearthed by Bavarian musicologist Jürgen May, that Babette made Nohl promise to publish the piece as 'Für Elise', whether in order to cover up her son's scandalous connection to Therese or to give her granddaughter unearned fame. Either way, she succeeds. Nohl returns the manuscript to Babette, who lives to be eighty-eight, dying in her Munich stairwell three days before Christmas 1880. Her son, identified as a 'Kapellmeister in Salzburg', is the sole heir. When he dies in 1896 there is no trace of a Beethoven manuscript among his relics. Rumour has it that Schachner took the 'Für Elise' sheet with him literally to his Salzburg grave, where Max Unger, the Nazi felon, failed to have it exhumed.

What can now be established is that Beethoven never knew anyone noteworthy by the name of Elise. Nonetheless, it is imprinted on his reputation. Millions in China know Beethoven only by this tinny piece of whimsy. Listen closely to the little piece. It begins in A minor, turning after ten bars into C major. The tempo is 3/8, a halfway waltz. The debutantes who dance with Beethoven know that he is famous, dangerous, unsuitable. They flirt and he winks with an ironic twist, wound around and around the 'Für Elise' theme to a point that is just two pursed lips short of kitsch, or a kiss. The girls might think they are breaking his heart, but he is smiling at them in 'Für Elise', waving – 'in remembrance of L. van Bthvn' – not drowning. Whatever we make of the piece, it is not 'Heartbreak Hotel'.

'Für Elise' is easy to play, too easy for pros. Artur Schnabel (1938) growls through it at two minutes and 43 seconds. A YouTube geek claims a world record at 1:15. The iconoclastic Russian emigré Anatol Ugorski (2014) drags it out over four unforgivable minutes. Online you will also find a Richard Clayderman orchestral version, a dubstep cartoon where Beethoven gets eaten by monsters, a heavy metal track, passengers tinkling it on airport pianos and a step-by-step tutorial by the Chinese mega-star Lang Lang.

Two cults come together here: the ear-worminess of 'Für Elise' and the global aims of a brand ambassador. Raised by a peasant father who ordered him to kill himself when he failed a Beijing audition at nine years old, Lang Lang made it to Philadelphia's Curtis Institute, where he was groomed for a Carnegie Hall career. He soon found other temptations. By his early twenties Lang Lang faced both ways, as a gala star in American concert halls and as an icon with posters fifty storeys high on buildings in Shanghai. Celebrity on this scale in China requires Party approval. Lang Lang ticked all the right boxes.

Thanks to the Lang Lang effect, an estimated fifty million Chinese children are learning to play the piano on locally manufactured uprights that their parents scrimp and save to afford. Walking through Shanghai in the late afternoon I have heard the relentless clamour of piano practice on ascending balconies.

Lang Lang was not solely responsible for this Chinese revolution. In October 2000 Yundi Li, aged eighteen, became the youngest-ever winner of the quinquennial International Chopin Competition. Victory in Warsaw gave Yundi world fame and a chance to seize the high ground from Lang Lang. Yundi played only Beethoven on his China tours, while Lang Lang played both classics and pops.

While Yundi eventually fell foul of the authorities, Lang Lang amassed endorsements. His life was a sequence of photoshoots in a white suit, a hoodie or a onesie. He played a piano named after him, kicked a ball at the Olympics, drove a Bugatti and flashed a Rolex. His wedding ceremony, to German-Korean pianist Gina Alice Redlinger, was held in the Palace of Versailles. Lang Lang was in the running to be the Sun King of classical merchandise. In China, he opened a gigantic CGI version of *The Lion King* at the Shanghai Disney Resort, accompanying an orchestra in 'Can You Feel the Love Tonight.'

Bling notwithstanding, Lang Lang's playing is serious. Unlimited speeds make him impressive in Rachmaninov and irresistible in Tchaikovsky, though his skills get stretched by subtler inflexions of the classical period. In Beethoven, Lang Lang registers emotion by an excess of head swaying and arm gesture. He seems to play at arm's length from the music. In 2019, Lang Lang adopted 'Für Elise' for a world tour. 'For me this piece is very romantic and very light, like a feather,' he proclaimed in a video tutorial. 'And some passages need to move people . . . Anyway, this piece needs to be like a real artistic work. You have to interpret it as a real masterwork.' Which, of course, it is not. Lang Lang's version of the piece is ten seconds short of the longest on record, interminable rather than indelible and surprisingly superficial. After his world tour, garbage trucks in the Taiwan capital Taipei begin to play an exceedingly slow 'Für Elise' recording as they pick up the night's leftovers. Put out your bins, there's Elise coming down the alley.

One morning, on a bullet train out of Shanghai, I catch sight of a nuclear family standing in the gangway. The father has farmer's hands, the mother is city chic. Their child is five or six years old. We get talking. They are from the north, near the Russian border. What are they doing so far from home? Entering a piano competition. 'What do you play?' I ask the boy. He mumbles two words. On third or fourth iteration, I recognise 'Für Elise'. I sing the opening phrase. 'Stop!' cries the child. 'You sang a wrong note.' Infants in China, I discover, are schooled in 'Für Elise'.

The Elise that never was.

32

Broken china

Piano Sonata No. 26, 'Les Adieux', Op. 81a (1809)

IN MARCH 1977 I ATTENDED AN ASIA-PACIFIC CONFERENCE OF television news chiefs in Hong Kong. As the youngest delegate, I was detailed to escort Japanese and Australian media barons on a nightly bar crawl. The notorious Kowloon bars had been cleaned up since the Vietnam war but the girls were still topless and extremely hardworking. I would count my guys back into their rooms, only for the girls to come giggling down the corridors, flourishing the executives' business cards and demanding compensation.

One evening, I excused myself from bar duty and crashed out in my room in front of the television. There were two Hong Kong channels and, if reception was good, you might just glimpse the People's Republic through a snowstorm of interference. I pushed the Beijing button on the TV set and could not believe what I saw. An orchestra on stage. A conductor walked on. He gave a beat. They played the opening of Beethoven's fifth symphony.

My ears popped. Under Mao Zedong's Cultural Revolution, Western music was banned. Mao's death six months earlier had left uncertainty but no policy shift. So what was Beethoven doing on China TV? I checked the date: 26 March 1977, one hundred and fifty years since Beethoven died. China had picked the anniversary to end its cultural lockdown. Rushing out, I banged on the doors of the world's news leaders, yelling that we had a huge breaking story here. 'Get over it, mate,' they said pityingly. 'Nothing changes that fast in China.' But it did.

Down the years, I was able to piece together some of what happened that night. A useful 2015 monograph, *Beethoven in China*, by Jindong Cai and Sheila Melvin, proved especially useful. It appears that Western music was not totally cowed by the Gang of Four. While Mao's wife, Jiang Qing, unleashed a pogrom against culture, some musicians were kept safe by other Party bigwigs. After his breakthrough China visit in February 1972, President Richard Nixon sent his favourite Philadelphia Orchestra to China as a goodwill gesture. Prime Minister Zhou Enlai retrieved an old friend, the conductor Li Delun, and ordered him to give a concert for the US Secretary of State. 'Kissinger is German,' said Zhou Enlai. 'You should play Beethoven.' Li Delun did what he could but the musicians had not touched their instruments in years. Kissinger wrote: 'there were moments when I was not clear exactly what was being played.'

With Kissinger gone, Li Delun asked if he could prepare more symphonies, to be held in readiness. Zhou and Mao died in 1976. The Gang of Four were arrested on 6 October that year. In January 1977 Li Delun applied for permission to give a public concert on the occasion of Beethoven's anniversary three months later. The Party havered, reaching a decision late on 23 March. The concert was announced two days later in the *People's Daily* but the content was so sensitive that Beethoven's name was given as 'Etc.' Li Delun had time to rehearse just two movements of the Fifth. Those of us who caught the concert on television had no idea of the terror that lay behind it. Later, I heard of a famous pianist who had his fingers broken, one by one, for refusing to give up names of other musicians, his 'fellow-criminals'.

Li Delun went on to form the Central Philharmonic Orchestra, leading a tour with Isaac Stern that was released as a documentary, *From Mao to Mozart*. Li died in October 2001, an unsung hero. China exploded into Western music. Today, eighty percent of the world's pianos are made in China and the country is growing five new orchestras a year. I return to China often and am impressed by its cultural evolution. The audiences I sit with are no less knowledgeable than those at Carnegie Hall and the musicians no less skilled. The students I teach at the Shanghai Conservatoire are as critical and inquisitive as any in Europe. China's hunger and enthusiasm for Beethoven can be overwhelming.

Three instrumental works stand out in our conversations, beyond the inevitable 'Für Elise' and the glimmering Moonlight Sonata, which has associations in China with lunar evocations in the eighth-century poet Li Bai. The third work that many Chinese know is the twenty-sixth sonata, titled 'Les Adieux'. Beethoven cast it in three movements – farewell, absence and return. These themes are also reflected by Li Bai in poems that Gustav Mahler drew from in 'The Song of the Earth'.

I heard 'Les Adieux' playing through open windows in Shanghai's French Concession, the city's most stylish section, laid out with rows of plane trees like Paris boulevards. The French connection runs deep in Shanghai. Joseph Kosma's autumnal lament 'Les Feuilles Mortes' ('dead leaves') is a perpetual hit. In the French Concession you wake up and smell the croissants with 'Les Adieux' playing on the radio. For some reason, no Chinese pianist has recorded 'Les Adieux'. On record, the Russians Gilels and Ashkenazy rule supreme.

33

Vita brevis

Piano Sonata No. 14 in C sharp minor, 'Moonlight Sonata', Op. 27/2 (1801)

I NEVER HEARD ANYONE PLAY THE MOONLIGHT SONATA LIKE Yundi Li. Good pianists take control of time when they play. Yundi does nothing so assertive. Rather, he loosens the bonds that connect you to the rest of your life, to the point where reality fades and you are left, like a twelfth-century Chinese painter, with a vast mountain and a tiny figure far below, which may be you. I have seen Yundi do this in concert and in private; I have even watched him do it on an accordion. He has an approach to time and place that is, in my experience, unlike any other.

The Moonlight Sonata is his signature piece. When he touched the first key in a publicity recital in a London fashion store, a chatter of Asian teens fell silent. Dark-haired, polite, inconspicuously dressed in brown suit and open shirt, Yundi Li made no grand statements. All he ever wanted was to play.

In two decades of jousting with Lang Lang, both changed record labels to avoid the other. Yundi, with a younger profile on Chinese social media, withdrew from Western tours and cultivated his local following.

On 21 October 2021, I awoke to a message that Yundi Li had been arrested by a police patrol in Beijng, accused of picking up a street prostitute. The alleged offence was a minor violation, carrying a maximum 14-day sentence, but state media launched a campaign of vilification. The editor of state-controlled *Global Times* wrote that the reaction was out of all proportion to the actual event. He was relieved of his job soon after. Yundi was cast into official disgrace.

What was really going on? The Chinese government was cracking down that year on citizens who had become too wealthy or famous. Yundi was either in the wrong place at the wrong time or had been singled out by officials in Beijing as a warning that no artist was too famous to be safe from the state. The fact that his arrest took place on the very day that the Chopin Competition was announcing its current winner in Warsaw was seen by some China-watchers as significant. Like the opening to Western culture on Beethoven's anniversary, the arrest of Yundi Li on Chopin Day was a signal to reverse the process, shutting China back into itself. Nothing more has been heard from Yundi Li since his arrest. Listen to the Moonlight on YouTube and you will hear the scale of the world's loss.

ꝫ

The Moonlight Sonata, originally known as '*Sonata quasi una fantasia*', reminded a poet, Ludwig Rellstab, of moonlight over Lake Lucerne. A publisher slapped a moonbeam on the cover and sales soared. The opening tune can be played by any child after two lessons. The Beatles quote it in their ballad 'Because' after Yoko Ono teaches John Lennon to play it backwards. The American pop star Alicia Keys plays it to packed arenas. No Beethoven work is easier to play badly. Few play it unforgettably. The Russian grandmaster Heinrich Neuhaus is at once profound and morbid, his skies full of dark omens. Gilels is sombre and fatalistic, Ashkenazy gently poetic.

The first prime minister of independent Poland, Ignacy Jan Paderewski, has his own take on the sonata. A leonine man with a blaze of coiffed hair, he recorded the Moonlight very, very slowly in 1906. Twenty years later, as a world figure, he repeated it, smarter and faster. His third attempt, in 1937, was done for a movie, *Moonlight Sonata*, starring Marie Tempest and Charles Farrell. The story? Young man woos heiress, whose parents object. A plane with Paderewski on board crash-lands in a nearby field. Parents see this as a sign from heaven since they first fell in love while listening to Paderewski play the Moonlight. Paderewski rises from wreckage. The lovers embrace. His playing outlasts the film.

34

Who's first?

Piano Concerto No. 1 in C major, Op. 15 (1795); Piano Concerto in E flat major, No. 0, WoO4 (1784); Rondo for Piano and Orchestra in B flat major, WoO6 (1793)

THE PIANO CONCERTO KNOWN AS BEETHOVEN'S FIRST IS WRITTEN after his second. Both are preceded by other concertos. Nothing is simple, the numbering is nonsense. Let's sort it out.

New to Vienna, he writes opus 15 at speed. 'Two days before the performance, four copyists sat in the hallway working from the manuscript sheets that he handed over to them one at a time.' A Czech musician, Václav Jan Tomášek, seethes with envy: 'His changes from one melody to the next avoid the organic, steady development of ideas . . . Such evils weaken his compositions, arising from an over-exuberant concept. The listener is often rudely awakened.'

Beethoven adds new pages and more instruments – clarinets, trumpets, timpani – trying out a revision in Prague, then changing more things. 'I do not claim it as one of my best, however, it would not disgrace you to publish it,' he tells a publisher in 1801.

Two artists command this concerto. In a 1958 Columbia recording, conducted by Vladimir Golschmann, Glenn Gould is the driver of a getaway car, taking corners blindfold on an icy road. At 06:15 in the finale he hits a patch of violent atonality and lingers out of key on the roadside, grinning at his death-defying naughtiness. Gould is a one-off, a self-made artist in life-enhancing music. Those who resent his liberties may share a lineage with the long-forgotten Tomášek.

Martha Argerich, eight years old, used to hide under a Buenos Aires piano at Friday night parties, snacking on buffet nibbles with Daniel Barenboim. In 2014 she toured this concerto with Barenboim's

West–Eastern Divan Orchestra. Argerich played no other concerto for a whole year. On the YouTube video she barely looks up at Barenboim; they know each other so well that each has the freedom to fly.

Beethoven left a 1784 E flat major concerto, numbered '0', in Bonn. Much of it sounds like Year 10 homework; in the second movement there is a glint of an idea. Mari Kodama (2019), with her husband, Kent Nagano, gives good account of it on record. In the even more obscure Rondo WoO6 there is a clear hint of the future Emperor Concerto. A Japanese-German pianist, Sophie-Mayuko Vetter, gave its record premiere in 2019.

35

Fallen star

Piano Concerto No. 2 in B flat major, Op. 19 (1795)

THE B FLAT CONCERTO USES THE KEY OF MOZART'S FINAL PIANO concerto, his 27th. Beethoven hawks it around at discount, telling a publisher 'this concerto I only value at 10 ducats'. Lacking clarinets, trumpets and timpani, its rondo-finale is Beethoven at his most playful.

William Kapell, America's first homegrown piano star, recorded this concerto in 1946. Kapell, twenty-four, had been imbued with American cultural cringe by his Texan teacher Olga Samaroff, ex-wife of Leopold Stokowski. He took lessons with Schnabel and crossed the road to knock on the door of Vladimir Horowitz, who refused to open. His admiration undimmed, Kapell shaped up to punch a *New York Times* critic who once gave Horowitz a bad review.

Kapell, said his widow, got 'pummelled by the critics for being weak in the classical repertoire'. In October 1953, while flying home from Australia, his plane crashed outside San Francisco, killing all on board. This Beethoven concerto, fractious in the central movement and gleeful in the finale, is Kapell's recorded epitaph. Schnabel, hearing it on the radio, mistook it for himself. Leon Fleisher said: 'He was probably the greatest American pianist who ever lived.'

Four years later, Glenn Gould entered the Soviet Union and enraptured its audiences. At the Leningrad Philharmonic, the chief conductor Yevgeny Mravinsky ducked out of his concert for fear Gould would play forbidden atonalities. The Czech Ladislav Slovák took over the Beethoven concerto in an account that is modern to the point of mayhem, wild in tempi and dynamics, aleatory in its excitements.

Other outstanding performances include Martha Argerich conducting from the piano for the only time on record (1983), Mitsuko Uchida deferring to conductor Kurt Sanderling (1998) and dominating Simon Rattle (2018) and the Russian Mikhail Pletnev, conducted by his DG producer Christian Gantz (2007). The Canadian Jan Lisiecki (2019) is the living, lyrical, orthodox opposite of Gould.

36

How to play

Piano Sonata No. 4 in E flat major, Op. 7 (1796)

HIS FIRST STANDALONE PIANO SONATA, ALMOST HALF AN HOUR long, is profuse with instructions. Where Mozart writes 'allegro', meaning lively, Beethoven prescribes *allegro molto e con brio*, extremely lively and spirited. Haydn uses 'largo', for broad and slow, Beethoven inscribes *largo con gran espressione*, grand and expressively so. He is taking control of how his work will sound. His pupils Czerny and Moscheles make a pedantic fetish out of his markings in future editions. Beethoven is concerned here with general mood.

The sonata, titled 'grand', alternates between exhilaration and contemplation, sidling off into forbidden little resolutions of B sharp into B flat. Some of the rhythmic shifts have a saucy swing. The first to play the work is a sixteen-year-old pupil, Anna Louise Barbara (Babette) Countess Keglevicz, who lives so close by that Beethoven turns up to teach her in carpet slippers. Most pianists treat this mid-20s work as Beethoven on the brink of greatness. The Italian Arturo Benedetti Michelangeli treats it without compromise as the finished object.

A tall man with a pencil moustache and ramrod posture, Michelangeli shunned publicity, society and his own country, choosing Swiss exile for a decade. After a concert he once said, 'so much applause, so much public. Then, in half an hour, you feel alone more than before.'

A graduate of the Milan Conservatorio at fourteen, he studied medicine to please his father and joined the air force when he could not avoid it. Twice married, his personal life is a closed book. Much admired as a teacher, he would sometimes dismiss a pupil after ten minutes, other lessons lasting over four hours.

No one captures the fullness of this sonata as Michaelangeli does in 1982, creating a narrative that extends from the storybook of a Schubert song to the unfathomable mute pauses of late Beethoven. This is piano interpretation at altogether another level. Something of Mihaelangeli's genius percolates through to his pupil Maurizio Pollini in his 2013 recording of this imposing sonata.

37

Eat like Beethoven

Piano Sonata No. 22 in F major, Op. 54 (1804)

GIVEN HIS DOMESTIC DISORDER AND CHAOTIC HOURS, IT IS A surprise to find that Beethoven maintains a healthy diet. The nearby woods abound in mushrooms and berries, the fields in root vegetables. The fish is fresh from the Danube (Beethoven favours pollock and pike-perch). Not much of a carnivore, he keeps a meat stew in a pot and a salami in the larder in case of sudden pangs. For carbohydrates, he likes pasta, especially macaroni, with cheese. Thursdays, he eats bread soup with ten hardboiled eggs. (Yes, ten.)

He drinks coffee first thing in the morning, 'prepared in a glass machine,' says Schindler. 'Coffee seems to have been his most indispensable food, and he prepared it as scrupulously as a Turk. Sixty beans were calculated per cup and he would count them out, especially when guests were present.' Evenings, with dinner, he drinks 'disgusting red wine' at the White Swan in the Neue Markt. He avoids the sickly-sweet late crop that they quaff in village taverns. His father may have been a drunk, but Beethoven is only once seen incapable. Intemperate in so many ways, he does not drink to excess.

The rest of his life is a mess. Here's an 1809 account from a French visitor, Louis Baron de Trémont:

> I think his apartment consisted of two rooms. In the first there was a
> closed alcove where his bed stood, but small and dark, so that he got
> dressed in the sitting room. Imagine the greatest filth and clutter there
> could ever be: puddles on the floor, a rather old grand piano with a thick
> layer of dust as well as manuscript and printed pieces of music. Beneath (I
> don't exaggerate) was an unemptied chamber pot. Beside the piano, a

small walnut table, used to often having its writing set knocked over, all sorts of ink-encrusted pens ... The seats, almost all wicker armchairs, bore plates with the remains of the previous night's supper, together with items of clothing, etc.

His sleeping alcove, according to Bettina Brentano, is 'a straw mattress and thin cover, a washbasin on a pine table, night clothes lying on the floor'. The piano-maker John Broadwood arrives in August 1817:

I was introduced to him by his friend Mr [Joseph Anton] Bridi, a banker at Vienna. He was then so unwell, his table supported as many vials of medicine and golipots as it did sheets of music paper and his cloaths so scattered about the room in the manner of an invalid that I was not surprised when I called on him by appointment to take him out to dine with us at the Prater to find him declare after he had one foot in the carriage that he found himself too unwell to dine out and he retreated upstairs again.

The composer Gioachino Rossini visits in 1822:

As I climbed the stairs leading to the squalid apartment in which the great man lived, I had trouble controlling my emotions. When the door opened I found myself in some kind of dark hole, as filthy as it was in a terrible mess. I recall above all that the ceiling, situated directly under the roof, showed wide cracks through which rain could pour in.

Why does Beethoven choose squalor when he can afford comfort? And why is he incapable of keeping staff for longer than a few weeks or months? Some believe he suffers from a rare neuropsychological condition, Diogenes syndrome, also known as senile squalor syndrome. The disorder is recognised by self-neglect, a filthy home, social isolation and compulsive hoarding of all forms of rubbish. It is an aggressive means of protecting personal space and avoiding intimacy. It may also be motivated by creating a disorder which only one person can resolve: the primary act of a composer.

The condition is not identified until 1975 (I lose a friend to it in 2020, during Covid). In Beethoven's case it may be an extreme reaction to deafness. He tells God: you want me isolated? I'll do better and drive everyone away.

The 22nd piano sonata, a dozen minutes long, is squashed between famous neighbours, the Waldstein and Appassionata. Although it shares manuscript dates with the fifth symphony, at no time do we suspect that they are concurrent. The sonata is quirky, jokey, ruminative, a bit basic in its humour. The Austrian-born pianist Anton Kuerti suggests that 'if the first movement is constipated, then the second movement suffers from the opposite ailment.'

Paul Badura-Skoda, recording on a Beethoven-era Erard, clunks about like bad plumbing. Hammer strikes string with a thud and there is no flowing ease between notes. Badura-Skoda's friend Jörg Demus sounds no better. Among modern readings on modern grands Jonathan Biss and Igor Levit, recording in 2018, are exceptional. Boris Giltburg (2021) is in a class of his own, tossing off great cascades with gleeful abandon. We shall never know why Beethoven needs an overflowing chamber pot beneath his stool in order to compose piano sonatas.

38

Fail better

Piano Sonata No. 21, 'Waldstein', Op. 53 (1805)

THE STAUNCHEST OF BEETHOVEN'S SUPPORTERS – COUNT Ferdinand Ernst Joseph Gabriel von Waldstein und Wartenberg – is a serial failure, a laughing stock among bluebloods. Early on, while attached to the Elector in Bonn, he forms a regiment to fight the French and sends it with British units to the West Indies, where his men fall sick and die. Waldstein stays in London, putting on amateur theatricals. Married to a Polish countess, he spends her fortune and applies for a post at the Congress of Vienna. Rejected, he retreats to an outlying home for destitute gentlemen. On the day he dies, word arrives that he has inherited a family fortune.

This wastrel of a Waldstein does more for Beethoven than any other benefactor. He pays for his Haydn lessons and gives him pocket money 'with such consideration for his easily wounded feelings that Beethoven assumed they were small gratuities from the Elector'. Beethoven repays him with the Waldstein Sonata, also known as *'L'aurore'* ('the dawn'). Waldstein, expecting a symphony, is furious and cuts him dead. Beethoven, seeing the ragged Waldstein some years later on the street, crosses the road with head held high.

The sonata is a huge leap forward, a technical breakthrough. The German biographer Wilhelm Lenz calls it 'an Eroica for the piano'. The three movements – quick-slow-dance – all begin softly. 'The first and last movements are among this master's most brilliant and original pieces, but they are also full of strange whims and very difficult to perform,' concludes an early review. Among the cascade of notes, the line of melody is limpid and transparent. Everything that Beethoven is about to do in his major symphonies is prefigured in this sonata. The colours he conjures from the keyboard seem to be limitless.

The Hungarian pianist András Schiff argues in a persuasive podcast that, from here on, Beethoven writes orchestrally for the piano. He throws out the middle movement, replacing it twice (the original is issued as Andante favori). He is in full flood and nothing will stop him now. Interpreters, daunted by his force, find quiet paths to the heart of his sonata.

Vladimir Horowitz, captured in his New York apartment (1956), evokes post-prandial coitus in the middle movement. Friedrich Gulda (1958) has similar thoughts in mind. The English pianist Solomon (1952) finds a redemption motif in the finale. Emil Gilels (1972) shapes each phrase to such distinction that the Finnish critic Vesa Sirén writes: 'Every time other great pianists start to play Waldstein, for at least a moment I wish they were Gilels'.

As for the Waldstein family, just before Christmas 2020 in the thick of global Covid lockdown, the Austrian ambassador in Stockholm presented a recital on YouTube of the Waldstein Sonata by the organist of the Catholic Church in Sweden. Her name? Elisabeth Waldstein, a descendant of the dedicatee.

39

Light my fire

The Creatures of Prometheus, Op. 43 (1801); Contredanses, WoO14 (1791–1800)

BEETHOVEN'S BALLET HAS A 28-NIGHT RUN AT THE BURGTHEATER and is his first large work to be performed in America (New York, Park Theater, 14 June 1808). It is neither dramatic nor very musical. Beethoven is lured in by Vienna's Italian balletmaster Salvatore Viganò, a nephew of the composer Luigi Boccherini. Viganò's wife, Maria Medina, drops out of the main role too late for anyone else to jump in. The ballet staggers along in fits and starts. Beethoven is relieved to receive a compliment from his teacher, Haydn: 'I heard your ballet yesterday and it pleased me very much.' Beethoven replies: 'O, dear Papa, you are very kind, but it's far from a *Creation* [Haydn's oratorio].' Haydn retracts: 'That is true. It is not yet a *Creation*, nor ever will be.' The evening is saved by the Eroica tune in the finale, drawn from Beethoven's Contredanses WoO14.

Viganò becomes balletmaster of La Scala, Milan, where he is known as 'the Shakespeare of the dance'. Percy Bysshe Shelley writes him an alternative script, *Prometheus Unbound*. Stendhal is another admirer. These are the beginnings of ballet as an art with an intellectual framework. *Prometheus* does not get danced much nowadays; the last London staging was a 1970 Frederick Ashton choreography, one of his weakest. On record, Arturo Toscanini (1939) is sententious, Riccardo Chailly (2009) tightly focused.

BEETHOVEN IMMERSED

40

No hero

Symphony No. 3, 'Eroica', Op. 55 (1805)

THIS MAY BE THE BIGGEST TURNING POINT IN THE HISTORY OF music. Albert Einstein would say: 'Before Beethoven, music was written for right now; with Beethoven, music starts to be written for eternity.'

The Eroica opens with the sound of someone being executed, out of sight in a nearby wood. Two shots: crack, crack. Beethoven is using music as it has never been used before, as a mirror of current events and a warning of worse to come. The symphony foretells occupation by a French army.

After the shots come cellos, augmented by short-bow viola flutters. The low strings reset pulses to normal, then a pair of hammer blows warn of terrors ahead. The second movement is a funeral march, the mother of all funeral marches from Chopin to Mahler, Samuel Barber to Arvo Pärt. The third movement is frenetic, edgy, at times boisterous. The finale, probably written ahead of the rest, recycles a tune from *The Creatures of Prometheus*, also previously used in a set of piano variations. Prometheus is a god. Beethoven is reaching for superhuman powers. The Vienna-born philosopher Ludwig Wittgenstein considers the Eroica 'beyond belief'. It is at once real and above reality.

The Eroica is twice as long as any prior symphony and twice as loud. Yet Beethoven adds just one instrument to the normal complement, a third horn. The grandeur of Eroica is all in the mind. The work is part illusion, part history in motion. Begun in a time of friendship with France, it ends with Napoleon's armies at the gates of Vienna. Beethoven is both reporter and interpreter, terrified eyewitness and ice-cold analyst, dutiful chronicler and creative artist.

He has to rename the symphony. Ferdinand Ries reports that Beethoven is intrigued at first by Napoleon who, like himself, is a provincial lad who leapfrogs all his superiors to become all-powerful First Consul and vindicator of the French Revolution. Beethoven, says Ries, 'held him in the highest regard and compared him to the greatest Roman consuls. I and many close friends saw this symphony on his table, fully scored, with "Buonaparte" inscribed at the very top of the title-page and "Luigi van Beethoven" at the very bottom. And nothing more.'

Then Ries tells Beethoven that Napoleon has declared himself Emperor. 'Whereupon Beethoven flew into a rage and shouted, "So he too is nothing more than an ordinary man . . . He will place himself above everyone else and become a tyrant!" Beethoven went to the table, took hold of the title-page at the top, ripped it all the way through and flung it on the floor. The first page was rewritten and . . . the Symphony entitled Sinfonia eroica.' The printed edition reads 'Sinfonia Eroica . . . composta per festeggiare il sovvenire di un grande Uomo (composed to celebrate the memory of a great man)'. Is this the memory of the Napoleon he idealised, or of Beethoven himself, humbled by his former naivety? Ries, who migrates to London, never knows.

The other unanswered question is how Beethoven, having conceived a symphony that celebrates heroism, turns in mid-creation to anti-heroism without, in any way, departing from his musical concept. This may be the moment when he discovers that music is susceptible to self-contradiction. To say one thing and imply another is a delineator of the greatest of minds. It leaves a masterpiece that is ever open to contemporary interpretation.

The first public performance, on 7 April 1805 at the Theater an der Wien, takes place two weeks after Napoleon proclaims himself King of Italy. In November the French Emperor occupies Vienna. In December, he crushes the remains of the Habsburg army at Austerlitz. Beethoven's prediction has come to pass.

≀

No two conductors beat the crackshots the same way. A sampling of YouTube videos from 1922 (Oskar Fried) to 2011 (Riccardo Chailly) reveals vast perceptual divergences. Arturo Toscanini and Fritz Reiner begin by clubbing a man to death. Herbert von Karajan fires long-range cannon. Some beat the opening with a double karate chop. Others stab like gangsters. Claudio Abbado performs a wide circular motion that sacrifices crisp precision for a numinous spirituality. In this, he consciously follows the symphony's most ethereal interpreter, a conductor who empathised so strongly with this symphony that he became its anti-hero.

Wilhelm Furtwängler avoided giving a beat. 'Too boring,' he said. Players in the Berlin Philharmonic had to guess when he wanted to start. One told me: 'We waited until we could wait no more; then we came in.' Another said: 'When the baton reached the third button in his waistcoat.' Wilfully vague, angular motions gave the music that flowed from Furtwängler's motions an aleatory spontaneity, an in-the-moment quality that others could merely envy.

A tall man with an unusually long face and limbs that looked as if they had been bolted on in a self-assembly kit, he concealed athleticism and virility behind a shambolic frontage. Outside the hall, he wore a battered hat and rumpled coat, adding to an impression of disorientation. We know that this was a calculated image. Furtwängler could, when required, give a precise beat and act decisively in his vital interests. On the death of the hypnotic Hungarian maestro Arthur Nikisch, Furtwängler seized both of Europe's best orchestras, in Leipzig and Berlin, before anyone else got a look-in. By his mid-thirties he was the high priest of the German concert hall. The son of a world-famous archaeologist, he was formidably well-read, imbued with philosophical pessimism. Conservative by nature, he performed Schoenberg under duress but eschewed Mahler; Hindemith was his type of modernist. Furtwängler composed much music of his own, none of it original.

Under the Nazis, Furtwängler flourished. As Hitler's favourite, he crushed rivals and inflated his fees. The Führer gave him a personal state pension worth forty million marks. He posed beneath swastika banners and, in one film shot, gave the Hitler salute. Joseph Goebbels grumbled that Furtwängler was forever interceding to rescue Jews, albeit at little personal risk. In a 1942 Beethoven essay, he uses supremacist Nazi terminology:

Nowhere in the whole of European music is there another composer [like Beethoven] in whom the pure-melodic and the pure-structural, the gentle and the severe, combine so perfectly in a single, living organism – no other music in which, to use the metaphor of the human body, flesh, bone and blood are so organically fused. The power that sweeps through this music is compelled by the inexorable force of a divine, rational will to obey the laws of organic life.

These dirty words – pure, inexorable, blood, obey – are drawn from Hitler's lexicon. Furtwängler embraced both the spirit of his time and place, and its criminal ideology.

In January 1945, tipped off by the slave-labour minister Albert Speer, Furtwängler abandoned his Berlin musicians to their fate and slipped away to Switzerland, where he had property and rich friends. In denazification hearings, dramatised in Ronald Harwood's play *Taking Sides*, Furtwängler denied any knowledge of genocide. He told Artur Schnabel that he never met any Nazis. His mission was to save German music from Nazism, for the benefit of German people who had never needed it more. Rejoining the Berlin Philharmonic in 1946, he made a torrent of recordings over the next eight years until his death in November 1954.

Furtwängler recorded Beethoven's Eroica no fewer than eleven times, each different, all imbued by a moment in time. With the Vienna Philharmonic in December 1944 he dances on the lip of a volcano. In 1952 Berlin he paints light onto a devastated cityscape. His uncanny knack of capturing a transient mood and infusing it into a symphony reaches its apotheosis in these two Eroica extremes, unsurpassed on record.

Herbert von Karajan, his Berlin successor, reconfigured the conductor as hero: elegant, accurate, elevated and all-controlling. Karajan filmed his concerts from many angles and edited them in his home bunker near Salzburg to present the conductor as master of all things. Karajan personified Germany's post-war ideal of technical progress and perfection – *Vorsprung Durch Technik*. He chose the Eroica to celebrate the Berlin Philharmonic's centenary in April 1982, a conductor-glorifying film that cannot be watched more than once without nausea.

The German conductor Hermann Scherchen, self-taught and batonless, drove the fastest Eroica of his time, just under 44 minutes, with Vienna Philharmonic musicians in May 1958. It is not just quick but quarrelsome, forcing naked aggression from the brass and unaccustomed edginess from the strings. It is rare to hear the Vienna Phil thrown so far off its stride and the experience is by no means unpleasant. Scherchen gets raw truths in the opening movement and querulous emotion in the funeral march. The finale is positively fractious, drawing blood from flutes. This is an Eroica for Beethoven sceptics, an anti-Eroica for a nuclear age, wilful, wanton and wasted. Scherchen once said: 'I would like to have a space that I can deactivate.' He was an important mentor for the Frenchman Pierre Boulez, who called him 'cyclonic'. Boulez, never a natural Beethoven conductor, did not record the Eroica.

Elsewhere, Erich Kleiber gives a convincing 1950 Eroica in Amsterdam. Ferenc Fricsay (Berlin, 1961) delivers an immaculate scherzo. Chailly (Leipzig, 2011) clips 50 seconds off Scherchen's record with something like Toscanini's whiplash speeds. Toscanini, in flight from Fascist Italy, opposed any political interpretation of the Eroica. In a 1937 BBC tape he can be heard declaring to the musicians: 'Is not Napoleon! Is not 'Eetler! Is not Mussolini! Is *Allegro con brio*!'

41

Stolen

Eroica Variations, Op. 35 (1802)

THE FAMOUS THEME THAT SETS OFF THE EROICA SYMPHONY finale is not by Beethoven. A Yale musicologist, Leon Plantinga, locates it in a piano sonata in F minor, opus 13, No. 6, published in 1784, by the Italian-British composer, pianist and publisher Muzio Clementi. It is unmistakably the same idea, written eighteen years ahead of Beethoven's. Curiously, neither composer remarks upon it.

Clementi prefers Beethoven to Mozart, who once called him 'a charlatan, like all Italians,' and stole a theme from his B flat major sonata in *The Magic Flute* overture. Clementi moves to London and buys the publishing house of Longman & Broderip. He marries an English Emma and sires an English dynasty, one that latterly includes an RAF air vice-marshal and a deputy governor of the Bank of England. London is good for Clementi but he needs new product and travels regularly to Vienna. In April 1807 he bumps into Beethoven and secures publishing rights in England for all his works. Beethoven calls it 'a really satisfactory arrangement' and praises Clementi sonatas 'for their lovely, pleasing, original melodies'. Schindler writes: 'Among all the masters who have written for piano, Beethoven assigned to Clementi the very foremost rank. He considered his works excellent as studies for practice, for the formation of a pure taste, and as truly beautiful subjects for performance.'

Beethoven likes Clementi's Eroica tune so much that he uses it in four different works and gets fifteen variations out of it in this set. The 14th is wistful, mystic, multi-meaningful. I am hooked on recordings by Gould (1960) and Gilels (1980) until an Italian friend, Valerio Tura, directs me to a lost genius. Tura writes:

I was a teenager, and I used to attend concerts at Teatro Comunale di Bologna. In 1970 an all-Beethoven piano sonata series was planned, and I attended . . . almost all of them, sitting (or most times standing . . .) in the 'loggione' (the 'paradise', where students could buy the cheapest tickets). The concert which I believe I will never forget, was a recital by prominent upcoming Italian pianist Dino Ciani, not yet thirty at that time. After quite a demanding programme (if my memory does not fail he played Pathétique and Pastoral sonatas, plus the Diabelli Variations in the second part), the demand of encore was loud, strong and insistent . . . he kept being called back, over and over, maybe a dozen calls, and in the end he sat back at the piano and played one more astonishing rendition of the entire Diabelli Variations.

Ciani's 1973 recording of the Eroica Variations is no less revelatory. The space between notes can be practically taken out and deep-frozen. Months ahead, after playing a Beethoven concerto in Chicago with Carlo Maria Giulini, Ciani died in a road accident in Rome, aged thirty-two. An irremediable loss.

42

Poles apart

Piano Sonata No. 12 in A, 'Funeral march', Op. 26 (1801); Orchestral version, WoO96 (1815)

FREDERIC CHOPIN DISLIKES BEETHOVEN. HE TELLS THE painter Eugène Delacroix: 'Beethoven is obscure and seems to lack unity – not, as some claim, due to wild originality (a quality they admire) but because he turns his back on eternal principles. Mozart never does this.' He calls Beethoven 'very vulgar'.

The timid Chopin feels safe with Mozart's preset patterns. He fears Beethoven's freedoms, his restlessness. Teaching Beethoven to students, he assigns the twelfth sonata as a tame exemplar. Then, out of its third movement '*Marcia funebre sulla morte d'un eroe*' ('funeral march on the death of a hero'), he creates the famed funeral march of his own B flat minor sonata.

Russians, exposed to interminable repetitions of Chopin's march at freezing state funerals, have skin in this sonata. The redoubtable Maria Yudina, who supposedly refused a prize from Stalin, is inimitably sepulchral in this sonata (1958). Yudina describes her own playing as 'only an endless, screaming sign of despair'.

Beside her, others are merely gloomy. Maria Grinberg gives a tenebrous reading. Sviatoslav Richter is introspective, Emil Gilels darkly submissive. The question arises: is there a Russian way with Beethoven? Certainly none of these artists could be mistaken for any Westerner, or even for a veteran emigrant like Horowitz or Ashkenazy. Living under Stalin clearly imbued their perceptions; other shared qualities can be ascribed to a common experience of Soviet Russia.

The commonality starts with language. There is no letter 'h' in Russian. Trivial as this might seem, Beethoven with a 'kh' is not Beethoven as experienced in English, French or German. Then there is the matter of priority. Stalin placed Beethoven on a pedestal and spoke of his 'revolutionary' character. Pianists were encouraged to display a positivist Soviet style in his sonatas. Some tried. Most, while absorbing state propaganda, found individual affinities in the music. Lacking access to Western editions, they made their own. Restricted to scratchy sound studios, they found technical ways of transcending audio limitations. Every Russian piano recording of the 1950s is a triumph of will over wretched machines. Yudina, a devout Christian, performed transubstantiation. Grinberg, a modernist, reduced her sound spectrum to bare bones. Richter and Gilels took opposite approaches, one granitic, the other gentle. Both worked with and against the same grim circumstances. A collective defiance arose: Russian artists create beauty on a tin can in minus thirty degrees. Nowhere is there such a concentration or continuity of Beethoven pianism. Set aside the big four and you still have Neuhaus, Nikolaeva, Bashkirov, Grigory Ginzburg, Oborin, Sofronitsky, Alexeev, Gavrilov, Naumov, Pletnev, Kissin, Sokolov, Berezovsky, Berman, Ovchinnikov, Shcherbatov, Lugansky, Zilberstein, Leonskaja, Postnikova, Neuhaus' son Stanislav, Afanassiev, Demidenko, Lubimov, Matsuev, Ugorski, Gerstein, Trifonov, Gugnin and Levit. And that's without listing all the artists who died unrecorded in Siberian camps. Russia learned Beethoven the hard way. The rest of the world can but listen in awe.

ॽ

Beethoven sells this sonata to a London publisher, Johann Baptist Cramer. Mannheim born, Cramer is Clementi's rival with a shop on Regent Street and a set of eighty-four études that all students of the time have to learn. Beethoven makes his sonata slightly easier to get a Cramer deal. He also licenses the third movement as orchestral music for a stage play, *Leonore Prochaska*, about a Potsdam woman who cross-dresses into army uniform to fight Napoleon. Wounded in the Battle of Göhrde in 1813, she is exposed as a female during field surgery. After weeks of agony, she dies aged twenty-eight. Despite Beethoven's music, Johann Friedrich Duncker's play never gets staged in Vienna.

43

Head or heart

Piano Sonata No. 27, Op. 90 (1814)

AS A YOUNG MAN, SVIATOSLAV RICHTER HUNG OUT AT THE Odessa opera house, coaching singers and learning the vocal repertoire by heart. In 1941, his father was shot as an alleged German spy. He never forgave his mother for her suspected role in his betrayal. Believed to be gay, Richter lived from 1943 with the soprano Nina Dorliak. While Oistrakh and Gilels were allowed to travel after Stalin died, Richter was not let out until October 1960 for fear he might defect or otherwise discredit the Soviet regime.

Gilels, from an Odessa-Jewish background, married the pianist Rosa Tamarkina, who came second in the 1937 Warsaw Chopin Competition. He won the Queen Elisabeth in Brussels in his own right the following year. His sister Elizabeth came third in the Queen Elisabeth violin contest (won by Oistrakh). Elizabeth Gilels married the violinist Leonid Kogan, who reported to a KGB colonel. Emil often partnered Kogan in recital, fearing his secret-state connections while occasionally using them for humanitarian purposes. Gilels is supposed to have sprung Heinrich Neuhaus from Lubyanka prison in 1944. He later fell out so badly with Kogan that he refused to pay a condolence visit to his own sister on her husband's death. Gilels, behind a mousy exterior, had an explosive temper.

After Rosa died, aged thirty, Gilels had a wartime affair with a Leningrad nurse, Bonya Hirshberg, a strong-minded woman who left him because she could not bear his tantrums. In 1947 Gilels married a poet, Farizet Almahsitovna Hutsistova, in what appears to have been a devoted union. She wrote of him:

He loved light, comfortable shoes, he laced them up quickly and attractively, with a special 'knot', bending down to one foot, then to the other, while sitting. He cleaned the shoes with a yellow, fluffy 'prop' with quick, short movements. He loved the summery Italian, almost a little dapper, as well as the 'serious' patent leather shoes. For the street he preferred English ones – made of waterproof suede. He chose shoes resolutely, quickly, trying them on, wondering if his foot didn't feel the slightest bit of discomfort . . . From the sound of the footsteps one could recognize his inner state.

Richter and Gilels competed in every aspect of life and work. When Richter gave the world premiere of Sergei Prokofiev's 7th piano sonata, Gilels grabbed the 8th. Richter's sonorities could be monochrome, austere. Gilel played with an unrivalled palette of colours. At the 1960 Tchaikovsky Competition, Richter gave top marks to the American Van Cliburn while Gilels went trembling to the Soviet ruler Nikita Khrushchev asking if he might perhaps be permitted to give first prize to a foreigner ('Is he the best?' said Khrushchev. 'Then give it!').

Each pianist had a personal way of contextualising Beethoven. Richter would twin a Beethoven sonata with the serialist Webern, Gilels with the Stalin-era Prokofiev. The pianist Yakov Zak noted that Gilels observed 'the pathos of distance'. His colleague Valery Afanassiev said Gilels 'knew how to shape and handle silence like no one else.'

Both men played the weighty 27th sonata as a recital opener; both recorded it twice. Richter, on a rattly piano in January 1951, delivers ever-expanding breadth of expression. 'I play for myself and the composer,' he said. Gilels, in an April 1957 London concert, opens with a brutal statement that melts in stages into a wonderfully consolatory resolution. In his 1974 DG recording, he produces exquisite sound in a reference performance. That two artists so opposite in temperament should flourish under totalitarianism is a testament to the capacity of great artists to work their way through the cracks in an iron curtain.

Schindler calls the first movement of this sonata 'a contest between head and heart' and the second a 'conversation with the beloved'. The music is written in the thick of lawsuits. Beethoven lets through nothing of his stress.

44

Red Square

Piano Sonata No. 23 in F minor, 'Appassionata', Op. 57 (1804–6)

VLADIMIR ILYICH LENIN IS THE BIGGEST FAN OF THIS SONATA. 'I know nothing that is greater than the "Appassionata,"' he tells the writer Maxim Gorky. 'I would like to listen to it every day. It is marvellous, super-human music. I always think with pride – perhaps naïvely – what marvellous things humans can do.'

Lenin is presenting himself as a leader who can stand back from ideology and marvel at mortal genius. He wants Gorky to consider him *kulturny*, a person of cultural sensitivity, and *chutkiy* – empathetic to human feeling. Such qualities, however, must never override the priorities of politics. Lenin continues:

> I can't listen to music very often, it affects my nerves. I want to say sweet, silly things, and pat the little heads of people who, living in a filthy hell, can create such beauty. These days one can't pat anyone on the head, they might bite your hand off. Hence, you have to beat people's little heads, beat mercilessly, although ideally we are against doing any violence to people. Hmmm . . . what a devilishly difficult job!

Lenin's Beethoven quotation – sometimes augmented with a coda 'If I keep listening to it, I won't finish the revolution' – lays the foundation of Soviet cultural policy. Art exists to elevate *homo sovieticus*, but not to the point where it moderates the cleansing violence of revolution. Culture must not be mistaken for humanity: in Communism, it is a useful weapon in the class war.

Soviet propaganda adopts Beethoven as a fellow-traveller. Stalin declares the ninth symphony to be 'the right music for the masses. It can't be performed enough and it ought to be heard in the smallest of our villages.' Beethoven's 'be embraced, you millions' serves as cover for Stalin's murder of millions.

How did culture become an instrument of state policy? A Russian classicist at the University of London, Dr Irene Polinskaya, offers this analysis:

Being *kulturny* was not a choice but a condition of social class. Lenin and Stalin grew up in families of *raznochintzy* – (midway) between the aristocracy and the peasantry. Culture for such people was an aspiration to higher status. Russian nobility, imitating its European cousins, educated its young in languages, music, literature and other refinements. If *raznochintzy* were to mix in noble circles, they had to be also educated in the arts. And with such education came the appreciation of its value. So, culture is not what Lenin chooses or rejects, it is part of him and hence of his internal conflict. The point is not that Lenin or Stalin cared about being perceived as 'cultured' but that they had to accept that culture was a fact of life . . . and since it could not be eliminated or ignored, they had to *make it work for the Revolution* . . . Had either Lenin or Stalin been from peasant backgrounds, they would never have heard of Beethoven and would have had nothing to say about that and would not have worried about being made soft by 'Appassionata'.

The Bolsheviks' failure to ban 'old' culture left a seed of beauty and softness, ultimately, of humanity . . . and allowed Russia and Russians to live through the Soviet experiment. In schools, reading Tolstoy, Chekhov and Dostoevsky and going to the Philharmonic on a monthly basis was a norm. Nowadays, pop culture and social media have replaced them. There is nothing in contemporary Russia that could foster an indigenous cultural revival.

The 'Appassionata' is named by a Hamburg publisher, August Cranz, ten years after Beethoven's death. The music is passionate in determination rather than emotion. Czerny calls it 'the most perfect execution of a mighty and colossal plan.' In the opening pages, the 'fate' motif of an unwritten fifth symphony flickers between the lines.

Beethoven's pupil Ries observes the work in progress on a long summer's day in the Vienna Woods:

> We went so far astray that we did not get back to Döbling until nearly 8 o'clock. He had been humming, and more often howling, always up and down, without singing any definite notes. When questioned as to what it was he answered, 'A theme for the last movement of the sonata has occurred to me.' When we entered the room he ran to the pianoforte without taking off his hat. I took a seat on the corner and he soon forgot all about me. He stormed on for at least an hour with the beautiful finale of the sonata. Finally he got up, was surprised that I was still there and said, 'I cannot give you a lesson today, I must do some work.'

Beethoven plays his 25-minute sonata at all his usual mansions, testing pianofortes to destruction with bulging fistfuls of bottom notes. 'The moment he is seated at the piano he is evidently unconscious that there is anything else in existence,' writes one cowed listener.

Artur Schnabel in this sonata is headlong, madcap, irresistible. Emil Gilels lets the music unfold organically in Berlin's Jesus-Christus-Kirche. Sviatoslav Richter resets the clock to his own erratic heartbeat. There is a 1947 Abbey Road performance by the Russian composer Nikolai Medtner, wayward and bleak, just how his friend Rachmaninov might have played it. Topping my reject pile are Vladimir Horowitz (capricious), Van Cliburn (unimaginative), Glenn Gould (over-imaginative), Evgeny Kissin (relentless) and Lang Lang (unfeeling). Among current interpreters, I am thrilled by the Argentine Ingrid Fliter and the Russian-German Igor Levit. But when all's said and done, it's Richter and Gilels who set the tone, unwittingly perpetuating Lenin's monolithic dictum.

45

Historically informed

Symphony No. 4 in B flat major, Op. 60 (1808)

MY FRIENDSHIP WITH NEVILLE MARRINER DEEPENED ONE JUNE evening in Kensington as the claret bottle on the low table between us went down with the reddening sun. I was trying to get Neville talking about how he discovered there was more than one way of playing classical music. 'It was around D-Day,' he reflected.

'You were in the Normandy landings?' I prompted.

'No, it was just before.'

Marriner, a volunteer in the Special Boat Service, got sent out at night to collect sand from French beaches so that geologists could assess their landing potential. It was a hazardous mission from which few were expected to return. 'We got the sand and were on our way out,' he recalled, 'when the German guns spotted us and opened up on our boat.'

Scraping back to England with shrapnel shredding one of his kidneys, Marriner woke up in hospital next to a mathematician called Thurston Dart, a polymath who intended to complete his music studies in Belgium after the war. Dart explained that music probably sounded different in Mozart's day. This came as a shock to Neville, who had been happily play-ing violin in the London Symphony Orchestra since he was sixteen and imagined this was what Mozart had intended. Dart told him Mozart wrote his music for simpler instruments, and at a decidedly lower pitch. Modern orchestras were missing the point, he maintained.

'Thurston was very grand but the style he was looking for suited my way of playing,' Neville decided, 'so after the war we'd get together, a few of us, twice a week, to try a different way'. His group, rehearsing in the Church of St Martin-in-the-Fields on Trafalgar Square, started with baroque Vivaldi, worked through classical music and finally reached Beethoven.

They had furious rows at almost every rehearsal. The pianist Christopher Hogwood stormed out when others refused to play at a lower pitch. Neville was the peacemaker, seeking compromise between a radical, grating sound and acceptable modern beauty. Leading from the violin, it took time for him to realise he had become a conductor.

'Pierre Monteux said to me one day [in the LSO], why don't you put down that violin and stand up to conduct like a man?' he reported. Neville began taking lessons with the man who had premiered *The Rite of Spring*, applying the imagined shock of the new back to Beethoven's era.

He was fortunate in his timing. Stereo had just come on stream and record labels were looking for new ways to sell classical warhorses. A grant from an Australian heiress enabled Neville's group to cut their first records. Vivaldi's *Four Seasons*, still a novelty on record, established their best-selling credentials. In time, Neville would make three hundred recordings, more than any conductor except Karajan. By 1960, the early music movement was going global, although Neville kept his seat as principal second violin in the LSO for the rest of the decade.

In Vienna, the aristocratic Nikolaus Harnoncourt underwent a parallel evolution. Descended from Habsburg emperors and now earning his living as Karajan's principal cellist, Harnoncourt spent his leisure hours in junk shops, acquiring medieval instruments and teaching himself how to play them. With like-minded friends, he formed the Concentus Musicus Wien as a skinny alternative to Karajan's big-band sound. When a Concentus record hit the charts, Karajan banned Harnoncourt from the Salzburg Festival and never spoke to him again.

HIP – Historically Informed Performance – was now spreading like measles. In Amsterdam, Gustav Leonhardt taught Bach on early keyboards; Frans Brüggen in The Hague favoured wooden flutes. An American in Paris, William Christie, revived Charpentier and Rameau. The Cologne-based Reinhard Goebel earned the nickname 'Ayatollah'. Soon, they all descended on Beethoven.

First to record the symphonies on period instruments were the Hanover Band, a conductorless ensemble based in Brighton. Bracing as sea air, their sonority was certainly different if not altogether pleasing. Next up was Hogwood with brilliant Decca sound and interpretations that felt routine on second hearing. The cultural philosopher Roger

Scruton complained that HIP was 'elevating musicology over music' and he was not entirely wrong. John Eliot Gardiner spouted more theories than he could possibly prove and others called Pinnock and Parrott, Kuijken and Clemencic, Herreweghe and Haim, kept sniping from the sides.

Mainstream conductors, feeling threatened, responded by assimilating period style into their regular practice. Claudio Abbado conducted his young Orchestra Mozart on instruments both ancient and modern. Simon Rattle and Vladimir Jurowski cut their milk teeth on the period style of the Orchestra of the Age of Enlightenment. François-Xavier Roth and Teodor Currentzis played both sides against the middle, where Neville Marriner held sway for half a century as the centrepoint of reasonable colloquium between ancient and modern sound.

The fourth symphony proved itself a good litmus test for HIP Beethoven on record, being riddled with outlandish approaches. Its understated, ultra-slow opening anticipates Schumann and Mahler. Hector Berlioz speaks of the symphony's 'heavenly gentleness'. Leonard Bernstein calls it 'the biggest surprise package Beethoven has ever handed us'. Carlos Kleiber, whose 1982 Munich recording is at once magical and wayward, claimed a repetitive viola motif in the second movement is Beethoven plaintively crying 'Therese, Therese'. The Marxist social philosopher Theodor W. Adorno astutely calls the symphony 'suspended time.' Shorter than the Eroica, the fourth is contemporaneous with the fifth symphony and the violin concerto. There are four movements: two slow, two fast.

Among the HIPsters, Hogwood is faintly pedagogic. Norrington and Harnoncourt hold a fire extinguisher to the Promethean conflagration. Gardiner is superficial, Brüggen abrasive. The Belgian Jan van Immerseel (2006) is slick and assured. Beside them, Neville Marriner's 1976 release sails serene – sensitive, supple, sleek, slow-quick-slow with never a moment of doubt. In the finale, Marriner draws together untied Beethoven laces like no one else.

I am also smitten by Yevgeny Mravinsky and the Leningrad Philharmonic in 1955. A decade after the siege of Leningrad, these musicians knew what it was to live under bombardment, as Beethoven did. Mravinsky's disciple Mariss Jansons turned bleak memories to autumnal reveries (2012). The Czech Rafael Kubelík shared homelessness and paradise lost in 1974 with fellow-exiles in the Israel Philharmonic. Furtwängler's June 1943 broadcast is dread-filled, crackling with audience coughs and air-raid warnings. Karajan's best take is in 1963 Berlin. Abbado, Rattle, Chailly and Ivan Fischer are all atmospheric. Bernstein, who heard this Beethoven symphony growing up in Boston more than any other, infuses his 1978 Vienna recording with Haydn-like lightness and lashings of wit. Above all, I prefer Marriner.

Neville was a fine conductor and a caring man. When I asked why he kept on touring past the age of ninety, he gave a weary smile and explained that some of his musicians relied on his famous name to get work, and without him they would starve. Sir Neville Marriner died at home on a Saturday night in October 2016, hours before leading another musical landing in Europe.

46

Early birds

Quintet in E flat, Op. 16 (1797); Wind Trio, Op. 87 (1794)

SYMPHONIES ARE NOT THE EASIEST WAY TO DIFFERENTIATE between modern and period sound. The skeletal lines of chamber music are better. There's a vigorous, old-style 1950s recording of the quintet for oboe, clarinet, horn, bassoon and piano led by the prodigious British hornist Dennis Brain, as plush as it gets. Contrast it with the Belgian period ensemble Octophoros in 2006 and Brain's team sounds winded. On period instruments everything feels free range, pitch and tempi, soft keyboard and astringent horn. Now contrast both of these with players of the Academy of St Martin-in-the-Fields and you will find perfect centre.

Beethoven's winsome wind trio attracts attention from the Boston period oboist Lani Spahr, who models her oboes on an instrument in the library at Yale and her cor anglais from the national museum in Lisbon. The benefits? Marginal. The virtuosic Heinz Holliger and François Leleux sound far better on modern reeds.

47

Post horn

Horn Sonata, Op. 17 (1800)

UNLIKE MOZART, WHO WROTE FOR HARP, GLASS HARMONICA, bassoon and anyone who paid for supper, Beethoven sticks on the whole to piano, violin and cello. He makes an exception with this sonata, written for a tour with a Czech hornist, Giovanni Punto, whose real name is Johann Wenzel Stich. Punto has invented hand-stopping technique, improving his control of horn tone.

The horn he plays is a piece of metal curlicued around itself and ending in an estuary-like bell shape. Punto changes notes by lip pressure and by sticking his hand in the bell. Beethoven writes this sonata the night before their recital at Vienna's Burgtheater. The middle movement is barely a minute long, a mark of Beethoven's disrespect. Punto cancels the tour on the second date.

Dennis Brain, a player whose serenity persuades Benjamin Britten to write his Serenade for Tenor, Horn and Strings, makes the signature recording, partnered somewhat dustily by Denis Matthews. Major composers – Hindemith, Malcolm Arnold, Gordon Jacob – write concertos for Brain. He is the one player in London whom Furtwängler asks for by name. Karajan books him for Mozart. Taking nothing too seriously, he performs a Leopold Mozart concerto on a garden hose.

In September 1957, driving home at night from the Edinburgh Festival, Dennis Brain drives his Triumph TR2 sports car into a tree on the A1, north of London. He dies instantly, aged thirty-six. The French composer Francis Poulenc mourns him in an inconsolably atonal Elegy for Horn and Piano.

Many horn players match Brain for virtuosity but none has his insouciance. The only player to deliver a comparable ear-baffling brilliance in

Beethoven is an obscure Soviet, Yakov Shapiro, partnered by Emil Gilels in 1951. All I can find about Shapiro is that he was born in Minsk in 1908 and was solo horn of Soviet Radio and the Bolshoi Theatre from 1943 until 1952. No date of death is registered. In this Beethoven recording, Shapiro blows rings around Gilels, playing just as he pleases and with a slight, improvisatory discoloration in the finale. Did the pair even rehearse beforehand? It's that spontaneous.

48

Blank pages

Piano Concerto No. 3 in C minor, Op. 37 (1801)

TOYING WITH HIS AUDIENCE, BEETHOVEN CASTS HIS THIRD concerto in the key of Mozart's 24th (K491) and with an opening theme of uncanny similarity. Most of the forty-minute work is still in his head when he first plays it. Here's an account by the Theater an der Wien concertmaster, Ignaz Seyfried:

'In playing the concerto movements he asked me to turn the pages for him; but – heaven help me – that was no easy thing. I saw almost nothing but empty sheet; at most on one page or other a few Egyptian hieroglyphs wholly incomprehensible to me scribbled down to serve as clues to himself; he played nearly all of the solo part from memory, since, as was often the case, he had not had time to put it all on paper. He gave me a secret glance whenever he reached the end of one of the invisible passages; my visible anxiety not to miss a vital moment amused him greatly and he laughed heartily over it at the jovial supper which we ate later.'

Consider his response to failure. Instead of slinking home as most of us would, he goes to dinner laughing 'heartily' in defiance. Does he not care what people think? Or is that the precise, stuff-you message he wants to project?

The concerto leaves enough of an impression for some rich men to request a second performance. Beethoven assigns it contemptuously to his pupil Ries, telling him to write his own cadenza and ripping it to pieces in his dressing room before the concert. Despite his intervention, the concert goes well and Beethoven is first to his feet to applaud. He is perfectionist, professional, generous, never knowingly predictable. The concerto matters greatly to him. He will return shortly to the C minor key for his fateful fifth symphony.

At the heart of the concerto, a slow largo, the pianist holds the pedal down to create a mood of blurred contentment. The work concludes with a mood-swing rondo, at once fiery and fretful. Great pianists cherish this work. Claudio Arrau records it eight times, Arthur Rubinstein six, Emil Gilels five. When Glenn Gould plays it at his 1957 Berlin debut the ultra-modernist critic, Hans Heinz Stuckenschmidt, proclaims him the most interesting pianist since Busoni, which is not altogether an exaggeration. Gould makes the weather in this music.

Arrau is heard best in 1957 with Otto Klemperer; Gilels is supreme in Cleveland with George Szell in 1966; Radu Lupu is breath-taking in 1981 with the Israel Philharmonic and Zubin Mehta. Also in contention are Michelangeli (1987), the feather-fingered Rudolf Firkušný at Salzburg 1963 and the ursine Yefim Bronfman in David Zinman's 2005 Zurich set. A 2021 performance in Geneva by the Russian Mikhail Pletnev takes the breath away with the pellucid transparency of his sound. The notes seem to come from nowhere, a trickle-down from the dawn of time. Pletnev, a Tchaikovsky Competition winner in 1978, went on to vest so much of his career in conducting the Russian National Orchestra that one can easily forget how original and overwhelming a pianist he can be. This Claves release is quite the most enjoyable C minor interpretation of the twenty-first century.

Women do a different C minor. Annie Fischer, with Ferenc Fricsay in 1957 Berlin, delivers a tempered eruption of Hungarian erudition, taking her bows in a cloud of smoke. 'The only times she did not have a cigarette between her lips was when she was on stage or asleep,' writes the violinist Györy Pauk.

Clara Haskil, a Sephardic Romanian, lived in pain from 1941 after a tumour removal in German-occupied Paris. 'Haskil nursed an inborn fear predominantly of playing the piano and secondly of her own mortality. It is in her playing that we became profoundly aware that time is indeed running out and at a frightening pace,' writes her pupil Peter Feuchtwanger. Haskil's November 1960 Paris recording of the C minor concerto with Igor Markevitch seems to use her own fragile heartbeat as a metronome in a performance that, like Einstein, redefines our conception of time. Weeks later she slipped on icy steps at a Brussels railway station and died, aged sixty-five. Charlie Chaplin says: 'In my lifetime I have met three geniuses: Professor Einstein, Winston Churchill, and Clara Haskil.'

Martha Argerich was sixty-three before she recorded this concerto. It achieves transcendental communication. In the finale, she overrides the conductor Claudio Abbado like a lover prioritising her own needs in coitus. Mitsuko Uchida (1986), Maria João Pires (2014) and Alice Sara Ott (2018), each in her own way, amplifies an impressive feminine chain of interpretation.

Wake me before dawn and the first Beethoven C minor that I would name is Arthur Rubinstein's. An irrepressible entertainer, Rubinstein records the C minor concerto with Toscanini, Krips, Leinsdorf, Ormandy and others, but the most singular of his qualities of generosity and continuity is heard in an avuncular 1976 concert with a young Daniel Barenboim conducting the London Philharmonic. Hear it now, and you'll think it's Barenboim playing the piano, such are the mysteries of musical transmission.

49

The one

Violin Concerto in D major, Op. 61 (1806)

WHEN MUSICIANS SPEAK OF 'THE BEETHOVEN CONCERTO', THIS is the one they mean. He may have written five works and more for piano and orchestra, but *the* Beethoven concerto is this, the one for violin against orchestra. Taking a dialogue between soloist and orchestra that evolved through Vivaldi, Bach, Haydn and Mozart, Beethoven doubles the duration, inserts confrontation and adds more orchestral weight than anyone thought the structure could bear. Like Gustave Eiffel's 'giddy, ridiculous' tower, his stubborn elevation stands every test of durability for all time to come.

Beethoven composes the violin concerto in the late autumn of 1806 alongside three string quartets, his fourth symphony and the G major piano concerto. He has French officers billeted in his house, which does not improve his mood. He is distracted, uncomfortable, irritated. As usual he fails to deliver the score until a day ahead of premiere, the night before Christmas Eve. The soloist Franz Clement is an experienced concertmaster and a composer in his own right, but Beethoven leaves him no time to learn the piece, let alone rehearse it. Clement is noted for 'delicacy, neatness and elegance', the antithesis of Beethoven. At one point, in rehearsal, Clement plays his violin upside down in protest.

The premiere is a fiasco. A writer in the *Wiener Zeitung* mentions discontinuity and disruption, urging Beethoven in future to 'make better use of his admittedly great talents'. The work unsettles from the start, five soft kettledrum taps. The soloist's entry is an apologetic intrusion as if the player is saying 'is it really my turn now?' The concluding passage in the finale runs so long that people think Beethoven is drivelling away, looking for an exit strategy.

Who wins? Some soloists claim the concerto is Beethoven's attack on his violinist father, but there is neither musical nor documentary validation for this theory. If the composer has any conflict in mind it is between citizen and society, between himself and a foreign occupation, between the powerless and the powerful. The work achieves apotheosis in a grudging acceptance of the world as it is.

He signs off the violin concerto and never writes another, seemingly convinced of its failure. Over three decades, a meagre handful of soloists perform it without success – Haydn's concertmaster Luigi Tomasini in Berlin, the Belgian Henri Vieuxtemps in Paris; Baillot (1828), Wiele (1829), Barnbeck (1834), Ulrich (1836), Gulomy (1841). London's Philharmonic Society is informed that violinists find it 'not a proper and effective development of the powers of that instrument.'

Until a kid in short pants shows how it's done. Joseph Joachim, brought to London by Felix Mendelssohn a month before his bar mitzvah, surprises his mentor by asking to play the Beethoven concerto. On 27 May 1844 'frenetic applause' greets his performance, with 'hearty cheering' from the orchestra. Tears glint on Mendelssohn's cheeks and a 'look of amazement' passes over the concertmaster's face. What has Joachim just done? One critic notes that he 'entered into the spirit and character of the concerto', treating it as a unique object, different from any preceding work and superior to all others in form and content. Even so, one has to marvel at the determination of a chubby-faced child to take on a concerto of this length and complexity and deliver it with such authority that comprehension and pleasure are the immediate outcome.

From here on, the concerto gets taken up by everyone, becoming a staple of cultural heritage, while Joachim founds an alternative model of violinist fame. Rejecting the Paganini career of crazy tricks and constant touring, he settles as concertmaster in Liszt's orchestra in Weimar, and then at the court of Hanover, becoming a Protestant to secure the post (when an unconverted Jewish musician is refused promotion in the orchestra, Joachim quits and moves to Berlin, where, at royal command, he founds a world-class music conservatoire).

His friends are great composers – Schumann and Brahms, later Dvořák and Bruch – all of whom consult him in the making of their concertos. Heavily bearded and opinionated, Joachim enjoys unique status in the violin works of the romantic period and a social respectability never accorded before to a concert soloist. This hard-won status would be tarnished in the 1880s when Joachim unaccountably accused his wife Amalie, with whom he had six children, of sleeping with his publisher, Franz Simrock. Brahms sided with the wronged Amalie and Joachim's attachment to great composers never fully recovered from divorce-court coverage.

Throughout Joachim's long life, the Beethoven concerto is one of his signature works, alongside those of Mendelssohn and Brahms. He writes two cadenzas for the Beethoven, one in 1852 and another in 1894, and these become the industry standard thanks to his claim to have redeemed it from failure. The cadenza, a passage of freedom in a concerto where the soloist can play what he likes, is concretised in the Beethoven concerto at Joachim's dictation.

Joachim's cadenzas prevail for half a century until a Viennese entertainer bounces up, twinkle-eyed and bushy-moustached. Fritz Kreisler's cadenzas are unabashed crowd-pleasers, flashy and hyper-romantic. Kreisler is the antithesis of Joachim, a womaniser and gambler who hoaxes the critics with fake-baroque encores and composes a Broadway operetta and a movie score. Wounded in the German trenches in the First World War, Kreisler is high-society's soloist par excellence until the Nazis come to power in 1933 and he emigrates to America, his name erased from German history and his works banned.

That creates a sudden problem when the Germans realise that the only two cadenzas that everyone plays for the Beethoven concerto are written by two Jews, Joachim and Kreisler. Amid embarrassment in Berlin, both are tacitly reinstated and continue to be performed in German concert halls and on radio throughout the Third Reich. The Kreisler cadenza is broadcast from the Philharmonie in the very last January 1944 concerts before it is bombed to rubble; the soloist is the Berlin Philharmonic concertmaster, Erich Röhn, the conductor Wilhelm Furtwängler, and the recording sounds more like Wagner's immolation scene in *Twilight of the Gods* than anything by Beethoven. In the history of classical recording, this performance is a titanic aberration, transfixing the listener with its political authenticity and musical perversity.

Joachim, who died in 1907, never left an audible record of the concerto. Kreisler made two recordings, in December 1926 with a Berlin orchestra conducted by Leo Blech, and in June 1936 with John Barbirolli and the London Philharmonic. Both are paramount performances, yielding undimmed pleasure on repeated listening. No recommendation list is complete without them and neither is ever surpassed in the relaxed sense of ownership that the soloist exhibits in the score.

Deutsche Grammophon's all-time best-sellers in the Beethoven concerto are the teenaged Anne-Sophie Mutter with Karajan in 1979 and the teen idol David Garrett in 2011, the former a prim and proper head girl, the latter a bad boy in ripped jeans; Britain's Nigel Kennedy vies with Garrett in public misconduct.

In the quiet carriage of this clattering train, Herman Krebbers, the long-serving Amsterdam concertmaster, gives a Dutch object lesson in putting the music first in a concerto and the player's personality last; Bernard Haitink is the empathetic conductor. Yehudi Menuhin's 1947 dialogue with Wilhelm Furtwängler crackles with unarticulated tensions on both sides. If only they could have spoken their minds, this might have been a performance for the ages.

How does one make a shortlist from two hundred recordings? Overwhelmed, I consult the Latvian violinist Gidon Kremer, a cerebral soloist with strong and sometimes quirky views. Kremer emails me his own quest for the ideal Beethoven concerto on record:

I became more and more desperate as time went by. Repeated listening added to my confusion. One day it seemed that my favourite was Zino Francescatti. On the next it seemed that Joseph Szigeti – especially with his authority and cadenza – won my heart. Then I again returned to the impeccable readings of Heifetz and Milstein. Their sheer perfection was a factor I could not ignore. I also had notions that the cadenzas by Szigeti/ Milstein and even Huberman deserve to be published as a kind of a bonus to the set of 'ideal recordings'.

And then . . . something unexpected happened. It came to me 'out of the blue'. As I explored the realms of YouTube, I discovered a recording which progressively intrigued and then overwhelmed me. Slowly it became not only my preference above all those I had spent weeks listening to, but clearly my choice. The discovery made my day! I felt relieved to recognise my own set of values and was able to dismiss the idea of being so fixed on my own reception of the concerto that none of other interpreters would ever be able to convince me. It was such a relief because my dissatisfaction with so many great interpretations which I certainly appreciated but did not love had taken me almost to the point of thinking that my listening abilities were very limited, that I was simply unable to differentiate clearly enough. I felt that I had failed to give a clear professional explanation. Why couldn't I pick out a favourite among so many jewels? Was I too snobbish? Too choosy? Too narrow-minded?

Like a dark cloud on a sunny day, all this frustration suddenly vanished. I had stumbled over one performance which gradually entered the space within me that I have called my 'soul'. Something else happened, too. There was something more interesting about the discovery itself. I became aware that many of the things that I had described as too disturbing for an 'ideal' reading suddenly became secondary considerations . . . Probably the most surprising element of my discovery was that the interpretation that I came across 'by chance' was totally unlike my own imagined 'ideal' reading of the work. What I appreciated, loved, adored – and despite the deficiencies referred to above, always will! – was the fact that this performance was the most personal one. It was not just a display of instrumental capacities at the highest level that was completely devoid of narcissism; it was genuine and very human music-making that also displayed the highest level of commitment to the creator. It simply matched my ideal notion of 'inspiration'.

So what was the recording that had dispelled the gloom of my indecision and brightened my day? For me the best, warmest, most human, most personal performance and the one most dedicated to music – one that everyone should listen to – is the live-recording of Ginette Neveu with the South-West German Radio Orchestra under Hans Rosbaud, dated September 1949, one month before, at the age of 30, she and her pianist brother died in an air crash while on their way to a concert tour in the USA. More than any other, this performance is filled with plenty of emotion (but not emotionalism), clarity and an individual approach. Re-releasing this unique document of a human soul audibly 'breathing' – literally and as well musically – would be a reminder of many things at once: the tragedy of life, the eternal power of artistic creations by geniuses, the multitude of possible approaches to a masterpiece (bearing in mind that next to it, the same set would include Diapason's own choice, a recording by David Oistrakh – Ginette Neveu's rival in the Wienawski competition, which she won!). To hear both of them playing the same cadenza would not be to enter them into another competition but would display something of the variety of different approaches to it. For me, the cadenza played by Ginette Neveu demonstrates the closest relationship to . . . Ludwig. Another reason why this, and no other recording, would be my choice.

Kremer is too humble to mention his own contribution to the concerto's evolution. In 1981, chafing at the conservatism of Soviet apparatchiks and American label executives, Kremer recorded the concerto for Philips with cadenzas by the wickedly original and unfailingly provocative Russian composer Alfred Schnittke. A modernist who blindsided the commissars by simulating Mozart passages in his scores, Schnittke pasted together a Beethoven cadenza out of clips of every major violin concerto from Bach to Alban Berg. This 'open window in the space of a composition' (Kremer's phrase) allowed the work to exist first as a chronology of concerto history and then as an artwork in its own right; ultimately as a gateway to a collagist, polystylist musical future. I loved it on first hearing and wrote an instant panegyric in the *Sunday Times*.

Mine, however, was a lone voice. Both Soviet and Western conservatives called it an abuse of Beethoven's masterpiece. *Gramophone* magazine grouched in its inimitable style and executives on Philips deleted the recording to avoid further offence (though it's now on YouTube). I still love the Schnittke cadenzas and wish more violinists would give them a try, instead of recycling Kreisler and Joachim like lobotomised parrots. At last, in summer 2020, the boutique BIS label in Sweden issued a new recording of the Schnittke cadenzas by a Russian émigré, Vadim Gluzman, which I find no less refreshing than Kremer's.

In summary, if only the most remarkable will do, I would urge you to choose from the following dozen: Kreisler (1926), Josef Wolfsthal (1929), Menuhin (1947), Neveu (1949), Oistrakh (1959), Milstein (1971), Mutter (1979), Perlman (1981), Kremer (1982), Janine Jansen (2009), Patricia Kopatchinskaja (2009) and Gluzman (2020).

50

Chips off

Concerto for Pianoforte and Orchestra in D, Op. 61a (1807); Romances, Opp. 40 and 50 (1798–1803)

THE LONDON PUBLISHER MUZIO CLEMENTI HAS A BETTER IDEA. He gets Beethoven to make a piano version of the violin concerto to give it a stronger chance.

> I agreed with him to take in manuscript three [string] quartets, a symphony [the Fourth], an overture [the Coriolan], a concerto for violin which is beautiful and which, at my request, he will adapt for the pianoforte, and a concerto for the pianoforte [the Fourth], for all of which we are to pay him one hundred pounds sterling. I think I have made a very good bargain.

Beethoven writes a cadenza for the first movement of the revised violin concerto with plenty of percussion and some extra riffs. He also makes copious corrections to Clementi's piano score, but no one wants to perform it. In his lifetime it is the only one of his substantive orchestral works that is a total write-off.

On record, there is a 1954 Vienna performance where the soloist is Helen Schnabel, Arthur's daughter-in-law. The interpretation is immersive, with moments of near-rapture in the slow movement. Elsewhere, Daniel Barenboim directs the work unconvincingly from the keyboard. Peter Serkin (Rudolf's son), playing with Seiji Ozawa and the New Philharmonia in his hippie phase, gives the work a subversive tweak, ambling along as if he's not sure he should be doing this square stuff, but liking it despite himself. It's a curiosity, and no worse for that.

Each of Beethoven's two romances for violin and orchestra has a catchy theme, followed by general adumbrations. David and Igor Oistrakh present an agreeable study in generational contrast. I enjoy Heifetz (1951), Menuhin with Furtwängler (1953) and Christian Ferras with Leopold Ludwig (1955) – the kind of aristocratic playing we may never hear again. Nathan Milstein (1975) is the acme of elegance. The technically challenged, stunningly beautiful Gioconda de Vito recorded the romances soon after marrying her EMI boss David Bicknell, but she's classier than you'd think. Anne-Sophie Mutter (with Kurt Masur and the New York Philharmonic) turns the Romances into coffee-morning chatter, low-level and inessential, a missed opportunity.

51

Black notes

Sonata for Violin and Piano No. 9,
'Kreutzer sonata', Op. 47 (1803)

ON THE MORNING OF 16 APRIL 1803, BEETHOVEN SEES A PAIR of acquaintances on the street, an aristocrat and his physician, and invites them to a rehearsal at Schuppanzigh's. 'We met a number of the best musicians gathered together,' writes the doctor, 'the violinists Krumbholz, Möser [of Berlin, and] the mulatto Bridgethauer who in London had been in the service of the Prince of Wales.'

George Augustus Polgreen Bridgetower is turning heads in Vienna. Son of an African valet in the Esterházy household, he wins Haydn's approval and, aged nine, is toured like Mozart. Haydn's London impresario, Johann Peter Salomon, gives him a booking. He plays at the royal Handel commemoration of 1791 and visits Brighton and Bath. The future King George IV pays for his tuition and employs him as concertmaster. He becomes a familiar figure in drawing rooms and watering places. I wonder if the producers of the Netflix costume drama *Bridgerton* did not unwittingly take the series' name from Bridgetower, a mixed-race violin virtuoso at the social apex of Regency London.

At twenty years old, Bridgetower sets off around Europe. He arrives in Vienna as the trees come into blossom. Everyone is whistling Beethoven's Spring Sonata. Beethoven is enchanted by Bridgetower and takes him under his wing. Bridgetower is handsome, flamboyant, charming. Beethoven asks if he'd like to play a new sonata with him. Bridgetower is up for it. Beethoven books an open-air concert in the Augarten on 24 May for eight a.m., the only slot he can get. At four-thirty that morning, Beethoven tells Ferdinand Ries to make the soloist a clean copy of the violin part; the piano part is still 'only sketched in here and there'.

Bridgetower has to squint over Beethoven's shoulder to see what he is supposed to be playing.

The sonata is neither short nor easy: forty-five minutes in three strongly characterised movements. Despite the unsocial hour, the concert attracts a flock of morning-coated dignitaries, among them Prince Esterházy, Count Razumovsky and the British ambassador.

Eighteen bars into the work, Beethoven, who has not slept a wink, leaps from his stool and cries 'Noch einmal, mein lieber Bursch!' ('Once more, my dear boy!'). He keeps his foot on a pedal while Bridgetower repeats a variation of his own. The slow movement goes down so well it has to be repeated, twice. During curtain calls, Beethoven presents Bridgetower with his personal tuning fork (now in the British Library) and inscribes his name on top of the new score: 'Sonata mulattica, composed by the mulatto Brischdauer, great fool and mulatto composer.' Elsewhere he names it 'sonata per una mulaticco lunatic' ('Sonata for a mad mulatto'). Rough and racial as his language might be, there is no mistaking his fondness for his debut recital partner.

We don't know what happens next, or why. An account appears fifty years later in the *Musical World*, by a British violinist, J. W. Thirlwell:

> In respect to the . . . Sonata, Bridgetower told me, that when it was written, Beethoven and he were constant companions, and on the first copy was a dedication to his friend Bridgetower, but when it was first published, they had some silly quarrel about a girl, and in consequence Beethoven scratched out the name of Bridgetower and inserted that of Kreutzer, a man whom he had never met.

Aside from one error of chronology – the rift occurs years before the sonata goes to print – the story has the ring of truth. The fact is, Bridgetower's name gets omitted from the printed edition. Why would Beethoven do that? 'Beethoven wasn't a roaring success with the ladies and it may have been that Bridgetower touched a raw nerve,' opines the violinist Richard Tognetti in a 2020 BBC documentary, implying that the rupture is triggered by sexual jealousy. Does Bridgetower flaunt his prowess? Is Beethoven offended on behalf of one of his beloveds? Does his rejection of Bridgetower make Beethoven a racist? The matter does not bother anyone for the next two hundred years.

On 25 May 2020 an African-American man, George Floyd, is asphyxiated on camera under a Minnesota policeman's knee. Protests erupt. The USA sees an estimated 10,400 demonstrations. Universities rush to 'decolonise' their curricula, public buildings are renamed and Winston Churchill's statue is defaced outside the mother of Parliaments. The death of George Floyd turns into a flashpoint for debating and righting racial and social wrongs.

A cry goes up to abolish Beethoven. 'Canceling Beethoven is the latest woke madness in the classical music world,' reports the *New York Post*. Beethoven, say a pair of podcasters, is 'a symbol of exclusion and elitism'. A Cambridge musicologist, Anna Bull, urges that 'classical music requires exclusionary practices', by which she implies that old composers should be arbitrarily replaced by young diversities. Andrea Moore, a Chicago musicologist, calls for Beethoven to be subjected to 'a year-long moratorium'. Philip Ewell of Hunter College, CUNY goes further than most. Ewell redefines Beethoven as:

> a metonym for the toxic combination that often happens when whiteness combines with maleness in the history of the United States. At times, especially in terms of power and impact, whiteness plus maleness has more or less always equated with power. And, when that power gets challenged, it really can lash out in horrible ways – up to and including violence, rape, and murder.

Beethoven, by Ewell's logic, is implicated in George Floyd's death. A can of worms has been opened. Didn't Beethoven call Bridgetower a 'mulatto', an insult denoting mixed race? And why does his ninth symphony proclaim 'all men shall be brothers', but not women? The President of the German Cultural Council, Olaf Zimmermann, issues a public apology for 'patriarchal structures . . . deeply entrenched in the pattern of artistic work'. Ban Beethoven now.

It is not easy to defend the innocent when they are dead, but let's try. We can prove that Beethoven has no prejudice. Blacks, whites or Jews, all are the same to him. He may even prefer outsiders. An authentic portrait, by Blasius Hoefel, shows his complexion to be swarthy and his hair frizzy. His jaw is square, his lips thick, his nose flat and his eyes dark. He is certainly not a typical Dutchman or German. Might Beethoven be Black? The supposition is first raised by a Wisconsin scholar, Dominique-René de Lerma, who traces Beethoven's maternal grandmother, María Josefa Poll, to a Spanish family that enters Holland around 1710. Many Spaniards have Moroccan-Islamic descent. Beethoven's mother has dark eyes and Mediterranean features. His own eyes are black. In Vienna, some call Beethoven 'the Spaniard'. His opera *Fidelio* is set in Seville. The South African novelist Nadine Gordimer titles a powerful short story collection of unbelonging *Beethoven Was One-Sixteenth Black*. She might well be right. Like the Russian poet Alexander Pushkin, whose great-grandfather was a slave, Beethoven passes easily in high society. Mixed race, in the classical era, is no big deal. It becomes so in recent times.

In June 2021, REMA – 'the representative network for Early Music in Europe' – calls a conference in Amsterdam under the title 'Beethoven is Black'. 'Is classical music a universal cultural value,' it asks, 'or does it represent Western imperialism and white supremacy? Can we decolonize classical music?' The keynote speaker is Chi-chi Nwanoku, a double-bass-ist in a period-instrument orchestra who, in the title of a BBC documen-tary, is intent on 'Reclaiming the Bridgetower Sonata'. Nwanoku, who is of Nigerian and Irish descent, is principled, personable and smart, an effec-tive activist, creator of Europe's first minority ethnic orchestra, Chineke! She says:

> When I was growing up, I had no role model in the classical music world who looked like me, people of colour, people of African heritage. I didn't even know that people of colour wrote classical music. So to hear that there was a virtuoso violinist that performed with Beethoven, no less, a piece that Beethoven actually wrote for him, it suddenly opened a door: *yes*, I did belong in an industry where I'd received many suggestions that it wasn't really a place for people like me.

Nwanoku seeks 'to restore Bridgetower to history', putting him on a pedestal as a potential role model for minority musicians. More than anything, she wants to see Bridgetower's name back on the frontispiece of the Kreutzer Sonata and she has no trouble finding support. Professor Christine Siegert, archive director of the Beethoven-Haus in Bonn, says: 'I would be so happy if there would be an edition really emphasising the importance of Bridgetower for this sonata because Beethoven has written it exactly for his musical skills.' The German violinist Anne-Sophie Mutter adds her endorsement: 'It is overdue that the work is called the Bridgetower rather than the Kreutzer.' A publisher, Peters Edition, agrees to put both names on its next printing. Nwanoku is 'so proud that major recognition is finally coming . . . it's the best result I could possibly have had.' BBC Radio 3, which commissions her crusade, can barely contain its righteous excitement.

What gets lost in this process is perspective. Works of music are hardly ever named after their first performer. If they were, the Brahms violin concerto would be 'the Joachim' and Elgar's 'the Kreisler'. There is neither logic nor historical precedent for renaming Beethoven's opus 47 after Bridgetower.

Nor is there social justice in 'restoring Bridgetower to history' when, according to the available evidence, the man in question does his best to escape it. Bridgetower, we know, returns to London in 1805, gives concerts, joins the Royal Society of Musicians and receives a degree from the University of Cambridge. A founding member of the Philharmonic Society, he is last seen at a concert in 1819, in the company of a 'Mrs Bridgetower', an English heiress. The couple take a grand tour to Paris, Rome and Vienna. When his wife's money runs out, Bridgetower settles on a poor street in South London. His death, aged eighty-one, is recorded in Peckham in February 1860; he is buried at Kensal Green.

Bridgetower lost his taste for fame. Having once hit the high notes with Beethoven, he prefers obscurity, showing no further interest in 'his' sonata. What happened in Vienna stays in Vienna. George Augustus Polgreen Bridgetower is a footnote in music, not a front page. The BBC documentary contradicts what little we know of his wishes. The only purpose of this campaign is to furnish the all-white classical music establishment with a fig-leaf of diversity.

It is now open season on Beethoven. Sample this from another BBC Radio 3 presenter, Corey Mwamba: 'The statement "Beethoven was Black" [is] a disruption of a very canonical way of thinking. It makes us think again about a culture that gives his music so much visibility. Had Beethoven been Black, would he have been classed as a canonical composer?' Come again? Had Beethoven's world thought of him as Black, would it have made any more difference to his reception than it did to Pushkin's?

Beethoven's 2020 bicentennial was embittered by further assaults of this kind. What we need to recognise and celebrate is Beethoven's mixed ancestry, a documented fact that refutes, at root, the Nazi myth that European culture is Aryan and white. The facts of artists' lives reveal that Western civilisation is not homogenous, never was. Beethoven is mixed-race, Cervantes is part-Jewish. A study of Picasso's abstract art reveals surprising affinities with medieval Muslim figures. Europe in Beethoven's time is a melting pot. That is what gives it an edge of genius and makes it a magnet for a multiplicity of talents. Art is never black nor white, and music is an amalgam of all the arts. Beethoven embodies that truth, far ahead of his time.

≀

With Bridgetower gone, Beethoven needs a new name for his sonata. He alights on Rodolphe Kreutzer, the best violinist in Paris, professor at the Conservatoire and concertmaster of the Opéra. Kreutzer, whose father is a German courtier at Versailles, is a pet of the Paristocracy. Beethoven has met him once in 1798 and thinks him 'a dear kind fellow who during his stay in Vienna gave me a great deal of pleasure'. He sends Kreutzer the sonata, and hears nothing back, not so much as a thank-you. Kreutzer finds the music, according to Berlioz, 'outrageously unintelligible'. Like most Napoleonic citizens, he has no high regard for German art. During a concert of Beethoven's second symphony at the Conservatoire, he storms out of the room, hands to his ears. He is self-satisfied, reactionary, closed-minded. Unwilling to play Beethoven's sonata, he defames it.

In doing so, Kreutzer earns himself immortality to die for. At the latter end of the century, in 1889, Leo Tolstoy writes *The Kreutzer Sonata* and gets banned in Russia and America. Tolstoy applies Beethoven's creation as a template for sexual desire – 'the swinish connection' – and its potential to wreck a loving marriage. The narrator, seeing his wife play piano for a violin-ist in Beethoven's Kreutzer Sonata, is consumed by feelings of male failure:

I was in torture, especially because I was sure that toward me she had no other feeling than of perpetual irritation, sometimes interrupted by the customary sensuality, and that this man, – thanks to his external elegance and his novelty, and, above all, thanks to his unquestionably remarkable talent, thanks to the attraction exercised under the influence of music, thanks to the impression that music produces upon nervous natures, – this man would not only please, but would inevitably, and without diffi-culty, subjugate and conquer her, and do with her as he liked.

Catching his wife eating dinner with the violinist, he pulls a dagger and kills her, letting the musician escape because 'it is ridiculous to run after one's wife's lover in one's socks.' Tolstoy, whose domestic life is arid, concludes the novella with an appeal for sexual abstinence in marriage.

Thirty years on, the Czech composer Leoš Janáček, in love with a chaste housewife, Kamila Stösslová, titles his string quartet *The Kreutzer Sonata*. Janáček, in his sixties, is miserably married; Kamila is a contented wife, semi-educated and half his age. By no means a femme fatale, she is plump, provincial, uninquisitive. 'You are so lovely in character and appearance,' Janáček tells her. Kamila worries about her dress. He explains Tolstoy's novella: 'I had in mind a poor woman, tormented, run down and battered to death just like the one Tolstoy describes.' Janáček's infatuation is fero-cious, Kamila's passivity inflames him. They play out an intense soap opera over eleven letter-filled years.

Janáček's *Kreutzer Sonata* quartet is a grenade that explodes with Beethoven fragments. Of the second quartet, 'Intimate Letters', he asks Kamila:

Did I write that? Those cries of joy, but what a strange thing, also cries of terror after a lullaby. Exaltation, a warm declaration of love, imploring; untamed longing . . . Confusion and high-pitched song of victory: 'You've found a woman who was destined for you.' Just my speech and just your amazed silence. Oh, it's a work as if carved out of living flesh.

Janáček dies that summer of pneumonia, Kamila seven years later of cancer. Janáček quotes Tolstoy: 'Music generally is a fearful thing . . . take, for instance, this Kreutzer Sonata, the first presto. How can that presto be played in a drawing room among ladies in low-neck dresses?' Janáček's quartets mingle temptation with terror. He calls Kamila, who is Jewish, 'my black gypsy, my negress'. She is his dark side, as Bridgetower is Beethoven's, an unbreachable innocence.

❧

In Beethoven's sonata the violin is in fight mode from the opening bars. Early in the finale it runs out of notes. The central theme-and-variations movement bursts its banks and floods with possibilities. Beethoven is wrestling, like Jacob with the Angel, until the break of dawn.

Among a hundred recordings, a dozen stand out. Jascha Heifetz and Brooks Smith (1961) set a land speed record. Jacques Thibaud and Alfred Cortot, in May 1929, are contemplative. Yehudi Menuhin and his sister Hephzibah (1934) are showy, squeaky, staid. Two Hungarian exiles give an elevated recital at the Library of Congress in Washington, DC on 13 April 1940, playing Béla Bartók's 1922 sonata and the 1917 Debussy sonata with Beethoven's Kreutzer. The performers are the violinist Josef Szigeti with Bartók himself at the piano. In the last half-minute of the Kreutzer's opening movement, there is a hush of loneliness and alienation, a pain of exile so acute one cannot move for fear.

Other good duos are Schneiderhan–Kempff, Oistrakh–Oborin, Grumiaux–Haskil, Szeryng–Rubinstein and Itzhak Perlman with Vladimir Ashkenazy (1974). Gidon Kremer with Martha Argerich (1994) are unmatched for ferocity and *tendresse*.

One film is historic. In July 1986, Nathan Milstein gives the last recital of his life. He is eighty-two years old and has been on stage for seven decades. His secret, he tells me, is to limit himself to thirty concerts a year, using the time in between to store up fresh experiences. I catch him one day watching the ice-dancers Torvill and Dean on TV. 'I can learn from them, too,' he beams. At an age when others suffer shaking fingers and memory loss, Milstein is immaculate, twinkling away on his Stradivarius and coming back for encores so long as there's still one hand clapping. I hear him in Switzerland a few weeks before this film and am blown away by his joie de vivre. He loves, he says, to surprise himself with music.

His Kreutzer Sonata with Georges Pludermacher, filmed in Stockholm by the British documentarist Christopher Nupen (on YouTube), is a world heritage monument of music at its most serene. Milstein stands in the spotlight, some distance from the piano, communing with his violin, enticing from it the sweetness that resides in a long, faithful relationship, charming it to stay with him to the end. Weeks later, he suffers a fall, injuring his left hand and ending his life on stage.

52

Rode ahead

Sonata for Violin and Piano No. 10
in G major, Op. 96 (1812)

WE ARE NOT DONE YET WITH KREUTZER. BEETHOVEN WRITES his next violin sonata for Kreutzer's arch-enemy, Pierre Rode. A concert-master who quit Napoleon's orchestra, Rode accepts five thousand silver roubles a year from the Tsar to raise violin standards in Russia. Kreutzer condemns Rode's playing as 'too cool'.

In December 1812 Rode reaches Vienna and Beethoven tailors a sonata to his 'cool' style. His pupil, Archduke Rudolph, advises that Rode has technical limitations and cannot let rip as Beethoven likes to do. Beethoven concedes: 'I have not hurried unduly to compose the last movement as, in view of Rode's playing, I have had to give thought to the composition of this movement. In our finales we like to have noisy passages, but R does not care for them – and so I have been rather hampered.' Rudolph plays piano at the private premiere at the Lobkowitz Palace and again in public on 7 January 1813. The reception is muted. It takes three years for the sonata to find a publisher. Rode, on his return to Paris, has no success in promoting Beethoven against Kreutzer's opposition.

The tenth sonata is the sunniest of his violin works. While writing it, Beethoven is racked with chest and stomach pains, barely able to leave the house. His finances have collapsed and his brother Carl Caspar is sick. Yet Beethoven smiles through twenty-five transcendent minutes. Menuhin, Heifetz and Oistrakh set the bar high on record. Itzhak Perlman and Vladimir Ashkenazy (1977) add a cuddly tone with clinical precision. The match between Gidon Kremer and Martha Argerich (1994) feels like watching Roger Federer play Novak Djokovic at Wimbledon, two champions who rely on the other to return as good as it gets.

53

Ars longa

Piano Sonata No. 13, 'Quasi una fantasia', Op. 27/1 (1801)

IN THE FIRST TWO YEARS OF THE NINETEENTH CENTURY Beethoven writes a quarter of all of his piano sonatas. To accommodate publishers, he submits them in batches of two or three. Both items in opus 27 are described by the composer as being 'like a fantasy'. They could not be more different from each other (the second is the Moonlight).

What does Beethoven mean by fantasy? The first sonata is fifteen minutes of unbroken narrative, dipping in and out of E flat major. The Swiss pianist Edwin Fischer calls it child's play. The Canadian Angela Hewitt wonders if Beethoven is playing hide-and-seek.

Schnabel treats the work as a joke. Glenn Gould sings the opening theme so loud you can hardly hear the piano; even sworn Gouldians consider this track an abomination. Peter Serkin plays it with the insouciance of the young Gould and the mature Gilels, a potent blend. Jonathan Biss (2016), son of violinist Miriam Fried, cracks into the first presto at way over safety speed.

I have listened to Daniel Barenboim play this sonata all my adult life. In 1967, at the opening of London's Queen Elizabeth Hall, Barenboim, aged twenty-four, performed all 32 sonatas and recorded them for EMI. That summer he married Jacqueline du Pré – in Israel after the Six-Day War – and began to conduct. The 13th sonata in this set starts at pedestrian pace and grows into a car chase, leaving the listener open-mouthed as Barenboim hot-foots it clean away.

Forty years later, as music director at the Berlin State Opera and a Middle East peacemaker, Barenboim returned to London to repeat the cycle at the Royal Festival Hall over eight nights. Extra seats were crammed onto the stage. I sat between two young women who, drawn by a media storm, had never heard Beethoven before. Barenboim played the sonatas, like Schnabel, in random order. He refused a BBC broadcast, fearing that critics would take him to task for Schnabel-like fingerslips. His studio recording of the fantasia is remarkable in many ways, not least as a testament to the things an artist learns in the course of a long, combative and very public life.

54

Comic timing

Piano Sonatas Nos. 16 to 18, Op. 31 (1801–2)

THIS SET ATTRACTS MERRY QUIPS. ALFRED BRENDEL WRITES that 'only the comic intent' makes the 16th sonata 'plausible'. Jeremy Denk feels it 'is not a serious piece with jokes in it . . . the whole edifice is laughing, laughing at its core'. Turn now to Charles Rosen, the best writer ever to play Beethoven for a living. Rosen says: 'The comedy of the sonata in G major opus 31 starts with the first bar, even before the first bar, in fact as the right hand enters a split second too soon before the bar line. The anomaly is making the right hand precede the left.' If your image of Beethoven is a huge cranium stuffed with gigantic thoughts, never ignore the possibility that he is out to have fun with the people who play his music.

Rosen tackles opus 31/1 with a kind of gimpy arrythmia, more crude than cruel, a caricature of disability with a subtext that music can surmount it. Rosen reads more into Beethoven than any performing musician. His Yale guide to the Beethoven sonatas (2002) is a blaze of original aperçus and wheeling insights. Taught by a Liszt pupil in New York, Rosen was a polymath who knew no bounds. Fluent in French and Italian cuisines, he was a bon vivant who relished luxury but adored the piano austerities of Pierre Boulez and Elliott Carter. He knew his way around architecture, art, literature and science. Apart from that, boy, could he play.

But piano was never enough for Charles. While rehearsing for his Carnegie Hall debut, he took a PhD in French literature at Princeton, also studying maths and philosophy. His study of *The Classical Style* brought offers of professorships, but Rosen took a room in Paris and, for some years, gave up music. At his death in December 2012, he was writing an essay on the English playwright William Congreve. He had a chortling, self-congratulating wit. Once in a BBC studio he argued with me about shrinking concert audiences. 'On occasion,' declared Charles, 'I have played for as few as fifteen people in a recital. Of course, twelve of them were Nobel Prize winners.'

In Beethoven, he banishes the image of a composer racked by deafness and replaces it with a fount of creative vitality, defeating adversity with every note, every page, every breath. His recordings of the late sonatas are a trifle remote, but in these opus 31 sonatas Charles Welles Rosen is peerless, rippling with humour and asperities, a world apart from the tombstone-faced Carnegie Hall recitalists he so volubly abhorred.

≀

In opus 31/2, 'the Tempest', Heinrich Neuhaus exposes musical sinews like a classroom pathologist. Maria Yudina is both tempest and ship, subject and object. Richter, at Carnegie Hall in December 1960, is a weatherman with the wrong forecast, announcing storms when all the eye can see is clear skies. Gilels offers qualified shelter. All are unsurpassable.

One other pianist you must hear is Käbi Laretei, fourth wife of the Swedish film director Ingmar Bergman. An Estonian refugee, muse for Bergman's film *Autumn Sonata*, Laretei plays the Tempest with icy gravitas. At 07:30 on the YouTube video, she plinks out a line from the finale of Beethoven's ninth symphony. Where does that come from? How come other pianists don't spot it? This is where interpretation becomes inspiration, revealing hidden clues in familiar music. Laretei divorced Bergman in 1969. After the death of his fifth wife she returned as his companion. Bergman died in 2007, Laretei in 2014. She is an uncommonly interesting musical explorer, on first-name terms with Hindemith and Stravinsky.

≀

Three minutes into the second movement of opus 31/3, Maria Grinberg dissolves a Beethoven phrase like a sandcastle in an incoming tide. Raised in Odessa, her father and husband murdered by Stalin, Grinberg played piano at ballet classes to stay alive. Although never allowed out of the Soviet Union (except once, to Holland) she recorded Beethoven in her sixties when almost blind. Playing from memory, she catalogued the 32 sonatas as a secret chamber of Soviet horrors. Maria Grinberg, a warning from history, died in 1978, aged sixty-nine.

The first pianist I heard in opus 31/3 was Arthur Rubinstein. A Polish-Jewish sybarite with an eye for ballerinas, Rubinstein hung out with composers – Debussy, Ravel, De Falla, Szymanowski, Stravinsky, Prokofiev. He seemed too frivolous to be a force in Beethoven, but in this sonata he turns inwards, pondering the spaces between notes as much as the music itself. He recorded opus 31/3 four times, the tempo hardly varying from one to the next. It is his Beethoven signature piece.

55

Fluff

**Piano Sonatas Nos. 19 and 20, Op. 49, 1/2 (1805);
Two Rondos, Op. 51; Variations, WoO80 (1806)**

THESE MINIATURES, EIGHT MINUTES EACH, ARE FOUND IN A
drawer by Beethoven's brother and peddled to a publisher. There is smart
stuff in the first sonata but the second is fluff, barely relieved by a pop-up
tune from his septet. Radu Lupu recorded them in 1977 in Decca's
Kingsway Hall with London's Underground rumbling through the wall.
Bearded, Romanian and introspective, Lupu made barely twenty recordings, of which these sonatas are expressionist marvels, closer to Schubert's
singing liquidity than Beethoven's solid tread. There is a silence around
Lupu that is quite surreal. In his only known interview, he says: 'Everyone
tells a story differently, and that story should be told compellingly and
spontaneously. If it is not compelling and convincing, it is without value.'
The two rondos and C minor variations meander down the paths of
Beethoven's woodland walks.

56

Cricket score

Razumovsky Quartets, Op. 59/1–3 (1806)

EIGHT YEARS AFTER BEETHOVEN'S FIRST BATCH OF STRING quartets, opus 18, he writes another set. In between, everything has changed. Even the notebooks he uses are smaller so that he can:

> carry them always under his arm or in his pocket . . . He was never seen without his scraps of ruled paper on which, as inspiration came to him on his walks or while visiting, he would scribble down his ideas. And with the altered size of his notebooks the character of his sketches was modified . . . Year by year the number of preliminary drafts and tentative sketches increased. Developments no longer occurred to him in their completed state; he would constantly correct details.

This is his method at the high noon of maturity. It helps that he knows who he is writing for. Four of his friends – Schuppanzigh, Louis Sina, Franz Weiss and Joseph Linke – are employed by Prince Andrey Razumovsky, the Russian ambassador. Knowing Schuppanzigh's pride in his status as leader, Beethoven gives the opening theme of opus 59/1 to the cello. The audience get the joke and have a chuckle at the jealous fat man. Beethoven makes another adjustment. Razumovsky, he is told, likes to sit in for Sina on second violin, so he makes sure the part is kept simple, not beyond princely fingers.

No ordinary diplomat, Razumovsky infiltrates the upper echelons of Vienna's cultural life. He marries Lichnowsky's sister-in-law and fills his palace on the Landstrasse with works by Raphael, Rubens, Van Dyck and Angelika Kauffmann. His gardens are a horticultural miracle, with statuary by Antonio Canova. He entertains lavishly through the course of the

Napoleonic wars, winning himself a seat at the top table of the Congress of Vienna. Sacked by the Tsar, Razumovsky converts to Roman Catholicism, remarries and spends the rest of his life in Vienna.

He makes one request of Beethoven: he wants a Russian folk song in each of his quartets. Beethoven obliges in the opus 59/1 finale and the 59/2 scherzo – the 'Slava' tune also heard at the coronation of Mussorgsky's *Boris Godunov* and in Stravinsky's *Firebird* ballet – but not in opus 59/3, where Beethoven either forgets or, more likely, rebels.

His notebooks reveal a disturbed state of mind. One jotting reads 'a weeping willow on my brother's grave', when both of his brothers are alive and well. Opus 59/3 has a funereal introduction. His anxiety levels are high.

Each quartet lasts half an hour. The first review reads: 'They are of great length and difficulty.' Asked for an explanation, Beethoven says, 'Oh, the [quartets] are not for you, but for a future age.'

Viennese string quartets set the style, notably the Barylli Quartet (1955) and the Alban Berg Quartet (1980). The Beethoven Quartet of Moscow, Shostakovich's favourite ensemble, are rough, gruff and in your face. Two recent recordings – the Spanish shimmer of Cuarteto Casals (2018) and the serene athleticism of the Parisian Quatuor Ébène (2019) – are formidable.

The Razumovsky Quartets enter sporting legend when England, having lost the first Test match against Australia in 1981, appoint a professional psychiatrist to captain the team. Mike Brearley is a good batsman, a fraction short of world-class. It is all he can do to stay alive while fearsome opponents hurl a red missile at him from 20 metres at ninety miles an hour. In between each ball, Brearley sings Beethoven. As a bowler thunders up to deliver, he hums the opening cello motif of the first Razumovsky Quartet. His surreal composure disconcerts the all-conquering Australians, sapping their confidence. England, with Beethoven at the crease, win the series by three Tests to one.

57

Harping on

String Quartet No. 10 in E-flat, 'The Harp', Op. 74 (1809)

HIS NEXT QUARTET SHARES A KEY WITH THE EMPEROR Concerto and the piano sonata 'Les Adieux'. You would not know from this quartet that he is writing under the French bombardment. Some artists are frozen by existential fear. Beethoven just carries on. In writing breaks, he jots 'memorial to Johann Sebastian Bach' in a notebook, followed by 'the servant's wages are due on the fourth'. When the shooting gets too close he takes rooms in the Golden Cross inn on the outskirts of Vienna and writes another quartet.

The 'Harp' opens with plucked passages, marked *sotto voce*. The second movement has a smiling melody. The third has a fifth symphony-like attack, while the finale produces wondrous catharsis. The quartet is composed in the year that Felix Mendelssohn is born and his family acquire the manuscript. The work has a decisive influence on Mendelssohn, who quotes it at the start of an E flat quartet that he writes as a teenager, the year after Beethoven dies.

Hungarians own this score. The Lener Quartet (1932) and Budapest Quartet (1936) play with a ferocious passion and an accent that tilts the music towards melancholy. Sándor Végh's quartet (1952) slopes even more to the left, wrongfooting anyone who thinks they know how this work is going to end. The Takács Quartet (2002) – Edward Dusinberre, Károly Schranz, Geraldine Walther, András Fejér – deliver a Decca session that has everything: penetration, fantasy, wit and perfect poise. The Bartók Quartet (2014) are also pretty good. There is no sound reason why Hungarians understand this quartet more profoundly than others, but the recorded evidence does not lie. The Takács crack it.

58

Deadly

String Quartet No. 11 in F minor, 'Il serioso', Op. 95 (1810)

WHEN I FIRST MET THE AMADEUS QUARTET THEY WERE IN advanced middle age and in no mood for banter. At our photo session, one of them burnt his jacket sleeve on studio lights and muttered about suing. The other three just grumbled. I wrote them up in a magazine article as 'the serious quartet', not yet realising that all string quartets are morose. Show me a smiling string quartet and I know they are about to break up. Over time, I got to know the Amadeus, meet their wives, hear their stories. Three Viennese Jews – Peter Schidlof, Siggi Nissel and Norbert Brainin – met as interned enemy aliens on the Isle of Man in 1940. On release, they met a London cello student, Martin Lovett. Their debut on 10 January 1948 at the Wigmore Hall came at a moment when Britain lacked good quartets and could not afford to import one.

After making two under-appreciated records for Decca, the Amadeus were snatched by Deutsche Grammophon. One of their first sessions in 1952 was Beethoven's 'serioso' quartet, played with the raw aggression of recent refugees at an impassive German studio crew. Their 1960 stereo retake, even more muscular, underlines a stubborn contrariness, unforgiving of past crimes, ungiving of cheap pleasure. They earned immense respect in Berlin and Vienna, with 'Il serioso' as their signature repertoire. (Others who excel on record in this work are the US Emerson Quartet and the Prague-based Smetana Quartet.)

In August 1987, soon after agreeing to re-record all the Beethoven quartets in digital sound, the quartet came to an end. Peter Schidlof – 'the one who was least often satisfied' – died of a heart attack on a Sunday afternoon in the English Lake District. The other three could not go on without him. A string quartet is for life.

The 11th quartet is Beethoven's shortest, barely twenty minutes long. It has either three movements or seven, depending on who is counting. Although Beethoven dedicates the score to the cellist Nikolaus Zmeskall 'as a proof of my continuing love . . . for I number you among my oldest friends in Vienna,' the music yields scant affection or warmth. It has a metronomic propulsion, a resistance to the ticking down of life's clock. Beethoven tells an Englishman, George Smart, that the work is meant for serious people, 'never to be performed in public'.

String Quartet No. 11 in F minor, Op. 95 (Arr. Gustav Mahler)

The week Gustav Mahler enters the Vienna Opera in April 1897, Gustav Klimt founds a Secession movement of rebel artists. Five years later Klimt opens his gold-topped Secession building around a Max Klinger sculpture of Beethoven, heroic and half-naked, with a frieze around the upper walls depicting a knight in golden armour whose features are unmistakably Mahler's. Among sixty thousand people who rush to the show, the Emperor Franz Joseph is said to be shocked by the disrespect shown to Beethoven.

Mahler, no respecter of reputations, outrages Vienna still further by fleshing out Beethoven's 'serious' quartet in a string orchestra version. The audience boo and the score languishes in archives until 1986. A first recording by the Vienna Philharmonic, conducted by Christoph von Dohnányi, adds little to our appreciation of either Beethoven or Mahler.

String Quintets, Opp. 4, 29, 104

Beethoven writes three works for string quartet with extra viola. Opus 4 (1795) is frothy, Mozartian; there's a fine recording by the Endellion Quartet with violist David Adams. Opus 29, dated 1801, has echoes of the first Razumovsky Quartet; the Amadeus nail it, with Cecil Aronowitz as plus-one. Opus 104 reworks an early piano trio. The Fine Arts Quartet with Gil Sharon do it justice on record.

59

Tick-tock

'The Eyeglass Duo', WoO32 (1796–7); Three Pieces for Musical Clock, WoO33a; Serenade, Op. 25 (1797/1801)

THE CELLO-PLAYING, BROTHEL-CREEPING BARON ZMESKALL IS a civil servant who steals paper from the Chancellery stationery cupboard for Beethoven to compose on. 'Duet for Viola and Violoncello in E flat major with eyeglasses obbligato' is Beethoven's joke that he has written Zmeskall's part very small in order to economise on state paper.

The German composer Paul Hindemith made a recording of the first movement with his cellist brother Rudolf, an exemplary piece of family music making in which the better brother reins himself in to accommodate the weaker. Hindemith is the inventor of *Gebrauchsmusik*, 'user-friendly' music for all to play at home.

The musical clock is a novelty item to be found on many Viennese mantels, including Mozart's. There is a flute-and-harp recording by Jean-Pierre Rampal and Marielle Nordmann, and a violin-piano pairing by Anne-Sophie Mutter and Lambert Orkis. The serenade, for flute, violin and viola, is pretty, flirty and fluttery. Sir James Galway and the London Virtuosi give an enchanting account.

BEETHOVEN IMMURED

60

Can't hear

Christ on the Mount of Olives, Op. 85 (1802); Elegiac Song, Op. 118 (1814)

IN OCTOBER 1802, BEETHOVEN ACCEPTS THAT HE HAS GONE deaf. Out in the fields with Ries he sees a shepherd tootling on a wooden flute, lips pursed and fingers flying, yet not one peep reaches his ears. He has been aware of losing his hearing for four or five years but this, he knows, is the end. He has tried a range of quack cures and given up. Ahead, lies silence. He is thirty-one years old.

He takes a six-month break among the vineyards of Heiligenstadt, on the outskirts of Vienna. In October they harvest the late vines. Beethoven drowns his anxieties of an evening in the heady aromas of new wine, as all around him men and women sway back and forth on wooden benches, clinking tankards. He cannot hear them, and sits alone. Back in his room he decides to share his predicament with his closest kin, his two younger brothers.

Relations between the Beethoven boys have never been easy. Carl Caspar works as a government clerk and uses Treasury notepaper to deal with publishers as Beethoven's agent. The publishers don't like that; it seems irregular and impertinent. They make out that Carl Caspar is dealing with them behind Beethoven's back. Ludwig issues a vigorous rebuttal: 'Although wicked people spread a rumour that he does not treat me honourably, I assure you this is untrue and that he always looked after my interests with integrity.' Privately, he worries that Carl Caspar is consorting with loose women. When Carl Caspar introduces Johanna Reiss as his fiancée, Beethoven can see that she is six months pregnant, but he agrees to the marriage in the interest of family harmony. Johanna is financially imprudent and there are constant tensions. But when

Napoleon bombs Vienna, it is in their cellar that he finds shelter and when Carl Caspar falls sick Ludwig undertakes to cover all of the family's expenses.

The third Beethoven brother, Nikolaus Johann, serves as an apothecary's apprentice and learns enough to set up his own pharmacy. He dispenses remedies for Beethoven's ailments, some of them unknowingly harmful. Johann grows quite rich and looks after Ludwig in his final illness. Bonded around a bad boyhood, Beethoven has no one who understands him better.

In deafness, he writes a confession known as the 'Heiligenstadt Testament' to his brothers. His distress is betrayed by two glaring errors on the page. At the top, he cannot remember Johann's name; at the bottom he misspells his own address. He does not know how and where to begin. Instead of breaking the news gently and appealing for love and understanding, he starts by attacking both of his brothers for lack of empathy and support. The Testament is a tough document, unsparing of himself and others. He begins:

For my brothers Carl and [ ] Beethoven.
    Oh you men who think me malevolent, stubborn, or misanthropic, how greatly you wrong me. You do not know the secret cause that makes me seem that way to you. From childhood, my heart and soul have been full of a tender feeling of goodwill [as] I tried to accomplish great things. But for six years now I have been hopelessly afflicted, made worse by senseless physicians, deceived from year to year with hopes of improvement and finally compelled to face the prospect of a lasting malady (whose cure will take years or, perhaps, be impossible).

His life is wrecked, he tells them, his work imperilled:

I was compelled to isolate myself, to live life alone . . . I could not say to people, 'Speak louder, shout, for I am deaf.' Ah, how could I admit an infirmity in the one sense which ought to be more perfect in me than in others, a sense I once possessed in the highest perfection, a perfection such as few in my profession have ever enjoyed. – Oh I cannot do it; therefore forgive me when you see me draw back when I would gladly have mingled with you . . . For me there can be no relaxation with my fellow men, no refined conversations, no mutual exchange of ideas. I must live almost alone, like one who has been banished.

At rock-bottom, he considers suicide: 'Such incidents drove me almost to despair; any more and I would have ended my life: only my art held me back. It was impossible to leave the world until I had brought forth all that I felt was within me.'

Staring into a soundless future, he sees no hope. Dreams of love and glory are over. He needs to make arrangements for his death:

> You, my brothers Carl and [he still can't remember Johann's name], as soon as I am dead, if Dr Schmid is still alive, ask him in my name to describe my malady, and attach this written document to his account of my illness so that . . . the world may become reconciled to me after my death. I name you two the heirs to my small fortune (if so it can be called); divide it fairly; bear with and help each other . . . I thank all my friends, especially Prince Lichnowsky and Professor Schmid. I would like the instruments from Prince L to be kept by one of you but not as a cause of strife between you . . . With joy I hasten to meet death . . . Come when thou wilt, I shall meet thee bravely . . .
> Ludwig van Beethoven
> Heiglnstadt,
> October 6th, 1802

The brothers may never see the letter. It is found in Beethoven's desk after his death and published by Schindler in 1828. The manuscript comes into the hands of the famed Swedish soprano Jenny Lind, who bequeaths it to the University of Hamburg, where it can be read to this day. Beethoven's hand is firm and legible, sloping slightly upwards. Errors aside, he takes control of his emotions and his destiny.

Nowhere in music is there an act of auto-analysis like the Heiligenstadt Testament, a composer exposing his agony. What is so striking about the Testament is how naked it is, how candid and how exemplary. He wants posterity to know of his suffering, perhaps to learn from it, but only once he is dead. He specifies that no one is to read it while he lives.

No sooner has he got the Testament off his chest than Beethoven packs up, heads back to Vienna and starts work on his next score. It is an oratorio, a meditation on Christ's last sleepless night before the guards arrive to arrest him for trial and crucifixion. A psychoanalyst might read it as transference, Beethoven imagining Christ's agony as his own, and vice-versa. Death is near, but music will endure:

Soon my torment will be over,
The work of redemption fulfilled,
Soon the powers of hell
Will be completely crushed and defeated.

Given the composer's circumstances, we might expect a masterpiece, the more so since this is the first major work that Beethoven attempts on a religious theme. But neither the oratorio form, nor the belief in redemption sits comfortably with Beethoven. Ambivalent, he delivers the work late for a Holy Week concert at the Theater an der Wien on 5 April 1803, a concert that also presents the first two symphonies, the third piano concerto and several arias. At five in the morning of the concert day he summons his copyist Ries. 'I found him in bed writing on *separate* sheets of paper. To my question what it was he answered *Trombones*.' Rehearsals begin at eight in the morning. There is a further afternoon rehearsal and the concert begins at six in the evening.

In the oratorio, Jesus is a tenor. The next biggest part is a soprano Seraph. There is no dramatic counterweight to Christ. The work is poorly received. Apart from a vogue in late nineteenth-century America, the oratorio is seldom revived. At a London Symphony Orchestra revival in January 2020, Simon Rattle hypes it up as 'complete heaven, something to wake up in the morning for'. A newspaper critic finds it 'gutsy rather than tragic'. Rattle's LSO Live release is worth hearing for Elsa Dreisig's soaring solos, one of them featuring that last-gasp trombone figure.

On record Jan Peerce and Maria Stader light up 1955 Vienna, conducted by Hermann Scherchen. Plácido Domingo, conducted by Kent Nagano, lacks colour. Apotheosis arrives in the form of Leif Segerstam, a wild-bearded Finn of retrograde views and chaotic habits. Segerstam called out a soprano for 'lacking balls' and titled one of his own symphonies 'when the cat came'. You will never hear a finer *Mount of Olives* than Segerstam's with the Turku Philharmonic. On the same Naxos album, Segerstam unearths an elegiac chorus song that sounds like, and might well be, a missing fragment of *Fidelio*.

}

How Beethoven lost his hearing is the subject of much speculation. His mother died of tuberculosis, a disease that may impair hearing. Did Beethoven catch it at her deathbed? In his mid-twenties he gets typhus. One variant, scrub typhus, brings a one-in-three risk of deafness. He visits 'bumbling doctors and medical asses' with stomach pains, which might be Crohn's Disease. He is treated with herbal folk remedies. Dangerously high levels of lead and iron are found in his blood at the post-mortem. His deafness worsens in 1805 after he is soaked in a storm. He suffers abscesses on his foot and jaw as his immune system weakens. Singly and severally, any of these complaints may be responsible for hearing loss. A likelier agent is a direct infection from a dirty finger inserted in his ear. The middle-ear bones are removed at autopsy. They might have revealed otosclerosis, a bone locking onto an inner membrane, stopping it from resonating: we shall never know.

No major composer before Beethoven shares the affliction, and very few after. The Frenchman Gabriel Fauré, the Czech Bedřich Smetana and the Englishman Ralph Vaughan Williams go deaf very slowly and late in life. None endures decades of silence.

Beethoven devises a system of communication by means of conversation books, in which he and his contacts jot down what they need to say. The method is unsatisfying and unrevealing of inner feelings. We have no idea how he copes.

While consulting widely on his deafness, I see a post on social media one morning from a Viennese composer, Albin Fries, stating he is giving up composing because he has gone deaf. I ask him to explain his situation in light of Beethoven's. As with all life-changing decisions, it turns out to be complicated.

Albin suffered severe hearing loss from childhood diphtheria. Despite the disability he became a professional musician, working as a pianist and repetiteur at the Vienna State Opera, one of the most pressured positions in the music world. His job was to help singers learn their roles and conductors to convey their ideas. 'Even as a student, I developed various tricks in order not to let another person notice that I understood very little of what was being said,' Albin tells me. 'In the opera, the daily fear began of not understanding the instructions of conductors and directors. Every interruption in a rehearsal raised my adrenalin but my fear immediately disappeared when I resumed playing.'

He played the piano for the most famous conductors. 'It was easy with Abbado and Kleiber. They let me decide where to start and trusted me completely. Solo rehearsals with singers went relatively well, although I could no longer hear the highest notes of the Queen of the Night [in the *Magic Flute*].'

At home, he composed Lieder that opera singers included in public recitals. Leonard Bernstein praised his piano sonata and the Vienna Opera commissioned a children's opera, *Persinette*. All was going modestly well until one bad year when deafness, marriage breakdown and a brutal blog review by an English academic brought him down.

'Suicide plans haunted me,' he reports, 'increasing with my divorce, my severe hearing loss and the devastating blog of a modernist English critic of my three songs sung by Elisabeth Kulman in the Wiener Konzerthaus. I waited for winter to arrive because I didn't want to die violently, but in harmony with nature. The main reasons for ending my life were my ears, loss of social contact, lack of zest for life, lack of success as a composer.'

Albin's resolution echoes Beethoven's in the Heiligenstadt Testament that deafness 'drove me almost to despair; any more and I would have ended my life.' A composer who has lost his life's purpose can see no way ahead. Beethoven pulled back in an act of defiance. Albin found fortuitous relief in a new relationship, early retirement from the opera and a decision to stop composing. 'I have withdrawn as a composer,' he tells me. 'I gave away my mistuned piano, destroyed most of my CDs, threw out thousands of manuscript pages of my works.' Deafness is the end of the line for a composer. Only Beethoven defeats it.

61

Spring time

Violin Sonatas Nos. 4–8, Opp. 23–24
and Op. 30/1–3 (1801–2)

BEETHOVEN FIRST SEEKS MEDICAL ATTENTION IN 1798: 'KNOW that my noblest faculty, my hearing, has greatly deteriorated. I beg you to keep the matter of my deafness a profound secret to be confided to nobody, no matter whom.' Tinnitus, a ringing or roaring in the ears, is indicated; or perhaps labyrinthitis, a lesion on the inner ear.

Ordered to take cold baths, he loses sixty percent of his hearing by July 1801. Much of the rest is gone within a year. In that time he writes five violin sonatas, numbered four to eight. The fourth, known as 'the wayward stepchild among Beethoven's violin sonatas', skirts the pond without diving in. We are halfway into the finale before Beethoven touches base. Notable recordings include a twinkling 1944 recital by Joseph Szigeti and Claudio Arrau, a nonchalant 1952 take by Jascha Heifetz and Emanuel Bay, and a solemn recitation by Wolfgang Schneiderhan and Wilhelm Kempff. The dry wit of Itzhak Perlman and Vladimir Ashkenazy (1977) overcomes the dull patches. Pamela Frank's American can-do on the violin (2011) offsets her father Claude's stern European pianism.

The fifth sonata, titled 'Spring', opens with a young couple in a sunlit meadow bursting with flowers, colour and fertility. We know what's on their mind but they are in no hurry to get to a private place. Melodic hints of the Pastoral Symphony blend with the composer's savouring of romantic innocence. This is a work of unaffected joy. The second movement, an adagio, is a declaration of love, open and utterly trusting. The last two movements are filled with faith in the future, whatever it might bring.

A 1927 Berlin recording by the Austrian-Jewish violinist Erika Morini, aged twenty-three, ripples with sensual awakening. The pianist, 'N.

Schwalb', is almost out of the sound picture. Morini gave her debut recital as a child for the Emperor Franz Josef. Her arrival at Carnegie Hall in January 1921 excited Jascha Heifetz, who asked for the secret of her staccato. Her fees soon exceeded his.

On the concert circuit she met and married an Italian businessman, Felice Siracusano, settling in New York. In 1961, she re-recorded the Spring Sonata, partnered by the Czech pianist Rudolf Firkušný, an adult conversation on love and hurt. Morini's life ended miserably. As she lay dying in hospital in October 1991, thieves ransacked her apartment, taking all her valuables. The 1727 Stradivarius, a gift from her father, has never been seen again.

Morini's antipode in the Spring Sonata is Rudolf Kolisch, brother-in-law of Arnold Schoenberg. Kolisch, aged seventy, reimagines the sonata as a structural problem that he alone can solve. It's a fascinating exercise, well worth a spin.

The sixth violin sonata winds itself around an opening theme of no arresting force. Have patience, because the middle movement turns into Eroica-in-motion. Perlman and Ashkenazy pick all the plums out of the pudding. James Ehnes and Andrew Armstrong (2017) achieve a balanced diet.

Sonata number seven goes for drama, with as much grandeur, rage and conflict as one of Shakespeare's Henry plays; all it lacks is a hero. Arthur Grumiaux and Clara Haskil (1956) offer an unhappy ending. Anne-Sophie Mutter, filmed in Paris with Lambert Orkis (2002), has certainty without fantasy. A 2020 festival performance by French violinist Renaud Capuçon with a young Englishman, Kit Armstrong, gets the tension just right.

The eighth sonata brings out the young wine, with hints of raspberry, mushrooms and rabbits. Capuçon (YouTube, 2019) is elevated by Martha Argerich's pianism. Augustin Dumay and his wife Maria João Pires have a picnic in a walled garden. Szeryng and Haebler evoke a pre-war tourist poster.

One historic duo cannot be surpassed. Fritz Kreisler and Sergei Rachmaninov played Beethoven tours. Kreisler is the jolly one, Rachmaninov the morose. One night in recital Kreisler loses his place in a sonata. Desperately improvising, he whispers, 'Where are we?' Rachmaninov, not missing a beat, growls 'Carnegie Hall'. Their performance here is joyful, mischievous and so close to symbiotic you cannot tell who leads and who follows. More than just the greatest Beethoven violin–piano pairing of all time, this is a prime act of musical intuition and transference. They know each other's intentions before a note is sounded.

62

Two to the power of five

Six Variations on an Original Theme in F, Op. 34 (1802); 32 Variations on an Original Theme in C minor, WoO80 (1806)

TWO WEEKS AFTER THE HEILINGENSTADT TESTAMENT, Beethoven is back in the best of spirits. He sends two sets of variations to Breitkopf & Härtel. 'Usually I have to wait for other people to tell me when I have new ideas,' he chuckles. 'But this time I myself can assure you that in both works the style is quite new for me.' Opus 34, he tells Carl Czerny, requires a 'pliant, refined and feeling style of performance.' Czerny, who turns himself into a plodding pedagogue, gives the work to children to improve their fingering. It becomes the bane of piano lessons. The main theme, of Lutheran gravity, gives way to a dancing arabesque in a different key, followed by a funeral march. Beethoven is as curious as we are to see where this is leading. After all what is a pianist supposed to do after playing his own funeral?

Wilhelm Kempff (1972) despatches the set with undisguised contempt. A young Claudio Arrau (1942) evokes unqualified lyricism. The Welshman Llŷr Williams (2015) has the sonority of a prayer-meeting. Angela Hewitt (2020) skips along a path to heaven.

Four years later, while composing the fourth symphony, Beethoven takes a morning to see how many variations he can squeeze from one eight-bar theme. The number thirty-two has symmetric significance. He achieves two to the power of five before losing interest. The Asperger-like Glenn Gould practically becomes Beethoven in this piece, which the film-maker François Girard envisages as a metaphor for his art in *Thirty Two Short Films About Glenn Gould* (1993). Gould's vitality, on video, is at once exhausting and inexhaustible.

Gould can also be disparaging. 'Beethoven's reputation is based entirely on gossip. The middle Beethoven represents a supreme example of a composer on an ego trip,' he declares, only to contradict himself. 'The grandeur of Beethoven,' says Gould, 'resides in the struggle, rather than in the occasional transcendence that he achieves.' Much the same can be said of the ever-wrestling Glenn Gould, who has never really received his due as one of the most insightful Beethoven interpreters.

63

Too easy by half?

Piano Trios No. 8, WoO39, No. 9, WoO38, No. 10, Op. 44; Triple Concerto, Op. 56 (1803–4)

PIANO TRIOS PROVIDE HIS FIRST SUCCESS. THE EIGHTH AND ninth date from the 1790s, the tenth consists of fourteen variations on an aria by Carl Ditters von Dittersdorf, 'Yes, I must leave her.' On record, the Beaux Arts Trio are exemplary.

Beethoven then attaches the piano trio to a symphony orchestra in the triple concerto. Almost unbalanceable on stage, he intends it for outdoor performance. In a rush to deliver, he omits flute, oboes, trumpets and timpani in the second movement. The finale is a helter-skelter *polacca*, pop music for a pub garden. The concerto is played only once in Beethoven's lifetime. As late as 1911 it is listed among 'lost works'. It clings still to the periphery of his output.

Among relatively few viable recordings, Bruno Walter employs principal players in the New York Philharmonic, John Corigliano and Leonard Rose, as soloists, alongside pianist Walter Hendl. Ferenc Fricsay's riveting 1961 account has Anda, Schneiderhan and Fournier. David Zinman's 2004 Zurich team presents Yefim Bronfman, Gil Shaham and Truls Mørk. The Beaux Arts Trio are in perfect accord with Bernard Haitink and the London Philharmonic (1977); completely irresistible is Martha Argerich (2019) with Ion Marin, the Hamburg Symphony, Tedi Papavrami (violin) and Mischa Maisky (cello).

But the recording you really need to hear is EMI's 1969 blowout with the top-fee conductor Herbert von Karajan and three Soviet exports: David Oistrakh (violin), Sviatoslav Richter (piano) and cellist Mstislav Rostropovich. Here's what Richter told the filmmaker Bruno Monsaingeon:

It's a dreadful recording, and I disown it utterly. Battle lines were drawn up with Karajan and Rostropovich on the one side and Oistrakh and me on the other. Rostropovich was falling over himself to do everything Karajan wanted whereas Karajan had a superficial and wrong-headed view . . . Among other things, the second movement was taken far too slowly. He held back the natural flow of the music. He was faking it, and neither Oistrakh nor I had any time for this . . . Suddenly Karajan decided that everything was fine and that the recording was finished. I demanded an extra take. 'No, no,' he replied, 'we haven't got time, we've still got to do the photographs.' To him, this was more important than the recording. And what a nauseating photograph it is, with him posing artfully and the rest of us grinning like idiots.

The results, far from awful, sound tense as a Cold War nuclear summit. Slava Rostropovich, the life and soul of any party that is not a communist one, is semi-subdued and Richter and Oistrakh lack magic. Three years later, the soloists got together again in Moscow with the underrated Russian maestro Kirill Kondrashin. This reading, grainily filmed, is gloriously free in spirit, each soloist pitching in with passion and a personal thumbprint. You'll never hear a better triple.

64

Ghostly

Piano Trios, Op. 70, 1/2 (1808)

IN 1954 THE CONCERTMASTER OF ARTURO TOSCANINI'S NBC orchestra decided that the maestro was losing his grip and it was time to get out. Daniel Guilet, a refugee from Lenin and Hitler, got a date to play Mozart trios at the Tanglewood Festival and went looking for a cheap pianist and cellist. The Beaux Arts Trio that came together for this occasion played on as an institution for fifty-three years. The last player standing in 2008 was Menahem Pressler, the pianist.

I first met Menahem in Ottawa, where we spent the night in a bar talking Brahms with the Emerson Quartet. Over breakfast, Menahem shared his life story. Born in eastern Germany in 1923, he was taught piano by a church organist. On Kristallnacht, the family store was destroyed but the Presslers' lives were saved by a teenaged neighbour who stood in SA uniform outside their door. In July 1939 they caught a train to Italy and a ship to Palestine. Grandparents, uncles, aunts, cousins who stayed behind were murdered in the concentration camps.

The Presslers opened a food store in Tel Aviv. Menahem's lunchtime job was to deliver sandwiches to offices. He stopped eating lunch and lost weight. Doctors sent him to a sanatorium, but nothing helped until Leo Kestenberg, former head of music for the state of Prussia, talked to him about the piano music of Beethoven and Busoni. A Russian émigré taught him Rachmaninov, a Frenchman Debussy. Menahem won a piano competition in San Francisco and leaped at Guilet's offer of a piano trio.

Since fees were meagre, the Beaux Arts would drive five hundred miles through the night across from one hall to the next, taking turns to sleep. They were the defining piano trio on record, as reliable as clockwork, if livelier. Schubert, Mozart and Dvořák were their calling cards, with

Beethoven close behind. Despite several changes of personnel, the timbre stayed mysteriously constant.

The first opus 70 trio in D major is known as 'The Ghost' for a spooky middle movement that reflects the witches' scene in *Macbeth*. The second trio, in E flat, has a melodic opening that disintegrates in rancour. Alternative recommendations include Glenn Gould with violinist Oscar Shumsky and cellist Leonard Rose (1960); Barenboim, Zukerman and du Pré in a 1970 television film; the Chung family – Myung-Whun (piano), Kyung-Wha (violin), Myung-Wha (cello) – in business suits; and the young Van Baerle Trio from Holland (2019).

65

Youngest son

Archduke Trio, Op. 97 (1811)

IN OLD-WORLD DYNASTIES, THE OLDEST SON INHERITS THE title and lands. The second is sent to the army, the third takes holy orders, the fourth becomes an adventurer and the youngest does something in the arts. In the ruling family of the Holy Roman Empire, Archduke Rudolph Johann Joseph Rainer, born 1788, is the youngest, least useful son of Emperor Leopold II and Maria Louisa of Spain. An epileptic child, he is given an infantry regiment to command but prefers to study with Beethoven. Rudolph plays piano and composes. Beethoven cherishes his company. When Rudolph leaves Vienna in 1819 to become archbishop at the Czech town of Olmütz, Beethoven sorely misses him, fearing rightly that they will never meet again. Beethoven dedicates two piano concertos to Rudolph, as well as the Hammerklavier and opus 111 piano sonatas, both of which prove beyond the capabilities of Rudolph's rheumatic fingers.

The Archduke Trio, named for Rudolph, also defeats him. Beethoven replaces Rudolph at the piano in the first performance in April 1814 with Schuppanzigh on violin and Linke on cello. At a repeat performance, Beethoven gives up playing for good. 'On account of his deafness there was scarcely anything left of the virtuosity,' reports Louis Spohr. 'In *forte* passages the poor deaf man pounded on the keys until the strings jangled, and in *piano* he played so softly that whole groups of notes were omitted, so that the music was unintelligible.'

The Archduke Trio is one of Beethoven's most sociable works. Early on there's a plucking cello passage, accompanied by a tutting on the piano keys, a tinkling of teacups. Beethoven dashes off the work in three weeks. The Japanese novelist Haruki Murakami applies the Archduke

Trio as an allegory of freedom in his conflictual creation, *Kafka on the Shore* (2002).

Alfred Cortot, Jacques Thibaud and Pablo Casals (1928) set the benchmark for vivacity. Barenboim, du Pré and Zukerman (1970) have fun. The Beaux Arts Trio are magisterial. A 2019 release by Hagai Shaham, Raphael Wallfisch and Arnon Erez has the semi-sweetness of slow-simmering Turkish coffee.

66

Render unto Caesar

Cantatas on the death of Emperor Joseph II (WoO88) and on the accession of Leopold II, WoO89 (1790)

ARCHDUKE RUDOLPH APART, BEETHOVEN AVOIDS POWER. HE does not want to be another Mozart, humiliated at court, or Salieri, courting favour. Early on in Bonn, in February 1790, he is required to acknowledge the death of the Elector's brother, the Holy Roman Emperor Joseph II. He writes two cantatas that earn Haydn's approval. A performance is arranged and hastily cancelled because the wind players are not up to scratch. Both cantatas go into a drawer and are not seen again until 1884.

The Joseph cantata is a simulacrum of public mourning, lacking personal investment. One aria eventually gives rise to 'O Gott! Welch' ein Augenblick' in Beethoven's freedom opera, Fidelio. The Leopold cantata opens with a rerun of Joseph's death before rejoicing at the acclamation of his heir. One chorus, 'Heil, stürzet nieder Millionen', anticipates the choral entry of the ninth symphony.

Clemens Krauss (1950) has dazzling wind solos from the Vienna Symphony Orchestra and superb vocalists in Ilona Steingruber and Alfred Poell. A 2020 set by the Finnish conductor Leif Segerstam is lusty, rumbunctious and stylistically incorrect to a celestial degree.

67

God knows

Mass in C, Op. 86 (1807)

Simple question: does Beethoven believe in God? The simple answer, based on his conversation books, is yes. 'I know well that God is nearer to me than others in my art, so I will walk fearlessly with Him,' he writes around the time of the Moonlight Sonata. He reads a book titled *God's Works in Nature*. In the Heiligenstadt Testament he appeals to 'Almighty God, you look down onto my innermost soul and into my heart and you know that it is filled with love for humanity and a desire to do good.' Elsewhere he jots: 'He who is above, O, He is, and without Him there is nothing.' Beethoven, for the Scottish Catholic composer Sir James MacMillan, 'saw his life and work as a mission and a vocation.'

On the agnostic side, however, he never goes to church, never receives communion, denounces the collusion of church and state, rails against abuses of clerical power and resolves his ninth symphony in universal brotherhood, not in God's boundless mercy. He seeks no commission from the Church and pays no dues. Haydn considers him an unbeliever.

Belief in God and mistrust of religion are not necessarily contradictory. The God Beethoven recognises is personal to him, present in nature and in mind. He does not seek God within confessional walls. Is his absence noticed? Dr Michael Lorenz of the University of Vienna argues that artists are absolved from church attendance: 'Nobody in Vienna cared because he was a foreigner, an artist, and not a member of a fixed community. To me it's quite obvious that Beethoven believed in a superior being.'

The issue arises in Beethoven's two great settings of the Mass. Are they devout, or detached? Verdi, Janáček and Britten, all of them declared atheists, have no inhibitions about writing a Mass. The form, in their mind, belongs as much to folk tradition as it does to a clerical hierarchy.

The Mass in C, commissioned by Prince Nikolaus Esterházy, follows the traditional form of Mass but adds female singers, anathema to the Vatican. The Kyrie is joyous, the Gloria restrained; the Credo is declamatory; and the Sanctus and Agnus Dei assail the heavens. 'Beethoven, what is it you have done again?' wails Esterházy, dismayed at the lack of Haydn-like piety. He concludes: 'Beethoven's mass is unbearably ridiculous and detestable, and I am not convinced that it can ever be performed properly. I am angry and mortified.' Others detect a therapeutic element in the work, 'a feeling of inner hurt which does not tear the heart but repairs it', in the words of E. T. A Hoffmann. If that is the case, Beethoven is healing the Viennese mind a full century before Freud.

Most of the best recordings are by non-believers. Sir Thomas Beecham, rude about God and Rome, pairs suberb English soloists – Jennifer Vyvyan, Monica Sinclair, Richard Lewis – with the soaring Polish bass Marian Nowakowski. Colin Davis steers an agnostic line. Richard Hickox is a tad too C of E for the Credo. John Eliot Gardiner simulates pagan energy. George Guest drives the Academy of St Martin in the Fields down the middle of the aisle with the Choir of St John's College, Cambridge, and soloists Felicity Palmer, Helen Watts, Robert Tear and Christopher Keyte. The supreme Mass in C (1971) is conducted in London by Carlo Maria Giulini with soloists Elly Ameling, Janet Baker, Marius Rintzler and Theo Altmeyer – easing from fast to slow, loud to soft, this world to the next. The only recording that comes close to its conviction is led by Günter Wand, conductor in Cologne, in Beethoven's native Catholic heartland.

68

Ah, men

Missa Solemnis, Op. 123 (1819–24)

WRITTEN PARALLEL TO THE NINTH SYMPHONY, THE MASS IN D is a massive undertaking – 'the greatest work I have composed so far'. In the Mass he uses solo voices from the start; in the symphony he reserves them for apotheosis. The Mass is for the glory of God, the symphony for mortal redemption.

'I remember his mental excitement,' writes Schindler, 'never before and never since that time have I seen him in a similar state of removal from the world.' He is in the grip of higher powers. 'From behind the closed door of one of the parlours we could hear the master working on the fugue of the *Credo*, singing, yelling, stomping his feet ... The door opened and Beethoven stood before us, his features distorted to the point of inspiring terror.'

Beethoven starts work in the summer of 1819 when Rudolph is made a cardinal-archbishop. He promises to finish in nine months. 'The day when a High Mass of mine shall be performed at the ceremonies for YIH [Your Imperial Highness] will be for me the most beautiful day of my life,' he writes, 'and God will inspire me so that my weak powers may contribute to the glorification of this solemn day.' But Rudolph's day comes round and he fails to deliver. Three more years elapse. His dither is out of character. Beethoven might show up late with rough sketches on a concert morning, but he always delivers. To miss a deadline altogether and by such a margin suggests that something has gone painfully wrong with Rudolph and he is paralysed with grief for the departure of a loved and sorely needed friend, the more so since there are few left that he can trust.

Beethoven has put his business affairs in the hands of a clerk, Franz Oliva, who works for the Jewish bank of Offenheimer & Herz. Oliva, with ideas above his station, invites Goethe to dinner. He resents Rudolph. As soon as the archduke is made an archbishop, he advises Beethoven to demand a salaried position at his cathedral. When no offer comes through, Oliva poisons the waters. In December 1819 he jots in Beethoven's book: 'Are you going to the Archduke again now & without compensation for your many troubles? Press for that which is owed to you.' Oliva whispers: 'everyone hearkens and hears' that Rudolph is homosexual, hinting that younger men have displaced Beethoven in his favour. He warns Beethoven that the archbishop won't pay his commission fee. 'Put an end to the Mass,' he urges.

Oliva moves to St Petersburg, where he is hired as adjunct professor of German literature, marries a Russian woman and fathers a daughter. The Austrian police issue a warrant for his arrest on passport irregularities. Oliva keeps plugging away at Beethoven, pestering him to sell the Mass to multiple publishers, all the while wrecking Beethoven's reputation for fair dealing. The Missa Solemnis is premiered in St Petersburg on 7 April 1824. Rudolph never gets to hear it. Beethoven sends him a copy with a quote from Goethe's *Faust*, 'from the heart – may it go again – to the heart', that hints at his own broken heart and regrets the distance that now separates them forever.

Blaming the Roman Catholic Church for taking Rudolph out of his life, in Missa Solemnis he turns defiantly to Protestant sources – to Johann Sebastian Bach's Mass in B minor and to Handel's *Messiah*, citing 'And he shall reign forever and ever' fiercely in the finale. Missa Solemnis is a slap in the face of clerical authority, a personal avowal of faith. It stands outside every recognised canon, 'an alienated magnum opus' in Adorno's telling phrase. Adorno, the most supple mind in twentieth-century musicology, gives up on the work as 'enigmatic and incomprehensible', all the while admitting that it 'contains little which does not remain within the confines of traditional musical idiom.' Beethoven succeeds in making an unfathomable mystery out of familiar, lip-worn liturgy. He refers to *Donna nobis pacem* as 'a prayer for peace, inner and outer', aligning his own ego with the state of the world. Beethoven keeps tinkering at the score, making small incremental changes until the week he dies.

Vienna first hears sections of the Mass as a prelude to the ninth symphony, a signal that Beethoven considers these twin peaks indivisible.

He takes care to rehearse two female soloists, one still in her teens. 'Jette Sontag and I entered the room as though entering a church,' writes Caroline Unger, 'and we attempted (alas, in vain) to sing for our beloved master. I remember my insolent remark that he did not know how to write for the voice, because one note in my part ... lay just too high. He answered, "Just learn it. The note will come."' Beethoven knows he is going beyond accepted norms: he expects the world to catch up, in time.

Half a century later, the *Musical Times* still protests: 'The work is impossible. No human lungs can endure the strain imposed by it.' Otto Klemperer demands: 'How do you translate into reality a work which doesn't take reality into account?' The work is neither worship nor opera. Falling between altar and stage, it requires an exceptional conductor to unravel its radicalism and present it with unequivocal conviction.

Toscanini in 1940 has the most outstanding soloists in Zinka Milanov, Bruna Castagna, Jussi Björling, Alexander Kipnis. Karajan marshals Elisabeth Schwarzkopf, Christa Ludwig, Nicolai Gedda, Nicola Zaccaria. Georg Solti in Chicago has the angelic Lucia Popp and Yvonne Minton. Bernard Haitink in Amsterdam (1978) and Munich (2015) can claim the best orchestra and chorus, along with an unforgettable concertmaster solo in the Benedictus. For all these glories, a certain elusiveness persists.

I attended the grand occasion of Salzburg's August 1991 memorial performance for Herbert von Karajan with the Vienna Philharmonic, choruses from Stockholm and Leipzig and a bank-breaking cast – Jessye Norman, Cheryl Studer, Plácido Domingo and Kurt Moll. Conducted by James Levine, the Mass collapsed for lack of humility.

In search of authenticity I consulted the conductor Nikolaus Harnoncourt, a great-great-nephew of Archduke Rudolph. Harnoncourt made it his mission to perform music in the spirit and on the instruments of its period. Unlike others in the early-music movement, he was not captivated by theory or ideology. 'Every musician can read the music, study the period and claim to be correct,' Harnoncourt told me. 'But for me the question is always why a composer wrote in a certain way. And that's what constantly interests me, the content not the form.'

A devout Roman Catholic whose brother was a priest in Graz, Harnoncourt approached Missa Solemnis as a mystery that called upon his entire skillset, practical, analytical and musical. Beethoven, he opined, had 'written failure into his score'. The conductor's task was to redeem the composer from his radicalism. Conservative in outlook, Harnoncourt attracted such forward-looking soloists as Gidon Kremer, Lang Lang, Thomas Quasthoff and Cecilia Bartoli. The search for musical truth must not be conducted along party lines.

On video, he can be seen floundering, his arms flailing behind the beat, his face reddening with stress. But players emote with him, seeking the essence. 'For me,' he said, 'the rehearsal starts with the content of a piece – what it means, how it can change the listener. I was an orchestral musician for seventeen years and what I missed was the question "why?"' His first two recordings of Missa Solemnis set out in search of an answer. He designated the third, in 2015, as his final release, if not the ultimate truth then the last grasp for it.

A man of unyielding honesty, Harnoncourt showed that a conductor does not need to be elegant, athletic or charismatic. 'As a cellist,' he'd say, 'you realise how few conductors are interested in the music. For most, the concert hall is just an arena where they perform masterly dressage as tamers.' His was a noble model of musical leadership: critical, collegial, informed, immersed and modest to a fault.

69

The conductor's concerto

Coriolan Overture, Op. 62 (1807)

As a child in Bonn, Beethoven is taken to the theatre to see *Hamlet*, *King Lear*, *Macbeth*, *Richard III* and *The Merry Wives of Windsor*. As a teenager he buys a German translation of Shakespeare and refers to it throughout his life. The slow movement of his first string quartet is based on *Romeo and Juliet*; the 'Ghost' trio, opus 70/1, is ascribed to *Hamlet* or *Macbeth*. There is a *Tempest* sonata and late-quartet hints of *A Winter's Tale*. He nicknames Schuppanzigh 'Falstaff' and refers to two other friends as gravediggers from *Hamlet*. Does Beethoven see himself as Hamlet: lonely, misunderstood, impetuous, fond of bad jokes, barely clinging to life? Shakespeare, he tells a Frenchman, is 'his idol'. He once considers composing an opera on *Macbeth*.

His Coriolan overture is written not for the Shakespeare play but for a drama by Heinrich von Collin, a civil servant. In Shakespeare, the ruthless general Coriolanus, hated by his own Roman people, goes over to lead their enemies, the Volsci. As he besieges Rome, Coriolanus hears his mother pleading for relief. In Shakespeare's text he asks the Volsci to 'cut me to pieces'. In Collin's, he falls on his own sword.

Collin's play is produced at Prince Lobkowitz's for one night only. Beethoven writes a triple whiplash opening that makes audiences leap in their seats. The overture is a maestro showpiece.

Arturo Toscanini (1947) covers it in under seven minutes. Herbert von Karajan (Berlin, 1965) is two minutes longer, with knife-edge entries and a line of beauty that turns suicide into an act of love. Slowest is Klaus Tennstedt at nine and a half minutes (1992), every second packed with incident. Richard Wagner once said that if Coriolan was all that Beethoven had ever written, it would stand alone as proof of genius. Listen to these three performances and you may well believe it.

70

The V sign

Symphony No. 5, Op. 67 (1804–8); Sonata
4-hands in D major (1796)

THE MOST FAMOUS FOUR NOTES IN THE WHOLE OF MUSIC ARE not conceived overnight. They are first heard in a four-hand piano piece from Beethoven's twenties, an esoteric rarity, seldom recorded (try the Dutch Jussen brothers' video on YouTube). The four notes pop up here and there in other sonatas, most clearly in the first movement of the 'Appassionata', where we hear Beethoven heavily pregnant with a symphonic phrase that is not quite ready to be born.

When the four notes finally sound out, twice across five bars at the start of the fifth symphony – g-g-g-E-flat, followed by f-f-f-Ddddd – they are freighted with a meaning that is, at once, forceful and obscure. We know something momentous is about to happen, but what? Beethoven's unreliable acolyte Schindler supplies a line from the composer: 'Thus Fate knocks at the door!' It's an evocative image, the so-called Fate motif, but is it what Beethoven has in mind?

Other solutions are proposed. It is: (a) the song of the Yellowhammer bird in the Vienna Woods; (b) a tune from Cherubini's *Hymne au Panthéon* (a John Eliot Gardiner theory); or (c) the landlady coming round to collect the rent. None of these explanations matches the expectation that Beethoven engenders with his stentorian opening. All we know for sure is that the theme has been in Beethoven's mind for years and that he delivers it with shattering effect. The fifth symphony is a demarcation line between the gracious classical symphony of Haydn and Mozart and something a whole lot more momentous.

The Fate motif will acquire political dimensions: as a sound of destiny in the 1848 uprisings; as a 1940 BBC Morse signal of V, for victory; and as a Chinese smoke-signal to end the Cultural Revolution. Beethoven opens music to limitless connotations.

The first to grasp the seminal shift that Beethoven has effected in this symphony is the Gothic-horror writer E. T. A Hoffmann, a man-about-bars immortalised in Offenbach's *Tales of Hoffmann*, Schumann's *Kreisleriana* and Tchaikovsky's *Nutcracker* ballet. Hoffmann, in the fifth symphony, declares the birth of the Romantic Age:

> When music is spoken of as an independent art . . . it is the most romantic of all arts, one might almost say the only one that is genuinely romantic, since its only subject-matter is infinity. Orpheus' lyre opened the gates of Orcus. Music reveals to man an unknown realm, a world quite separate from the outer sensual world surrounding him, a world in which he leaves behind all precise feelings in order to embrace an inexpressible longing . . .
>
> Mozart and Haydn, the creators of modern instrumental music, first showed us the art in its full glory; but the one who regarded it with total devotion and penetrated to its innermost nature is Beethoven . . . Beethoven's music sets in motion the engine of awe, of fear, of terror, of pain; and awakens that infinite yearning which is the essence of romanticism . . . What instrumental work by Beethoven confirms this to a higher degree than the profound Symphony [No. 5] in C Minor, a work that is splendid beyond measure. How irresistibly does this wonderful composition transport the listener through ever growing climaxes into the spiritual realm of the infinite. Nothing could be simpler than the two-measure main idea of the first Allegro, which, in unison at first, does not even define the key for the listener. The character of apprehensive, restless longing contained in this movement is made even plainer by the tuneful secondary theme.

Hoffmann ascribes the tension to an opening theme 'that does not even define the key' yet hangs around like a dental nerve awaiting extraction. Berlioz argues that the symphony is 'the first in which Beethoven gave wings to his vast imagination without being guided by or relying on any external source of inspiration.' Which is another way of saying that it is the purest of pure music, altogether without an agenda.

After a propulsive allegro con brio, the second movement is consolatory, the third admonitory and the finale exhortatory. Two centuries of scholarly exegesis cannot explain how it coheres into so captivating and coherent an entity. The stated key of C minor closes out in C major, which ought to send us home smiling but for the nagging of those opening notes which, in case you missed them, Beethoven hammers home again as a rhythmic pattern four times more in the score. It's not fate banging at the door, it's the composer drilling at your tooth. Nowhere else does he have to work so hard to make himself heard.

The first performance of the fifth symphony takes place in the second half of an overstuffed four-hour concert on 22 December 1808, featuring premieres of the fourth piano concerto, sixth symphony, the aria 'Ah, perfido', two movements of the Mass in C and the catastrophic Choral Fantasy. Beethoven, in an excess of nervous energy, knocks two candles off the piano, nearly setting the house alight. Genius that he is, he has no idea how to make himself presentable.

The symphony is made a cornerstone of concert repertoire by Felix Mendelssohn in Leipzig, Franz Liszt in Weimar, Gustav Mahler in Vienna, Artur Nikisch in London. In 1840s Boston, the fifth and sixth symphonies are performed in concert more than any other orchestral works. Nikisch, a wizard-like maestro, chooses Beethoven's fifth as the first symphony ever to be recorded. Forty Berlin Philharmonic strings and brass players crowd around a horn in a boxroom, alert to their conductor's fast-pulsating beat. The Nikisch recording remains, to this day, a textbook demonstration in pacing a Beethoven symphony.

Arturo Toscanini at La Scala (1920) takes the fifth at a crisp trot. Bruno Walter and Otto Klemperer make wholesale textural alterations. Walter downplays the opening thrust to accrue tension gradually. Klemperer gets the Philharmonia violins to play pizzicato at the end of the second movement and repeats the exposition in the finale, making the work feel less wild. There is a 1928 recording by the Staatskapelle Berlin where the conductor, Richard Strauss, slows down the strings until the players' fingers practically fall off. Wilhelm Furtwängler can be heard in full moral ambivalence – triumphalist in June 1943, defeatist in 1954. Among Herbert von Karajan's dozen recordings, his 1954 blast with an orchestra of British ex-servicemen pullulates with mutual resentment. Karajan's Mauser machine-gun opening notes are deemed illuminating by the critical consensus until, twenty years later, a less prescriptive contender turns up.

In June 1975, Deutsche Grammophon releases the fifth symphony with Carlos Kleiber and the Vienna Philharmonic. Kleiber, forty-five, has yet to make his name with any major orchestra. His father, Erich Kleiber, was an anti-Nazi musician who migrated to Argentina and never recovered his European career. Erich did all he could to dissuade Carlos from taking up the baton. Carlos, egged on by his mother, only wanted to conduct works that Erich had made his own. The family tensions must have been electrifying. Erich put in a word to get Carlos a first apprenticeship with a Vienna opera company before taking his own life in a Swiss hotel in January 1956. His American wife, Ruth Goodrich Kleiber, died in 1967, also by her own hand.

Carlos, sensitive to his father's fate, avoided the career ladder. After spells as second conductor in Stuttgart and Zurich, he refused other positions, maintaining a freelance existence. Karajan joked that Carlos conducted only when his fridge was empty, and for the highest fee. He demanded one hundred thousand Deutschmarks to conduct an orchestral concert in Germany, plus a top-of-the range Audi saloon. Often as not he cancelled, leaving the Vienna Philharmonic on the eve of a Japan tour, saying, 'I'm off into the blue.' Not many months passed before they implored him to come back. 'No conductor had such high standards,' said the violist Manfred Honeck. Carlos Kleiber was the real deal.

Ski-lodge handsome and fluent in English, Spanish, German and Italian, he made love to divas and movie stars while tenderly devoted to his wife, Stanka, who lived far from the musical fray on top of a Slovene mountain. Carlos, while cultivating friendships with select musicians, held himself delicately apart from those he conducted. In rehearsal he would leave notes on the musicians' stands in the interval rather than criticising them aloud. Famous conductors sneaked in to his rehearsals to see what they could learn. Simon Rattle remembers sitting with Bernard Haitink in a box overlooking the Covent Garden podium to watch Carlos conduct *Otello*. At one point in the first act Haitink leant over and said, 'I don't know about you, but my studies are just beginning!'

Acknowledged by his mid-sixties as the maestros' maestro, he suddenly gave up conducting, for reasons never specified. Stanka died in 2003 and he was diagnosed that year with a treatable form of prostate cancer. The next summer Carlos Kleiber committed suicide, alone on the Slovene mountain; he was seventy-four years old.

His recorded legacy, though small, is quintessential – Berg's *Wozzeck* and Johann Strauss' *Fledermaus*; Brahms' fourth symphony; Vienna New Year's Day waltzes; *Tristan und Isolde* from Bayreuth. His crowning achievement is Beethoven's fifth symphony in Vienna, which explodes like a cluster bomb on the innocent musical mind. 'One of the most glorious accounts of the Fifth Symphony I have ever had the pleasure of hearing,' was *Gramophone*'s initial verdict. Fifty years on, the *New Yorker* maintained:

> [Kleiber's] Fifth – it's pretty much the consensus view – is the greatest modern recording of the piece. When Mahler conducted the New York Philharmonic, in the early twentieth century, he tried to get the orchestra to play the opening chords with the proper weight. Well, with Kleiber, you certainly hear it – not just weight, but, as the movement goes on, speed, elegance of phrasing, perfect unanimity, and awesome power.

Re-listening to Kleiber's Fifth, I am stunned by the opening rat-at-at-taat, a fate fuelled by fury. The andante yields brief relief, like a coffee in an interrogation room. The third movement, led by strings and horns, reprises the symphony's opening theme, played pizzicato; the finale attains apotheosis. Everything about this interpretation is right in a way that defies verbalisation and yet appeals to almost every musical person who hears it. Very rarely on record is such rightness achieved – Radu Lupu maybe in a Schubert sonata, Gilels in the Beethoven's G Major Concerto, Flagstad in Strauss' Four Last Songs, Horowitz in Chopin.

Is this, then, the best-ever symphony on record, as most critics seem to think? Before we can approach a conclusion, we need to consider the father-son connection which cuts to the very heart of whether conducting is a transmissible skill or an innate talent. There are a handful of other father-son maestros – the Latvians Arvīds and Mariss Jansons, the Estonians Neeme and Paavo Järvi, the Italians Marcello and Lorenzo Viotti, the American Damrosches, the Sanderlings, the Masurs, a few more. In no instance is the transmission on the elevated altitude that the Kleibers attained in performance (I saw Carlos twice) and on record.

Before endorsing Carlos Kleiber's Fifth as the *ne plus ultra*, I listen once more to Erich's performance with the Concertgebouw in 1953. Erich is taut and tough in his opening tempo, the andante measured, the scherzo restrained and all power held in reserve for a lightning-strike finale of devastating, irremediable savagery. Assessing the symphony page by page and movement by movement, I find Carlos compelling throughout, while Erich overwhelms at the close. It is as if Carlos wins every battle, only for his father to win the war. All we can do is marvel at two unique and discrete miracles of symphonic interpretation.

Few others come into my reckoning. Solti in Chicago (1975) delivers vigour and vitality with the loudest orchestra on record. Gardiner with his all-standing Orchestre Révolutionnaire et Romantique (2016) keeps string players bouncing on the balls of their feet. David Zinman with the Zurich Tonhalle (1997) fuses period and modern practice. Mariss Jansons with Bavarian Radio on tour in Japan in 2012 gets clarity, coherence and humanity from Germany's most flexible orchestra. When all's said and done, it must be Kleiber, one or the other.

≀

In a series of lectures given at Trinity College Cambridge in 1927 and published under the title *Aspects of the Novel*, the English novelist E. M. Forster defines rhythm as a pre-requisite for anyone writing a story. He splits this into two types of rhythm – common and unattainable, like the opening of Beethoven's fifth symphony. Here's what he has to say:

> What a literary man wants to say, though, is that the first kind of rhythm, the diddidy dum, can be found in certain novels and may give them beauty. And the other rhythm, the difficult one – the rhythm of the Fifth Symphony as a whole – I cannot quote you any parallels for that in fiction, yet it may be present.

This comes tantalisingly close to the heart of the mystery. Forster, a capable pianist and constant afficionado who remarks elsewhere that 'Beethoven's Fifth Symphony is the most sublime noise that has ever penetrated into the ear of man', understands that Beethoven has cracked one of the secrets of creation in the opening of this symphony. That it is a Eureka moment. The symphony exists. The rest of us can conduct or play or hear it but we cannot repeat Beethoven's revelation: we cannot find a rhythm that is as right and true and necessary as the one that throbs beneath the midpoint work of Beethoven's contribution to musical life on earth. Fight or fail, the best a conductor or a writer can hope for is to convey a simulacrum of that deep secret. Fidget or enjoy, the best a listener can glimpse is a faint shadow of the enigma.

And so we keep trying.

71

Callous

'Ah, perfido!', Op. 65 (1796/1808)

THE ARIA THAT OPENS BEETHOVEN'S OVERSTUFFED DECEMBER 1808 concert proves unexpectedly controversial. Written for Mozart's favourite soprano Josephine Duschek with text by the vogueish librettist Pietro Metastasio, it hits a wall of incomprehension and goes back into the drawer. Beethoven's belief that it contains the best of him is not shared by singers, who fear for their top notes and their image. The singer's attack on her lover verges on man-hatred:

> Go, wicked man! Go, run from me,
> You won't escape the Gods' wrath.
> If there is justice in Heaven, or mercy,
> They will jointly punish you!
> I foresee my vengeance;
> I enjoy it already;
> I see lightning flash around you.
> Ah no, ah no, stop, Gods of vengeance!
> Spare his heart, strike mine!
> He has changed, I am the same,
> Living through him as I did, I would now die for him!

Recordings by Frida Leider (1924), Kirsten Flagstad (1937) and Birgit Nilsson (1958) have Wagnerian pathos. Inge Borkh (1956) takes us into Richard Strauss territory, a psychological thriller with a twisted ending. Janet Baker (1977), her voice gleaming like brass, assures us that the woman is reasonably sane.

There is one recording you must hear. This is the only extant Beethoven track by Maria Callas, so far as anyone knows. Callas made her stage debut as Leonore in *Fidelio* in August 1944, singing in Greek in an Athens amphitheatre packed with German occupation officers. She swore never to sing *Fidelio* again and was true to her word, but now, in December 1963, she was turning forty, her voice and life in tatters. Her shipowner lover Onassis treated her with contempt, she had been banned from the Metropolitan Opera and she was being needled by European critics for a shrill edge to her formidable sound. She had just one last run of *Tosca* to sing at Covent Garden, followed by *Norma* in Paris, and then her diary was bare and she would never appear again on an opera stage. Before that happened, she wanted one more blast at Beethoven.

Going into studio with Nicola Rescigno and an indifferent Paris Conservatoire orchestra, Callas made '*Ah, perfido*' eternally her own, freezing the blood with an opening shriek at the faithless male. This could be a blood-dripping vengeance monologue from *Norma* or *Anna Bolena*. She is going to die, but she will take that wicked man down with her. As she switches from fire to velvet, there is a wobble in her voice, but it hardly matters. Callas knows her Beethoven and maintains emotional control. This is Callas at her best, and her last. She died in her Paris apartment, aged fifty-three, in September 1977.

72

Car crash

Choral Fantasy, Op. 80 (1808)

BEETHOVEN WRITES A TWENTY-MINUTE PIECE FOR PIANO, chorus and orchestra the night before a four-hour concert. It is a sketch for the eventual ninth symphony, conceived without need or joy. He calls it an 'improvisation for piano with gradual entrance of the orchestra and finally a choral section and finale.'

Schindler claims it 'simply fell apart'. Czerny says that Beethoven shouts 'wrong, badly played (do it) again!' Seyfried reports: 'At first he could not understand that he had, in a manner, humiliated the musicians. He thought it was a duty to correct an error that had been made and that the audience was entitled to hear everything properly played, for its money. But he readily and heartily begged the pardon of the orchestra . . . and was honest enough to spread the story himself and assume all responsibility for his absence of mind.' 'During the finale,' writes Moscheles, 'I perceived that, like a runaway carriage going downhill, an overturn was inevitable.'

A solo piano intro resembles the Emperor Concerto finale, but as the orchestra joins in, followed by chorus, it seems Beethoven has no idea where he is going. At six minutes we hear a hint of the ninth symphony chorus. Ries captures the moment: 'We experienced the fact that one could easily have too much of a good – and even more, a powerful – thing.' The text is banal beyond words:

> . . . Do accept, then, you beautiful spirits
> Joyously the gifts of art;
> Love and strength are joined together
> God's favour is man's reward.

Daniel Barenboim (1968) plays the introduction with a forced solemnity, as if blending the Ten Commandments with the Sermon on the Mount. Alicia de Larrocha brings gravitas in Riccardo Chailly's Berlin account (1986); Menahem Pressler is respectful with Kurt Masur in Leipzig (1994). Alfred Brendel and Bernard Haitink (1977) are sane and stable. The young French pianist Bertrand Chamayou sparkles in a 2019 concert. Best of all is Martha Argerich with Seiji Ozawa (Berlin, 2018), a law unto herself.

73

God's flower

Piano Sonata No. 15, 'Pastoral', Op. 28 (1801)

IN BEETHOVEN'S 15TH PIANO SONATA, NAMED BY A LONDON publisher, the left hand starts with a low D note, played twenty-four times in as many bars and sixty in all. It reminds us of the groundbass used by late-baroque composers like Antonio Vivaldi in 'pastorale' style, an undercurrent drone. 'Pastorale', in baroque terms, is a calming, reassuring mood. The publisher is pitching this sonata to amateurs as being easy to play.

The standout recording is by Murray Perahia, a Sephardi New Yorker from a Salonika-Greek family. The soft-spoken Perahia (the name means 'God's flower') won the 1972 Leeds Competition, playing no louder than a whisper. His Beethoven is at once shy and strong, frugal and radical. In a 2008 recording, he turns left-hand rumbles into a Scandi-noir plot. His andante movement anticipates Chopin's funeral march, and the rest tingles with possibility. Perahia made this recording for his sixtieth birthday year, intending to follow up with more Beethoven. Sadly, his plans were thwarted by a persistent thumb injury and little Beethoven has been heard from him since.

Elsewhere, Maurizio Pollini's trademark thoughtfulness sounds self-absorbed. Alfred Brendel is schoolmasterly. Wilhelm Backhaus is dogmatic. Dino Ciani is sabotaged by a tinny piano. Maria Grinberg bangs out the groundbass with a mallet.

Emil Gilels, in one of his last DG sessions, takes the breath away with surreal beauty. Gilels lived in fear of his KGB minder. 'Look, my hands are shaking,' he told an Israeli conductor. 'How do they want me to play a concert?' In October 1985 during a routine Moscow hospital check-up, he died unexpectedly, aged sixty-eight. Medical incompetence was alleged but never prosecuted. Gilels' playing of the Pastoral is out of this world. He fell three short of completing a Beethoven sonata cycle on record.

74

Hell on earth

Symphony No. 6, 'Pastoral', Op. 68 (1808)

WHEN I WAS TEN YEARS OLD, THE PASTORAL WAS THE ONLY symphony I knew. It was played by my stepmother on her mono gramophone in our sitting room. The record featured Bruno Walter with musicians of the Columbia Symphony Orchestra. I see the names unblurring on the label as each side of the LP unwinds to its conclusion.

I hated this recording, and for reasons I dared not express. My stepmother was a Hitler refugee with emotional disturbances who married my father for financial security. She was in her late forties, a failed infants' teacher, a short woman in shapeless clothes, with a hair-trigger temper. Apart from loving music, chiefly Beethoven's sixth symphony, Mozart's *'Eine kleine Nachtmusik'* and Wagner's *Flying Dutchman*, she exhibited few endearing qualities. Her voice squeaked like an unoiled gate. Her cooking was tasteless, her outlook joyless, her rare smiles menacing. She got me a piano teacher and hit me if I skimped on practice. She hit me for many other sins, and for none. Orphaned of my mother, I had landed in a suburban, semi-detached house with a father who was mostly absent and a woman who demanded that I call her 'Mother'. When I refused, she hit me, as expected. No point complaining. A child learns to adapt, hangs on for a day of redemption.

Seeing people cross the road at the sight of her, I understood she was probably unhinged, or at least bad company. It was up to me to protect my unwell father and myself from the worst of her wrath. One way of doing that was by sitting with her while listening to the Pastoral Symphony, which evoked fond memories of her girlhood in Munich, a cultured capital where Generalmusikdirektor Bruno Walter presided over classical performance at a most exalted level. When anyone uttered the name

'Bruno Walter' her face took on a pious mien. She never tired of listening to Walter's recording of the Pastoral Symphony. Woe betide the phone caller (or me) who interrupted her beaming immersion in these bucolic reminiscences.

Behind my bedroom door, I swore at her, her music, her bloody maestro, the gramophone, the sitting room, its patio and the unendingly long garden lawn that she ordered me to mow. Most of all I cursed myself for buying her this record as a placatory birthday present, an act of craven hypocrisy on my part.

She began taking me to concerts at the Royal Festival Hall where, in the upper rows, I would be ripped apart between musical awakening and an intolerable revulsion at her presence beside me. I loved music, hated my neighbour. Beneath the outing lay a form of mental torture. Recognising that I had perfect pitch, she used my musicality as a weapon against my father, who could not sing a note. Each time I went with her was a calculated distancing from my poor Dad, who suffered a couple of strokes and spiralled into decline, for which I felt some guilt.

I saw legends on stage – Klemperer, Rubinstein, Boult, Tortelier, Kempff – but my torment became so unendurable that, after a couple of years, I stopped going to concerts and, indeed, listening to classical music. It took a nervous breakdown in my twenties for me to achieve a state of mind where I could listen to music without rage and allow myself to fall in love with a woman without fearing that she would turn into a younger version of my stepmother.

In common with every abused child, I thought my experience was unique. Those terror years between ten and sixteen left me solitary and suspicious, self-doubting and self-protective. Once I was away from home I ceased contact with my stepmother, who lived to be a hundred. I never held it against my father for bringing her into our lives; the poor man thought he was doing the best for me. If I held anyone to blame it was members of our family and community who saw what was going on and looked the other way. As with music, it took years before I could fully engage as an adult with family and community. Why am I sharing these memories in a book about Beethoven? Because, as soon as I read a brief biography in the local library, I empathised with his experience of a brutal parent in an indifferent environment. How did one escape?

In 2019, I was sent for review a study of Shostakovich written by a British broadcaster, Stephen Johnson. A few pages into the book, Johnson (whom I did not know) describes his experience of growing up with a violent, bipolar parent while discovering an unlikely place of safety in this furious symphony. Shostakovich lived a dual life under Stalin, outwardly compliant, inwardly screaming. Johnson endured a parallel duality. 'I had to lock myself away to avoid destabilising Mother and thus prevent the unspoken catastrophe that would surely have followed. If I could have voiced the commandment I unconsciously repeated to myself during that period, it would have been: "I must not feel, I must not feel". Except in music.'

I yelped on reading this passage, both with feeling for the child in Johnson and in me and with relief at our survival, his and mine. Johnson again: 'Violent reversal was always just around the corner. I remember one occasion where, after some misdemeanour on my part, she suddenly wheeled around brandishing a pair of scissors like a knife and hissed, "you're lucky you didn't get these in your *back!*"'

The Shostakovich symphonies that he borrowed from the library brought Johnson hope of relief. Shostakovich, under Stalin, found refuge by expressing in music what no one dared say in words. When Johnson's mother was finally carted off to a mental home, it felt to him as if his own Stalin had died. His wife told him: 'Living with your Mother must have been like that symphony'.

When I managed to leave home at sixteen, I found myself – literally found *myself* – in another land, a new language, different heat and light, with no threat at my throat. My life began again. I learned how to live and slowly to love, even though parts of me were so injured that I could not hear the Pastoral Symphony on the radio without wanting to throw up. This music had meaning for me, and at several deeper layers.

My stepmother, raised in the *Wandervogel* fad of hiking on mountain tracks, would drag me along on Sunday mornings for ten-mile schleps around the Home Counties with sandwiches in a rucksack and a Ramblers' Association map in hand. I was not asked if I wanted to go; I was there to serve her cult. Every moment I spent walking in meadows was an infinity of sodden misery. It rained with English inevitability and I prayed to God to send a hurricane or a nuclear strike to end my forced march. I fantasised about my stepmother being gored to death by a bull or bitten by a venomous adder. I hoped some farmer would shoot her for trespass. I untied my bootlaces, trying to break an ankle. Squelch, squelch went my boots in brown bilge until, out of a grey skyline, a Victorian steeple came in sight and there were only two more churches to go before we reached the station and a train back home. I loathed England's green and pleasantness. I failed Geography at school, intentionally so that I never had to read a map again.

Every country ramble had the Pastoral Symphony as soundtrack. Trudging and symphony were conjoined in a horror movie for which Beethoven had written the script: *Pastoral Symphony, more an expression of feeling than painting. 1st movement: pleasant feelings awaken on arriving in the countryside. 2nd: scene by the brook. 3rd piece: merry gathering of peasants, interrupted by 4th: thunder and storm, yielding to 5th: salutary feelings combined with thanks to God.*

No thanks from me, I can tell you. Decades later, once I was familiar with the wonders of symphonic music, I recognised Beethoven's sixth symphony as the precursor of pastoral marvels by Schumann, Brahms, Bruckner, Elgar, Vaughan Williams, Roussel, Sibelius – above all by Gustav Mahler, whose first symphony became central to me as Shostakovich's eighth was to Johnson. Mahler, as a boy, hid in a forest from violence at home. Researching his life, I walked the woods where he hid and heard the east wind blow the opening A of his symphony through the treetops. Mahler left home about the same age as I did. He made his way in the world, 'ever an outsider, never accepted'. As head of the Vienna Opera, he set Elysian performance standards, encouraging others to treat music as a flexible art, taking liberties with printed scores, including his own. 'Make it work,' he told the young Klemperer. 'If it doesn't work, change the score – you have a right, no, a duty, to change it.'

Mahler's most trusted interpreter was Bruno Walter, whom he had trained as a conductor from the age of eighteen. This presented an obstacle to my initial ventures into Mahler. Listening to Walter I could not forget that he was my stepmother's personal deity. He was also authoritative in Mahler. If I was to give a fair and reasoned account of Mahler's works I would have to overcome my aversion to the ultra-smooth Bruno Walter.

I grasped from his autobiography that Walter was not quite as he seemed. Walter was not his real name, for starters. He changed his surname from Schlesinger (too Jewish) and got himself baptised to advance his career. 'He was a Christian and a very good one,' his daughter maintained. He befriended the Munich archbishop who, as Pope Pius XII, negotiated a concordat with Hitler's Germany. Digging a little deeper I found that behind his cover of bourgeois propriety, Walter was a sexual predator who kept a mistress, the singer Delia Reinhardt, and seduced the teenaged daughter of his neighbour, the writer Thomas Mann. I did not need to know much more to conclude that Walter was not the paragon my step-mother imagined. He was an emotional whiteboard who shed no tears at his wife's death, nor at his daughter's murder by a jealous husband. His only capacity for feeling was a tsunami of self-pity when Hitler expropriated his personal wealth and drove him into exile.

Walter's murdered daughter was known as Gretel, my stepmother's name. By some auto-analytic quirk of Freudian free association that knowledge liberated me of any prejudice against him. I was finally able to assess his work with critical objectivity, both in Mahler and in Beethoven's Pastoral Symphony, of which he was an exemplary performer, perhaps the one closest in spirit to Mahler's interpretative ideas. Listening to Bruno Walter and the Pastoral Symphony was a sign that I had flushed away most of my trauma, once and for all.

Walter's first recording, dated Vienna 1936, is athletic, brisk, kitsch-free, well-rounded, exemplary. Mahler's brother-in-law Arnold Rosé was still concertmaster and the nightingale song in the finale echoes the one in Mahler's first symphony. I could imagine that Mahler made the Pastoral sound more or less like this, memorably so.

Walter's second recording of the Pastoral, in Philadelphia with America's best orchestra in 1946, is a total sellout – a Disney cartoon of country life as seen from a family Buick on an interstate highway. His third recording, made in Hollywood in 1962, wobbles at the very precipice of kitsch while surveying the grandness of the Belvedere gardens. The *Spectator* critic Richard Bratby speaks of its 'deep warmth and compassionate, lived-in style from a conductor I find it impossible not to love.' I cannot bring myself to love him, but I recognise Walter as a maestro for all seasons, one who delivers flawless technique and depth of experience without being in the slightest bit troubled by human consequences. Music is not a field of moral philosophy. Like water, it is neutral until humans pollute it with extraneous substances. Walter was human, all too human.

Klemperer (1957) takes three minutes longer than anyone else in the first movement of the Pastoral, taut as a tripwire. He strips the brook of babble and the peasants of schmaltz. His storm has Shakespearian menace and his nightingale has stolen the crown jewels. Klemperer's countryside is certifiably unsafe for city dwellers. This is reverse Mahler, admonitory and ominous.

Among other contenders, Herbert von Karajan has a rare and spectacular stumble in his 1963 Berlin cycle, recasting Beethoven's landscape as a tourist trap. Erich Kleiber finds fragile delicacy. Carlo Maria Giulini, raised in the Tyrolean Alps, runs out of oxygen at 10,000 feet. Riccardo Chailly directs an *Othello*-like storm. Klaus Tennstedt expresses a childlike wonder in the brook. I listen to their diversities with wonderment. My Pastoral past is now another country.

{

In writing this memoir I lay myself open to criticism from purists who maintain that a critic must stay out of the picture, assessing the music only on substantive merit. I make no apology for the digression you have just read. I cannot write about the Pastoral without declaring a personal interest any more than a financial journalist can report on a company in which he has shares. To withhold that information, painful as it may be, would be partial and dishonest. It would also diminish the impact that music has on each of us, on our inner selves.

While rewriting this chapter for the thirty-fifth time late one night I had a flash memory of a great Mahler scholar I had known with a similar dilemma. Kurt Blaukopf, a law student, left Vienna in 1939. He spent ten years in Jerusalem, eventually repatriating to Vienna in the 1950s as a professor of music sociology. Aware that there was no credible Gustav Mahler biography in post-war Europe, he applied himself to writing one. It was not an easy task, either in accessing the information or in assessing it. Blaukopf writes:

My love for Mahler was not constant. There were years when I turned
away from his music. The detachment gained by this – which arose partly
from a misunderstanding of Mahler and partly from a change in my incli-
nations – proved useful in the end, for it enabled me to understand the
fickleness of public favour . . . the interplay between artist and society
and . . . the changing position of the work of art in its social context.

This confession, written in 1968, stayed with me ever after, striking a
note of honesty in a field flattened by hagiolatry. A biographer approaches
a subject out of love and admiration. To discover while telling the story
that one's feelings have changed, that the subject is no longer attractive
and might even be loathsome is a horror that most biographers suppress.
Blaukopf's candour is rare, the more so for being made in the realm of
classical music, where presenters gush day and night over the genius of the
stuff that earns them their living. By admitting there were times he disliked
Mahler, Kurt Blaukopf gave the rest of us licence to step back and take our
blood pressure, daily if necessary, in relation to the music we discuss. It is
a permission that is not confined to critics and biographers.

Composers, too, can feel ambivalence. Mahler would tell an orchestra
to perform his symphony 'one day this way, the next day different.' That is
where interpretation begins. Immersed in Mahler, I was encouraged by
Blaukopf to face up to my own ambiguities. 'Doubtless I am beginning to
tire the reader with such minutiae,' writes Blaukopf. 'This is done deliberately, for I should like to arouse his sympathy for the despondency which
sometimes overtook me during this work. There are all too few facts I
could consider safely established; nearly every document I took up
produced doubts. I was particularly suspicious of certain sentences which
recur almost verbatim in a variety of publications . . .' – a warning from
history to the present cut-and-paste school of music biography.

Blaukopf takes us to the heart of Mahler, to his self-questioning and his
intermittent self-hate, to the fluidity of his music and, at the next stop, to its
relevance. I learned from Blaukopf that it is all right for a biographer to expose
his own history and feelings and shortcomings – as Mahler did in his music,
and Beethoven to some extent – so long as that exposure takes us closer to an
appreciation of the composer and his work. Kurt Blaukopf, a hero of biographical truth, died in Vienna at the end of Mahler's century, in June 1999.

75

Lola's finest hour

Egmont, Overture and Incidental Music, Op. 84 (1804)

IN THE SUMMER OF 1839, THE WILDLY POPULAR HUNGARIAN pianist Franz Liszt takes charge of Bonn's faltering plan for a Beethoven monument. On holiday in Pisa, Liszt commissions a Florentine sculptor in marble, Lorenzo Bartolini. The burghers of Bonn, preferring bronze, turn to a dusty professor from Dresden, telling him Liszt will pay. Liszt makes a lead donation of ten thousand French francs to the Beethoven commemoration campaign and hits the road to earn the rest. Frenzies of Lisztomania erupt. Matrons faint as he mounts the stage and their husbands cough up gold doublets for his appeal. His relationship with Marie d'Agoult, with whom he has three children, collapses under the strain.

The monument unveiling is set for August 1845. Queen Victoria and Prince Albert promise to attend, along with King Wilhelm IV of Prussia. The composers Berlioz and Meyerbeer arrive from Paris, Spohr and Moscheles from Vienna; Schumann and Mendelssohn stay away, fearing a Liszt circus. Bonn suddenly realises it has no performing space large enough for the concerts. Liszt dips into his pocket once more and pays for a temporary festival hall.

Rhine steamboats discharge thousands of tourists into the town. Hotels are overwhelmed and the beer runs dry. Liszt puts on a concert lasting four hours that ranks among the great classical disasters. Wilhelm IV arrives late and demands a repeat of all that he has missed. Six hundred guests fight over tables at the Golden Star Hotel. Liszt gets up to restore order and is just getting attention when heads turn to the next table where two legs, naked to the hips, are dancing on high heels. 'I'm a guest of Mr Liszt,' cries Lola Montez.

Into every artist's life, a little Lola must fall. Lola, described as a 'Spanish dancer', is neither Spanish nor much of a dancer. Her real name is Elizabeth Gilbert and she is an Irish-born English girl whose fortune is predicated on her protuberant upper half, which she wiggles at princes and kings. Liszt, after a night with Lola, locks her in a hotel room while he makes his escape. When she turns up in Bonn to steal his Beethoven bash he is altogether discombobulated. Liszt has done the most any musician could to honour Beethoven. He leaves Bonn 'tired, discouraged and nearly bankrupt'. In September 1847, aged thirty-five, he retires from the piano circuit and settles with a princess in provincial Weimar. In time, he takes holy orders in Rome and vows to sin no more.

Lola, after Bonn, alights upon King Ludwig I of Bavaria. Ludwig demands to verify by palpation that her breasts are real and, satisfied, sets her up in Munich as his state mistress. This arrangement lasts about a year until the 1848 revolution topples Ludwig and turfs Lola out of town. She sails to New York where, aged thirty-nine, she dies of syphilis. Lola is the original rockstar groupie. She deserves a monument in her own right. As for Bonn, it is so affronted by the 1845 bash that, for Beethoven's centenary in 1870, it pointedly disinvites Liszt.

All that remains of the 1845 festival, apart from the statue, is an item from the closing concert which includes, among varied arias and concertos, Beethoven's 1810 overture to Goethe's play, *Egmont*.

Egmont is a Dutchman who fought his country's Spanish occupiers. Liszt inserts the piece as a reminder to Bonn of Beethoven's Iberian and Netherlandish origins, his cultural and racial difference. Egmont, thanks to Liszt, becomes ever after a classical curtain raiser for great occasions.

Arthur Nikisch's 1913 recording with the London Symphony Orchestra is a cracker. Willem Mengelberg (1926), Dutch as it comes, administers blunt thrusts. Wilhelm Furtwängler (1947) fuses slow sentiment with fierce bluster. Bernstein pitches midway between Broadway and Brahms. Ferenc Fricsay conjures Lisztian paprika in a poignant 1958 reading. Klaus Tennstedt (1982) tells a bedtime story to a grownup lady. Christian Thielemann (2005) blends Wagnerian freakishness with Hansel-and-Gretel horror, the stuff of Gothic nightmares.

76

The apostle

Liszt/Beethoven: The Nine Symphonies
(transcribed for piano) (1837–64)

LISZT SAID THAT, AS A BOY OF ELEVEN, BEETHOVEN KISSED HIM on the forehead. In Weimar he kept a Beethoven piano in his living room. On tour from Russia to Ireland, Baltic to Balkans, he played many of the Beethoven sonatas as well as solo-piano transcriptions he made of the nine symphonies. People in towns without an orchestra were thus introduced to the symphonies. These piano scores, writes the Liszt biographer Alan Walker, 'dispel the popular view of him as a showman, taking other composers' works and turning them into a fireworks display for his own glorification. The act of self-denial ... suppressing his own creative impulses in the interests of Beethoven's music, has few parallels.'

The symphonies for piano have been extensively recorded.

1st symphony The French-Cypriot pianist Cyprien Katsaris recorded in 1980s sub-optimal sound. Idil Biret's 1985 Brussels set is likewise blighted. Jean-Louis Haguenauer, at the University of Indiana, Bloomington, is clear and bright though not terribly interesting (2020).

2nd symphony In St Martin's Church, East Woodhay, in Hampshire, Konstantin Scherbakov delivers muscular, pocket-sized Beethoven in a translucent acoustic, an appealing combination.

3rd symphony, 'Eroica' The Frenchman Georges Pludermacher offers Napoleonic magniloquence. Gabriele Baldocci goes for Italian braggadocio. Katsaris is my first choice.

4th symphony Alain Planès, a Pierre Boulez aide, adds pointillist modernism to the performance, sounding as if John Cage were playing Beethoven on prepared piano. Highly listenable, if not quite Liszt or Beethoven.

5th symphony Hold your hats. Glenn Gould plays Beethoven's fifth symphony with grit and grandeur on a honky-tonk piano. Gould's recapitulation of the opening theme ought to be taught in every conducting course. And if that's not surprise enough, the period-piano expert Paul Badura-Skoda somehow finds colours to spare in the upper register.

6th symphony, Pastoral Glenn Gould is a good companion in the first movement and an absolute terror in the storm. Ashley Wass conjures a bucolic atmosphere from an 1820s fortepiano in an English country house. Martha Argerich plays a new four-hand arrangement (by Selmar Bagge) with her Greek student Theodosia Ntokou. The fascination in their 2020 Warner release lies in Argerich's gestural transmission of Beethoven mannerisms to a responsive, if headstrong, pupil.

7th symphony The most phenomenal hand I ever shook belonged to Ronald Smith, an Englishman in pebble glasses who played unplayable Busoni and Alkan. Smith, who was going blind, carried a huge amount of music in memory. What we hear in his Liszt/Beethoven 7th is a pianist as prodigious as Liszt paying homage to Beethoven at his greatest. You won't breathe.

8th symphony Yury Martynov, of Moscow's Tchaikovsky Conservatory, recorded the full set in September 2013 at an austere Dutch church in Haarlem. The sound works exceptionally well in the light-footed eighth symphony.

9th symphony The Ninth cannot be fitted in a matchbox and no recording of the Liszt score is entirely convincing. There is a super-slow 2009 take by the Italian Maurizio Baglini, but I prefer a 2008 four-hander by Leon McCawley and Ashley Wass, two young Brits in a rush.

Liszt issued three versions of his Fantasia on motifs from Beethoven's 'The Ruins of Athens' – for solo piano, two pianos and piano and orchestra. In the last, he keeps the piano under wraps for ages, before letting in the soloist with a 'Dervish Chorus' and the 'Turkish March'. It's fun and frisky and possibly self-mocking. Among scant recordings, I would recommend Egon Petri (1938), a Dutchman with Liszt-like hands, and the Russian Grigory Ginzburg (1904–61), a Liszt specialist whom the Kremlin never allowed to tour abroad.

77

Look, one hand

Piano Concerto No. 5 in E flat major, 'the Emperor', Op. 73 (1809)

THE FIRST THING A CHILD SEES IN THE EMPEROR IS THAT ALL the action is in the pianist's right hand: why is that? This is the largest orchestra assembled for a concerto, yet in the second movement one of the flutes, the clarinet, both trumpets and timpani have nothing whatsoever to do. Why is that?

The opening movement is twenty minutes of imperial bombast. The music is in Beethoven's happiest key and the contrasts between piano and orchestra are better developed than before. Beethoven refuses to licence soloists to play their own cadenzas: this time, every note is justified and no more are needed.

The private premiere is given at Prince Lobkowitz's in January 1811 by Beethoven's pupil Archduke Rudolph, the son of an Emperor playing an Emperor concerto. The first public performance is a triumph in Leipzig, where the tripping finger rhythms of the preliminary dance themes prove irresistible. Whatever the concerto is called, it allows the pianist plenty of room for personal expression.

The Indian novelist, Rukun Advani, describes the concerto in *Beethoven Among the Cows* (1994): 'There was an immense, impassioned, ordered turbulence about the music which set in perspective everything else in life and made it seem the highest cathartic interruption within the general desirability of silence.' At the close of the 2010 movie *The King's Speech*, the Emperor's slow movement signifies King George VI's satisfaction at his triumph over a debilitating stutter.

The Nazis stamped this concerto with a swastika. Wilhelm Backhaus met Adolf Hitler on a plane in 1933 and was made head of a *Kameradschaft der Deutschen Künstler* (Fellowship of German Artists). In September 1936, he was Hitler's guest at the Nuremberg Rally, where he swore that 'nobody loves German art and especially German music as glowingly as Adolf Hitler.' Backhaus recorded the Emperor eleven times in all. Elly Ney, a dewy-eyed Hitlerite who took part in Nazi 'cultural education' camps, recorded the Emperor totemically during a 1944 Berlin air raid. Walter Gieseking – who said: 'I am a committed Nazi. Hitler is saving our country' – recorded the Emperor in Berlin in January 1945. Wilhelm Kempff, who entertained Nazi leaders within an hour's drive of the Auschwitz smokestacks, recorded the Emperor with a doctrinaire Nazi, Peter Raabe, in 1935 and again with Ferdinand Leitner in 1961. The Swiss Edwin Fischer, who took Schnabel's dates in Berlin, recorded with Wilhelm Furtwängler in 1951 – fluid, relaxed and unaccountably smiling.

Artists are no better at politics than the rest of us. They make decisions that they come to regret or deny, maintaining that, in any event, whatever ideology they espoused never had any impact on their music. There is no way of telling by listening to their recordings if Backhaus was more of a Nazi than Gieseking, or if Fischer ever discussed racial politics with Furtwängler. The fact that the Emperor was embraced by the Nazis does not reflect on its content, rather on their warped perception of it. Or so we tell ourselves.

On the opposite side, Dame Myra Hess, who kept music alive in National Gallery recitals during the London Blitz, recorded the Emperor in 1952 with a governessy rustle, as if to reclaim the moral high ground. Gina Bachauer, Greek and Jewish, recorded it in 1962 with Stanisław Skrowaczewski and the London Symphony Orchestra, a truly blessed reading.

Hélène Grimaud (2007) has the lightest of touches. Mitsuko Uchida (1999) plays the adagio faintly above susurration. Hardly any other women come into the reckoning. Missing are Martha Argerich, Wanda Landowska, Maria Yudina, Ilona Kabos, Annie Fischer, Ingrid Haebler, Moura Lympany, Alice Sara Ott, Yuja Wang, Maria João Pires and Angela Hewitt. The Emperor is a male domain.

The performance I have admired longest is Artur Schnabel's 1942 take, with Frederick Stock and the Chicago Symphony. Schnabel bullies the piano, the conductor and the musicians with a Beethoven-like gruffness until, in the finale, he beams in messianic benediction. Arthur Rubinstein (1976), conducted by Barenboim, is another reference point. Rubi pauses now and then between notes as if to relight his cigar. Emil Gilels in Cleveland with George Szell (1968) and Claudio Arrau with Klemperer (1957) are transcendent. Arturo Benedetti Michelangeli and Carlo Maria Giulini at the Vienna Philharmonic (1979) act like unruly Italian tourists with a flustered Austrian landlady. Rudolf Serkin, Murray Perahia, Pollini, Brendel, Ashkenazy, Solomon, Buchbinder, Glenn Gould are all outstanding. Time to draw the line. Ashkenazy and Haitink (1974) cannot be faulted. They are simply magnificent.

78

Turkish delight

The Ruins of Athens, Opp. 113–4,
King Stephen, Op. 117 (1811)

NOTHING TERRIFIES THE AUSTRIAN EMPIRE MORE THAN A Hungarian breakaway. Every few years Vienna does something to show Budapest it cares. In 1808, the Emperor builds a new theatre in Pest. Named the German Theatre, it opens in February 1812 with a play by August von Kotzebue and music by the greatest living composer.

In the play, Greek gods moan about the Turkish occupation, a political jibe that is missed by censors and audience alike. Beethoven's music functions like a film score, accentuating highlights and covering dull patches. Right in the middle of the play, Beethoven slams in a Turkish march from his opus 76 piano variations, a total showstopper. He gets to write music for another Kotzebue play, *King Stephen*, about Hungary's founding monarch.

Kotzebue comes to a sticky end, assassinated for obscure reasons by a theology student in 1819. The theatre in Pest burns down. Beethoven's music is reworked in 1924 by Richard Strauss and Hugo von Hofmannsthal as an allegory of post-war Austria, the rump of a fallen empire.

The best *Ruins* recording is by Bernhard Klee with the Berlin Philharmonic Orchestra and RIAS chorus (1970), every note given full value. I never saw the point of the King Stephen overture until quite recently, when a March 2021 concert by the Geneva Chamber Orchestra on the Claves label, conducted by Gábor Takács-Nagy, demonstrated how frisky the Hungarians must have felt on receiving an externally sanitised slice of their own cherished heritage. This performance combines mischief, rebellion, loud jubilation and reckless mockery of Austro-German musical pomposity. The accents are so acute it hardly sounds like Beethoven at all. It makes you wonder why more conductors don't take such liberties with his non-binding tempo markings.

79

Top of the Pops

ONCE OR TWICE A YEAR SOMEONE PARADES A CHART OF THE most popular classical music of all time, as selected by experts/listeners/ data scientists/record critics/a man on the Clapham omnibus. Singly or severally, these surveys reflect little more than the playlists of radio stations and the promo schedules of record labels.

The Classic FM Hall of Fame has been topped for eleven years running by Ralph Vaughan Williams' *The Lark Ascending*, alternating with concertos by Rachmaninov and Bruch. In the Beethoven year of 2020–21, the ninth symphony came in at number 5, the Emperor Concerto at 7, Pastoral Symphony at 14, Moonlight Sonata at 15 and fifth symphony at 17, just nudging out John Williams' movie score *Schindler's List*.

A broader survey registers the concerts notified to the Bachtrack website each year. According to Bachtrack, Beethoven was the most played composer in 2019, featuring in one in seven concerts worldwide, a total of 20,535 events. The Eroica was played most often, but no other Beethoven work figured in the top ten. The survey lacks data from China and South America.

For want of a reliable measure of Beethoven usage, I applied to the orchestra that has been most entwined with his music. The Vienna Philharmonic Orchestra, at its formation in 1842, contained musicians whose parents had played with Beethoven. A sense of ownership persists. I asked the orchestra's present archivist, Dr Silvia Kargl, which Beethoven works had been played the most. She replied, slightly bemused, that no one had ever asked that question before. Over the course of a weekend Dr Kargl and her colleagues collated for me every single Beethoven work played by the Vienna Philharmonic over the course of 180 years. Here, then, is the official top twenty of Vienna's most performed Beethoven works, with one score withheld for further consideration.

1. NN
2. Symphony No. 5 in C minor, Op. 67 – 354 times
3. Symphony No. 3 in E sharp major, Op. 55 – 323 times
4. Symphony No. 6 in F major, Op. 68 – 234 times
5. Egmont Overture, Op. 84 – 205 times
6. Symphony No. 9 in D minor, Op. 125 – 204 times
7. Coriolan Overture, Op. 62 – 189 times
8. Symphony No. 8 in F major, Op. 93 – 171 times
9. Symphony No. 4 in B major, Op. 60 – 162 times
10. Symphony No. 2 in D major, Op. 36 – 146 times
11. Symphony No. 1 in C major, Op. 21 – 135 times
12. Leonore Overture No. 3, Op. 72a – 117 times
13. *Fidelio*, Op. 72 (in concert) – 107 times (at the Vienna State Opera from 1869: 950 times)
14. Violin Concerto in D major, Op. 61 – 84 times
15. Piano Concerto No. 4 in G major, Op. 58 – 76 times
16. Piano Concerto No. 5 in E flat major, Op. 73 – 76 times
17. Piano Concerto No. 3 in C minor, Op. 37 – 66 times
18. Missa Solemnis, Op. 123 – 55 times
19. Piano Concerto No. 1 in C major, Op. 15 – 40 times
20. Overture, *The Creatures of Prometheus*, Op. 43 – 27 times

There are some surprising omissions, among them the second piano concerto; two romances for violin and orchestra; the triple concerto; the Choral Fantasy; and the Consecration of the House overture which gets trotted out whenever a new hall is inaugurated. The fourth piano concerto comes ahead of the supposedly more popular fifth and three orchestral overtures are heard more often than the critically important violin concerto. These, however, are nerdish caveats. What the Vienna Philharmonic plays is decided independently by its players. When the orchestra travels, it takes on board the wishes of local promoters while preserving its innate traditions. The chart above is as close as we can get to determining Beethoven's popularity in Vienna down the generations.

The astonishing discovery here is that the Beethoven work that received most play in the history of the Vienna Philharmonic is a symphony that has no name and never makes the headlines, a work that Richard Wagner dismissed as 'no better than dance music'. Thanks to Dr Kargl I can reveal that the seventh symphony, with 382 performances, is by some margin the Beethoven work that the Vienna Philharmonic has played most in its history.

Is that still the case? I asked Dr Kargl for Beethoven performances from 2000 to 2022. The frequency is virtually the same. Here's the twenty-first-century top ten:

1. Symphony No. 7 – 71 times
2. Symphony No. 3 – 64 times
3. Symphony No. 6 – 59 times
4. Symphony No. 5 – 53 times
5. Symphony No. 8 – 45 times
6. Symphony No. 2 – 33 times
= Piano Concerto No. 3 – 33 times
8. Symphony No. 9 – 31 times
9. Symphony No. 1 – 28 times
10. Piano Concerto No. 4 – 27 times

My next call was on Carnegie Hall which, from opening in April 1891 to its March 2020 Covid closure, has been America's benchmark concert venue. I put the question of Beethoven usage to Carnegie Hall president Sir Clive Gillinson. As in Vienna, no one had asked it before. Since Carnegie Hall hosts solo recitals as well as symphony concerts, the list is slightly more varied but the top places are pretty much the same:

1. Symphony No. 5 – 328 times
2. Symphony No. 7 – 301 times
3. Piano Sonata No. 23 in F minor, Op. 57, 'Appassionata' – 297 times
4. Symphony No. 3 – 284 times
5. Leonore Overture – 282 times
6. Violin Concerto in D major – 248 times
7. Egmont Overture – 236 times
8. Piano Concerto No. 5 – 215 times
9. Piano Concerto No. 4 – 192 times
10. Piano Sonata No. 21 in C major, Op. 53, 'Waldstein' – 187 times

11. Piano Sonata No. 32 in C minor, Op. 111 – 186 times
12. Piano Sonata No. 31 in A flat major, Op. 110 – 182 times
13. Symphony No. 6 – 181 times
14. Piano Sonata No. 14 in C sharp minor, Op. 27, No. 2, 'Moonlight' – 178 times
15. Piano Sonata No. 30 in E major, Op. 109 – 176 times
16. Coriolan Overture – 169 times
17. Symphony No. 9 – 160 times
18. Symphony No. 8 – 159 times
19. Sonata for Violin and Piano No. 9 in A major, Op. 47, 'Kreutzer' – 147 times
20. Symphony No. 1 – 146 times

Two symphonies, the fifth and seventh, jostle for top spot. The second piano concerto, and the second and fourth symphonies, are dropouts. The ninth is fairly scarce, no doubt for reasons of cost. New York is less keen than Vienna on the Pastoral. It goes crazy for the 'Appassionata'. It hears the seventh symphony at least twice a year, on average.

So what makes the seventh more playable than any other symphony? I put the question to conductors. Their responses range from technical appreciation to mild dismay. The Hungarian conductor Ivan Fischer tells me:

The special popularity of the seventh symphony may be due to the second movement which is in fact a masterpiece with a simple rhythmical pattern on one single note, an E, repeated over and over. This symphony also has an extremely effective finale with off-beat accents, which makes us feel that Beethoven invented repetitive music, or even rock music.

Sir Simon Rattle recalls:

When I met Mrs Furtwängler at the Brendels' house many decades ago, they were talking about how I should make my debut with the Berlin Philharmonic: she said of course you MUST play Beethoven 7 as it is the easiest success piece, never fails. There is a truth in what she said. Although very hard and unsatisfying to rehearse, it has its own life in performance

and its peculiar insanity tends to infect the performers, irresistible fire. I
save it for special occasions.

Riccardo Chailly, music director of La Scala, Milan: 'I have no rational
answer. In my experience the ninth has been more frequent. My personal
choice would be the fifth, an absolute ice-breaker.'
Franz Welser-Möst, steeped in Vienna's Beethoven, responds:

I don't perform it a lot because it's done soooo often and orchestras are
tired of it. I think the reason for being the most performed is the drive it
has in all movements. It would be interesting though when it started to be
the most performed. Has it to do with the overall development of speed
and fascination of mechanical things, the railways . . .?

Leonard Slatkin gives a practical perspective:

At a basic level, it is technically the easiest to conduct. There are no surprise
tempo changes, it is the most straightforward of all the symphonies. Unless
the conductor is a supreme idiot, it is almost always successful with the
audience.

This is not to minimize the difficulties in the piece. Just getting the
dotted rhythm in the first movement to be accurate is tricky even with the
best of orchestras. There are lots of decisions to be made but for various
reasons, there are simply fewer traps than the others in the form. For me,
the sixth was the hardest.

The seventh is also one of those pieces that you can slot in when there
is a difficult work elsewhere on the program. One time, in Minneapolis
during a summer concert, there was only one rehearsal and I found myself
with only ten minutes to rehearse the 7th. Telling the orchestra to put their
instruments down, I spent the time telling them which repeats we would
observe, how I wanted certain rhythmic figures played and more or less,
what the tempos would be. To this day, I think that was the best Beethoven
7th I ever did.

Fabio Luisi, music director of Zurich Opera and the Dallas Symphony,
finds several reasons:

1. Presenters, especially in Asia, always ask for this symphony (together with Tchaikovsky 5 and Mahler 1) because of the popularity. Beethoven is cheaper for travelling orchestras, no harps, no percussion, no extra instruments like double bassoon or English horn. Therefore a win-win.

2. It is a relatively simple symphony to hear (not the best Beethoven), lively, joyful, not too long.

3. It doesn't require extensive rehearsals since orchestras know it well and play it often.

4. It evokes positive, joyful thoughts, it's indeed very positive (we musicians appreciate most the second movement – which really IS the best Beethoven – not so much loved by audiences).

In my personal opinion, none of Beethoven's symphonies is the best Beethoven (maybe the 8th is an aspect of best Beethoven when he is self-ironical and full of fantasy), except parts of the Eroica, of the fourth and of the sixth, but never an entire symphony (although I admit the historical importance of all his symphonies, especially the Eroica). They are not to compare with the last quartets or the last piano sonatas or Missa Solemnis or the violin concerto or the 4th piano concerto. Those are the best Beethoven. And some violin sonatas. But this is strictly personal and I know that many musicians would vehemently oppose.

Although this is a random sampling of senior maestro opinion, the consensus appears to be that the seventh symphony is not innately popular but derives its frequency from other factors, such as cost and convenience. Asking around a wider circle of musical friends, I failed to find any who named the seventh symphony as their all-time favourite Beethoven work. On discovering that it is the most performed, some agreed with Ivan Fischer: 'I guess it has the most successful finale, which creates an unusual enthusiasm among listeners.'

But the data do not lie. If the non-agenda seventh symphony is more popular than the Eroica and the Ninth, it may be a sign that audiences prefer a score without a storyline. The seventh resists sales talk yet still sells out. That could be a positive outcome. It is a victory for music, pure and simple, and an opportunity to cancel the marketing budget and revise the education programme.

All my life, Beethoven has been pitched to kids at school as a bag of coloured bonbons – 'Für Elise', the 'Moonlight' Sonata, 'Rage over a Lost Penny'. These sticky bits underestimate a child's appetite for fantasy and awe at something big. No young life is changed by small stuff. Forget 'Für Elise'. Play an infants' class the finale of the seventh symphony and you may open their minds beyond all imagining.

80

Edge of seat

Symphony No. 7 in A major, Op. 92 (1813)

GREAT MINDS ARE LIT UP BY THIS GREAT WORK. EMILY BRONTË and Samuel Beckett play it on their pianos at home; Edward Albee quotes it in *Who's Afraid of Virginia Woolf*; Jacques Loussier writes jazz variations; Isadora Duncan choreographs it. A grey-and-white ultra-stark design for a seventh symphony ballet by Ben Nicholson, now at the Tate Gallery, is a landmark of British modernism. Wagner dances it in his drawing room as Franz Liszt plays the piano. Beethoven calls it 'one of my most excellent works'.

Brontë bought a five-octave piano in London that she played every day. In her eight-volume anthology of piano music she turned most to Beethoven's fourth, sixth and seventh symphonies, in the last-named to its second movement. The literary scholar Robert K. Wallace finds that 'the emancipating power of a work like the Seventh Symphony was bound to appeal to the woman who created Heathcliff'. Wallace believes Brontë took Heathcliff's features from 'Goethe's celebrated reference to Beethoven as "an utterly untamed personality"'. Brontë biographer Stevie Davies agrees that 'in style, texture and vision [*Wuthering Heights*] has strong affinities with [Beethoven]'. Charlotte Brontë writes of her sister's 'peculiar music – wild, melancholy and elevating'. Novelist and composer share isolation, self-immersion and an absorption with infinite expanses.

Beckett wonders why 'the sound surface of Beethoven's Seventh Symphony is dissolved by huge black pauses so that for pages on end we cannot perceive it as other than a dizzying path of sounds connecting unfathomable chasms of silence'. He might well be describing his own *Waiting for Godot*. Living in Paris, he plays piano and attends many concerts. He likes Beethoven's seventh symphony for being 'less buttoned up' and can tell the difference between conductors: 'Mr. Furtwängler, like the good Nazi he is, cannot tolerate mysteries, and it was rather like a fried egg, and, if you prefer, like a foot put in it, that he presented this music.' At one point, Beckett toys with writing a play about Beethoven's deafness.

Beethoven composes the seventh at Teplice in the summer of 1812, a turning point in European history. He conducts it at the end of the following year in a Vienna benefit concert for wounded soldiers, together with the eighth symphony and 'Wellington's Victory'. Beethoven is now totally deaf. Louis Spohr notes at rehearsal:

> He jumped into the air at the point where according to his calculation the forte ought to begin. When this did not follow his movement he looked about in a startled way, stared at the orchestra to see it still playing pianissimo and found his bearings only when the long-expected forte came and was visible to him. Fortunately, this comical incident did not take place at the performance.

The second movement receives shouted demands for an instant encore. The finale makes merry with an Irish jig he recently transcribed for a London publisher. A repeat concert is arranged, granting Beethoven some relief from financial worries.

The score's four-square movement raises illusions of straightforwardness. Nothing could be further from reality. The American conductor Leonard Slatkin finds a host of problems that he enumerates for me:

> The choices about length of notes, articulation and balance are critical. Even the first chord is up for grabs. Is it short and aggressive or longer and noble? In the introduction, can we always sustain the main tune with all those semi-quavers going on at the same time?
>
> The main body of the movement has one of Beethoven's trickiest rhythms to bring off successfully. It is usually notated as a quaver, followed by a semi-quaver rest and then another quaver in the 6/8 meter. This is the same rhythm that the timpani plays in the Scherzo of the Ninth. In fact, I always tell the orchestra to think of that instrument in order to play it correctly. Just think tim-pani, tim-pani.
>
> There is controversy about the tempo of the 2nd movement. Every conductor I know has struggled with this and changed their minds over

and over. George Szell called this, along with the 2nd movement of the Schubert Ninth, the two most difficult pieces to start conducting. What to do about those repeats in the Scherzo? It can be a bit boring to perform the same music three times. An equivalent problem pops up in the Finale.

I will not get into adjusting for balances, where the winds and strings need to take breaths, or how loud the triple fortes should be. This is the first time the composer utilized that dynamic. Therefore, should all the double fortes that precede it be of lesser volume? Choices, choices, choices.

Slatkin's ideal recordings include Szell, Giulini and David Zinman, none of whom, however, displace Arturo Toscanini's 1935 concert with the BBC Symphony Orchestra: 'It grabs me in a way that no other performance does. The balances are amazing, even with the limited technology of the time. Edge of your seat listening at its best,' says Slatkin.

To anyone who grew up in America in the 1930s and '40s, Toscanini's fame rivalled Frank Sinatra's. More than just a renowned conductor whose every concert was publicised by the NBC network and heard on millions of living room radios, he was seen as a defender of Italian democracy and a proponent of scriptural accuracy in classical scores, a fundamentalist myth that would fray by degrees once his scores were opened posthumously for inspection at the New York Public Library.

Where Toscanini stuck most to the letter of the score was in Beethoven and his authority in the symphonies stands unchallenged by note-picking critics. Toscanini's reputation rests heavily on his Beethoven. What puzzles me is why these recordings are so unenjoyable. It is not just the crabby NBC studio sound (though that doesn't help). Something of the pulsation of his performances strikes me as inflexible, as do the binary decisions that he makes at bends in the road. Toscanini was lauded in America for a 1939 Eroica of whiplash precision, a 1940 Missa Solemnis with unrivalled cast and a 1952 ninth symphony with an overwhelming finale. Against these exceptional, though uncomfortable, concerts I am inclined to agree with Slatkin that the seventh symphony he performed in a 1935 BBC studio exhibits Toscanini at his most exhilarating and irresistible, not least because the UK musicians come freshly surprised to his exacting charisma.

Toscanini aside, I conduct a quick survey of critical friends. Many prefer Wilhelm Furtwängler's 1943 Berlin concert; 'the most urgent and exciting, not a single note played routinely,' writes the former Decca chief Costa Pilavachi. The Spanish critic Luis Sunen recommends Pablo Casals in 1969: 'some minor imperfections but pure vitality, pure joy with a conductor who was ninety-two years old.' The Tel Aviv critic Amir Mandel advocates René Leibowitz with the Royal Philharmonic Orchestra in 1961, a performance that brings out an astonishing array of pastoral colours.

Arthur Kaptainis in Montreal swears by Leopold Stokowski's fabulous Philadelphians in 1927: 'Every bar alive in the first movement. The Allegretto is made an Adagio, in phrasing if not tempo, but it is mesmerizing. Fine madness in the finale.' The Chicago pianist Lori Kaufmann says, 'Put on George Szell and the Cleveland Orchestra and I guarantee you will hear notes that you never knew existed in this piece.' Concertmaster Eoin Andersen favours Nikolaus Harnoncourt with the Chamber Orchestra of Europe. Myself, I admire the exuberance of Daniel Barenboim's West–Eastern Divan Orchestra in Buenos Aires and a polychromatic firecracker by Libor Pešek and the Slovak Philharmonic, both released in 2020.

The Danish conductor and violinist Nikolaj Znaider opts for Erich Kleiber's 1950 age-of-austerity Amsterdam emanation, poised on a knife-edge of destiny. 'His sense of proportion and ability to elicit differentiated gestures for every motif is, to me incomparable; on top of which, his elegance, exuberance and own sense of wonder at the music is so intense and moving,' says Znaider. Carlos Kleiber's 1975 recording is so calisthenic it makes us leap from our armchairs. Few symphonies achieve such interpretative variety.

BEETHOVEN IN TROUBLE

81

Losing it

Sonata for Piano No. 28 in A major, Op. 101 (1815)

EARLY IN 1813 BEETHOVEN FINDS HIS BROTHER CARL CASPAR in a bad way with tuberculosis. Although the disease plays cruel tricks of simulated recovery, there is not much hope. Beethoven takes financial responsibility for his brother and his family – on one condition. He requires Carl Caspar to sign a declaration giving him sole custody of his son. The dying man signs an affidavit:

> Inasmuch as I am convinced of the frank and upright disposition of my brother Ludwig van Beethoven, I desire that after my death he undertake the guardianship of my son Karl Beethoven, a minor. I therefore request the honourable court to appoint my brother mentioned to the guardianship after my death and beg my dear brother to accept the office and to aid my son with word and deed in all cases.
>   Vienna, April 12, 1813

Nowhere in this deed is it mentioned that the boy has a mother. Beethoven blots out his brother's wife, believing she got pregnant in the first place to entrap him, 'an indication as much of his immorality as of his folly'. Johanna, to be sure, has her shady side. Her own parents accuse her of fraud and her friends of deception over the sale of some pearls. In 1811 she is convicted of embezzlement and sentenced to a year's jail in leg-irons, a term reduced to one month after her husband appeals to the Emperor. Marital relations are stormy; Carl Caspar once stabs her through the hand with a table knife in front of Ludwig, who claims: 'I warded my brother's anger away'. Beethoven is not, however, a reliable or impartial witness. Beethoven hates Johanna and Carl Caspar clearly loves her, faults and all, as does their son, Karl.

Johanna is neither dumb, nor poor. She owns a house outside Vienna and, as Beethoven will learn to his cost, she can play the grieving widow to a gullible court. Beethoven, having lent 1,500 florins to Carl Caspar, bursts in one night during dinner, shouting at Johanna, 'You thief! Where are my notes?' Carl Caspar leaps up to defend his wife and swears that he 'never wants to see that dragon in my house again.' Beethoven, seeing him next in the street and, shocked by his condition, calls a cab and showers him with kisses all the way home.

Carl Caspar dies on 15 November 1815. His will reveals a last-gasp codicil granting joint care of his nine-year-old son to his wife and his brother. 'God permit that the two of them be harmonious for the welfare of my child. This is the last wish of the dying husband and brother,' he writes. A fortnight later, Beethoven goes to court to claim sole custody.

What follows is a four-year battle, desperate, brutal and financially attritional. It upsets Beethoven so much that, for the only time in his life, he is unable to compose. Between three works of 1815 and the crashing Hammerklavier of late 1818 there is a black hole. The workaholic composer who hammers his piano for an hour on waking each morning is preoccupied with court appearances and affidavits. Advantage sways back and forth. Johanna tells the court that Beethoven is persecuting her because she refused his sexual advances. Beethoven retorts that she is 'a depraved person'. While Karl is with Beethoven, Johanna hides behind trees, dressed as a man, so that she can see the boy during school breaks. Beethoven removes Karl from school and beats him for infringements of discipline. He sends him to a priest for moral instruction. He has no experience of living with a child, let alone raising one. Karl runs back to his mother. Beethoven employs a private eye to spy on Johanna and her contacts.

She seems to be on the point of winning full custody when Beethoven's spies report that she has given birth to an illegitimate daughter, which does not go down well in court. She names the child Ludovica, after her brother-in-law, perhaps a conciliatory gesture. Karl is returned to Beethoven. He hangs out late at night. In 1826, aged nineteen, he shoots himself in a botched suicide attempt. He then joins the army to get away from his loving, maladroit uncle.

Beethoven is drained. He needs someone to care for the boy and provide a stable home. There is a candidate at school, the spinster sister of

Karl's headmaster, who likes the boy and admires his uncle, but Beethoven cannot countenance marriage without love. He is unable to cope on his own, nor can he keep a housekeeper for more than a few months. He can barely hear a word. He knows better than anyone how unsuitable he is for the role of adoptive father. Doubt seeps in. He permits himself to express sympathy for Johanna. 'Even a bad mother is still a mother,' he tells Karl. Johanna may not be lying when she claims that Beethoven has sexual feelings for her. It would be traditional, indeed biblical, for a man to wed his brother's widow. Does Beethoven, in his anguish, consider it? In the 1994 film *Immortal Beloved*, Johanna is depicted as Beethoven's secret love, with Karl as their son, a wholly spurious speculation.

⸎

Cataloguers give opus 101 as the end of his middle period and the Hammerklavier as the start of late Beethoven, but neither fits the slots they are given. Opus 101 is elusive. The opening is happy-go-lucky. After four minutes it fades to neurosis, everything restless, nothing resolved. The slow movement is jerky, chaotic, disturbing. The finale ends at the very bottom of the keyboard, as if Beethoven is sinking lower than he has ever gone before.

Wilhelm Kempff treats the sonata as Meissen china, sipping delicately. Walter Gieseking is dyspeptic, disapproving. The Hungarian Géza Anda adds Bartók-like aggression to the finale. Annie Fischer breaks your heart in the slow movement and stubs the pieces with her cigarette. Argerich, Ashkenazy, Gilels and Pollini are impressive.

I am drawn to Dina Ugorskaja, a fugitive from Russian prejudice who settles in Germany. While her father, Anatol Ugorski, records for DG in Berlin, Dina moves to Munich and teaches in Vienna. Stricken with cancer, she dies in 2019, aged forty-six. Dina recorded four Beethoven sonatas for a small label in April and May 2013, intuiting the composer's lament for lost youth and his helplessness in the fight for his nephew. Hers are some of the most affecting expressions to be found anywhere in the entire Beethoven discography.

⸎

On Beethoven's death, Karl inherits his estate. As he is still a minor, a court official, Jakob Hotschevar, is appointed his guardian. Hotschevar is a distant cousin of Johanna's, a para-legal who represented her in custody hearings only to condemn her 'far from praiseworthy moral conduct'. Happily reconciled with his mother, Karl marries and has four daughters and a son. He works as an estate manager, living comfortably until his death, aged fifty-one, in 1858. Johanna asks Franz Liszt to sell her copy of the Heiligenstadt Testament at a London auction. When it fails to reach her asking price of fifty guineas, Liszt makes up the deficit from his own pocket. Johanna dies in her eighties, in 1869. Karl's son, Louis, migrates to America, where he changes his name to Van Hoven and winds up working for the railroad company in Detroit. He is the end of the Beethoven line.

82

Ashes to ashes

Sonatas for Violoncello and Piano Nos. 4 and 5, Opp. 102/1 and 102/2 (1815); 'Brauchle, Linke' Canon, WoO167 (1815)

ON NEW YEAR'S EVE 1815, ARRIVING FOR A PARTY, BEETHOVEN sees his patron's palace go up in flames. Count Andrey Razumovsky, the Russian ambassador in Vienna, employs a string quartet that has given many Beethoven premieres. Without a house, he cannot maintain a quartet. Schuppanzigh, the leader, goes to Russia to work for the Tsar. The others scrabble around for employment.

The cellist Joseph Linke, gregarious and gossipy, tells Beethoven he has landed a post as tutor to Countess Marie Erdődy's children at her estate on the Jedlesee, five miles north of Vienna. Beethoven, who has known the countess for years, cadges a summer invitation. Marie Erdődy has a second musician in residence, Johann Xaver Brauchle.

Separated from her husband, Marie is a 'very small, pretty, delicate lady of twenty-five . . . afflicted since her first confinement with an incurable malady'. She takes opium for pain control. Beethoven calls her his 'father confessor' for her patience in listening to his woes. They bond over a bad joke he makes about Linke, when Beethoven says the cellist could start bowing on the left ('linke') bank of the Danube and end up on the right. He composes a canon on the names of Brauchle and Linke, a dinner-table amusement for two or four voices, lasting half a minute. He writes one cello sonata in late July, a second in early August.

Beethoven is one of few men Marie can trust. She is being spied on by her Hungarian ex-husband and, she thinks, by the secret police. Anxious, she shuts the lakeside house and moves to Croatia, then on to Italy where, one morning in Padua, her fourteen-year-old son August drops dead of a brain seizure. Beethoven, mourning his own brother Carl Caspar, writes to Marie:

> Nothing is more painful than the quick unforeseen departure of those who are near to us . . . I have the deepest sympathy for your irretrievable loss. Perhaps I have not written you yet that I have not been well for a long time, to this reason for my long silence might be added the care for my [nephew] Karl whom I had often contemplated as a companion to your dear son. I am seized with grief on your account and on my own since I loved your son.

Meeting Linke in a Vienna café he learns that Marie's household staff informed Italian police that August's death was brought on by tutorial beatings at the hands of Brauchle. Her daughter Mimi, in whose room August died, tries to kill herself by swallowing her mother's opium. Her ex-family in Hungary claim that Brauchle raped Mimi before plotting August's murder to stop him inheriting the Count's title.

Marie returns to Vienna and takes an apartment on the Kärntner Strasse. In 1820, anxious again, she moves to Munich, where Brauchle joins her, together with his wife. Her relationship with Brauchle is now outwardly respectable. In Munich, Marie's daughter Mimi gets a dog. They call it Fidelio, after Beethoven, their constant friend.

When Beethoven dies they find Marie's portrait inside his desk. Might she have been a belated Beloved? Rumours fly but there is not a shred of evidence to support them. The letters between them, fond and friendly, are mostly about music and maladies. In the 1994 film *Immortal Beloved*, a ravishingly beautiful Marie Erdődy is played by Ingrid Bergman's daughter, Isabella Rosellini. Marie, in life, was too sick to be seductive. For much of her time with Beethoven she was confined to a wheelchair. Her beauty is embedded in a pair of summer cello sonatas.

The sonatas are published in 1817 without dedication; Marie's name is added to the next edition. The first sonata, in C major, takes a quarter of an hour. The second, in D major, is twenty minutes long. The analyst Martin Cooper writes:

Both show a combination of characteristics which do not appear in any earlier works of Beethoven's with anything like the same consistency or concentration. In fact, these two sonatas are the earliest examples of what we come to recognise as a new style, the style of the Third Period.

Beethoven's themes have grown large, and largely unsingable. Raptures – in the fifth sonata adagio, for instance – are brief. Pleasure cedes to pain. The fourth sonata opening is as hard to get right as the fourth piano concerto. The French pair of cellist Gautier Capuçon and pianist Frank Braley (2016) judge it well.

Bad performances abound. Yo Yo Ma and Emanuel Ax are a match made in label hell, Ma going for the headline quote, Ax for invisibility. Jacqueline du Pré is so remote from the mike she gets swamped by Daniel Barenboim's piano. Gregor Piatigorsky and Arthur Rubinstein might as well have phoned in their solo parts for all the contact they make with each other.

Enough, though, of horrors. Cellist Leonard Rose takes us with pianist Leonid Hambro into the heart of the dark fifth sonata in a 1953 Library of Congress recital. In its slow movement Beethoven tries out the language of his last piano sonatas. A cry at around 4:30, reminiscent of his song 'Ah, perfido!' melts despair to resignation. Each listener is reminded of his or her mortality. Mischa Maisky and Martha Argerich (1995) are incontestable.

83

Sally in our Alley

25 Scottish Songs for Voice and Piano Trio, Op. 108; 25 Irish Songs for One or Two Voices and Piano Trio, WoO152; 32 Irish Songs for One or Several Voices and Piano Trio, WoO153–4; 26 Welsh Songs for One or Two Voices and Piano Trio, WoO155 (1809–1818)

A LETTER ARRIVES FROM EDINBURGH IN JULY 1803, REQUEST-ing six sonatas. Beethoven wants 300 ducats. The publisher sticks at 150. That seems to be the end of the matter. But Beethoven, more organised than he looks, keeps the correspondence on file. A year later he reopens negotiations with George Thomson, Clerk to the Board of Trustees for the Encouragement of Art and Manufactures in Scotland. Charged with civilising his country's image, Thomson twins the national poet Robert Burns with leading composers.

A village teacher's son, bespectacled and high-collared, Thomson is earnest, energetic and pedantic. He plays violin in a neighbourhood orchestra and sings vigorously at social occasions. Knowing what might sell in London, he brings six hundred songs to print between 1793 and 1841, a triumph of enlightened public sponsorship.

He sends Beethoven twenty-six songs, 'more or less defective and exceptionable', all requiring instrumentation. Beethoven declines his revised terms, noting that 'Mr Haydn was given a British pound for each air'. Negotiations drag on three more years before Beethoven, in the siege of Vienna, accepts a package deal for fifty-three songs. With war disrupting the postal service, he writes out every song in triplicate and sends each packet by a different route. Three years pass before the full set reaches Edinburgh, where Thomson, delighted, prints them on the best quality paper and engages Scotland's leading illustrators to make the volume beautiful, exclusive and collectable.

He pays Beethoven for 179 songs in all over nine years. Beethoven enjoys the haggling but draws the line at some of Thomson's more fanciful demands. 'I cannot bring myself to write for flute,' he says, 'as this instrument is too limited and imperfect.' Speaking no English, he communicates with Thomson in bad French. But he insists on knowing the meaning of each song before he composes it; when Scottish burns run dry he takes on Welsh and Irish airs. Thomson selects only 'the plaintive and lively kind, unmixed with trifling and inferior ones'. When sales flag he assures Beethoven that 'he composes for posterity'. Thomson lives into his nineties, long enough to see his granddaughter Catherine marry the wildly successful London novelist Charles Dickens.

Very few of the songs find their way onto records before the 1970 Beethoven bicentenary prompts labels to revive them in big boxes. Divas don't know where to go with them – high road or low? Janet Baker splits the difference in 'Bonnie Lassie, Highland Lassie' while her partners – Yehudi Menuhin, Ross Pople and George Malcolm – fall into a loch. The American tenor Robert White treats 'Sally in our Alley' as a music hall song (his partners are Yo-Yo Ma, Ani Kavafian and pianist Samuel Sanders). Some ballads, such as 'Sunset' and 'The Shepherd's Song', come over as fine as any German art-song. Thomas Allen gives them full value. Fischer-Dieskau is too solemn. But I do like Julie Kaufmann in 'The Sweetest Lad was Jamie'.

Pathos and poignancy commingle in the Irish Songs. Victoria de los Ángeles and Fischer-Dieskau evoke a pre-exilic emerald idyll. Walter Scott's poem 'Return to Ulster' is particularly fetching. Among twenty-six Welsh Songs 'Love Without Hope' is a gem that could have been written by Schubert. The Four English Songs contains an exquisite chamber setting of 'God Save the King'.

ξ

Variations on 10 national airs for flute or violin/piano, Opp. 105 and 107 (1818–9)

IN THE END, BEETHOVEN GIVES UP HIS PRINCIPLES AND WRITES for flute. The Scottish ballad 'Bonny Laddie, Highland Laddie' leaps out in full vigour, followed by a high-kicking Ukrainian dance. The French flute virtuoso Patrick Gallois is the pick of a limited pack, recording with pianist Cecile Licad.

84

A friend in deed

'Wellington's Victory', Op. 91 (1813)

THE MOST EMBARRASSING THING BEETHOVEN EVER WROTE IS this inexcusable rabble-rouser. What is Beethoven's excuse? 'I did it for a friend,' he says.

The friend is Johann Nepomuk Maelzel, inventor of the metronome, a tick-tock machine that indicates musical speeds. Beethoven is the first to insert metronome markings in his scores, boosting Maelzel's sales. Maelzel repays him with an improved ear-trumpet, in exchange for which he demands endorsements. Maelzel has created a 'panharmonicon', a spring-powered machine that mimics the sounds of a military band. Maelzel tells Beethoven he has sold one in Paris for a hundred thousand francs. He could sell even more if Beethoven were to compose something for the thunderous organism.

It is June 1813 and the Duke of Wellington has just crushed Napoleon's brother Joseph Bonaparte at the Battle of Vitoria in Spain. Beethoven jots: 'I must show the English a little what a blessing there is in "God Save the King"'. He mixes it with 'Rule Britannia', and the French march '*Malbrouck* [Marlborough] *s'en va-t-en guerre*' in the panharmonicon extravaganza and dedicates the score to the English Prince Regent, the future King George IV.

Having packed his music into Maelzel's machine, he makes a human version for symphony orchestra which he premieres in December 1813, together with his exalted seventh symphony. 'Wellington's Victory' is a terrific success, raising huge cheers from the crowd and a charitable fortune for wounded Austrian soldiers. Artistically, it is junk: blasts of battlefield noise, interspersed with cringe-making anthems. On record, Karajan fails to redeem it in optimum Berlin Philharmonic sound. Morton

Gould conducts a Cecil B. DeMille-style version with the New York Philharmonic.

Maelzel comes to a sticky end when lawyers issue claims to the metronome on behalf of an Amsterdam organ builder called Winkel. Despite testimonials from Beethoven and Salieri, Maelzel loses the first round in court. He sails in 1826 for the United States and on to Cuba and Venezuela, dying on board ship in July 1838. The American novelist Nathaniel Hawthorne summarises the cornucopia of his known inventions:

1 The automaton speaking figures, which articulate certain English and French words, in the hands of any person; 2 the panharmonicon a magnificent instrument, composed of all the pieces, rich, various and powerful as they are, of an entire military band; 3 the animated diorama of the cathedral at Rheims a large and most superb representation of the kind; 4 the automaton trumpeter, of the size of a man; and whose clarion notes cannot be equalled by those of any living performer the time from the nature of the mechanism, being absolutely perfect; 5 the equestrian automata; 6 and the automatous slack rope dancers, which go through all the difficult feats and surprising evolutions, both of 'horse and foot' of the circus or amphitheaters, and with an agility, ease and gracefulness, so true to nature, as scarcely to be credited by those who have not witnessed them; 7 the melodium, whose very name attests how exquisitely it is attuned to 'sweet sounds;' 8 the automaton charlatan, never exhibited, we believe, in America; 9 the metronome, or musical timekeeper, patented in Europe; and 'last not least,' that unique and most masterly combination of music, mechanism and design.

85

The pits

'Germania', WoO94; 'Des Kriegers Abschied', WoO143; 'Abschiedsgesang an Wiens Bürger', WoO121; 'Kriegslied der Österreicher', WoO122 (1814); 'Der glorreiche Augenblick', Op. 136 (all 1814)

ANOTHER PIECE OF TRASH THAT HE COMPOSES PROCLAIMS THE superiority of the German race. 'Germania' is a number in a propaganda opera by Georg Friedrich Treitschke to which all Viennese composers are expected to contribute. Treitschke is director of the Theater an der Wien and Beethoven owes him a favour for having revised the text of *Fidelio*. Treitschke is also a noted lepidopterist but he cannot write a poem to save a butterfly's life. His text is puerile:

Germania, Germania,
How bright you stand right now.
Mists envelope your great head,
The old sun might have been stolen,
But God, the Lord, came to your aid.
Let Him be praised, and Heil to thee, Germania.

Beethoven reports of the premiere:

It was a rare assembly of outstanding artists . . . Each, inspired by the sole thought of contributing something for the benefit of the Fatherland, worked together without thought of rank and in subordinate positions to bring about an outstanding performance . . . The leadership of the whole crowd fell to me only because I composed the music. Had it been by someone else, I should have been as willing as Hr. Hummel to take my place at

the great drum, since we were all filled solely with the purest feeling of love
for the Fatherland and with the joy of giving of our powers for those who
had given so greatly for us.

This is as low as Beethoven sinks into nationalism, and he does not
wallow there for long. He disputes Treitschke's use of Latin and tells him:
'I shall not be the slightest bit offended if you want to have it set to music
again by Gyrowetz or someone else, though I prefer Weinmüller. For I lay
no claim whatever to it. At the same time I refuse to allow anyone else,
whoever he may be, to alter my compositions.' That sounds more like
Beethoven. 'Germania' is five minutes of wasted time. The least odious
recording is by Andrew Davis in 1996.

In 'Des Kriegers Abschied' ('the fighter's farewell'), a baritone pledges
himself body and soul to the Fatherland; Hans Hotter sings it with righteous fervour in the thick of Hitler's war. In 'Abschiedsgesang an Wiens
Bürger' ('farewell song for a Viennese citizen'), Beethoven sends a civil
servant off to war with incoherent words and music. 'Kriegslied der
Österreicher' ('an Austrian's war song') opens with the words 'A great
German Volk are we . . .'

Somewhat better, the cantata 'Der glorreiche Augenblick' ('the glorious
moment'), by Salzburg surgeon Alois Weissenbach, delivers beautiful
soprano solos with orchestra and chorus. Ignore such declamations as
'Heil, Vienna! Heil und Glück!' and this is not a bad piece. It was first
recorded in 1997 by the St Luke's Orchestra in New York with a young
Deborah Voigt as one of three soloists.

§

Opferlied, Op. 121b (1824); Tremate, Op. 116 (1802–14)

BEETHOVEN TINKERS WITH A SACRIFICIAL SONG FOR SOPRANO, chorus and orchestra for three decades. Reminiscent of Mozart's 'Priest's Chorus' in *The Magic Flute*, the poem, by Friedrich von Matthisson, is 'to be performed with intimate, devout feelings, quite slowly', says Beethoven. The text is utterly vile. A child is sacrificed to the gods in exchange for the donor receiving everlasting youth and beauty. The closing words '*Das Schöne zu dem Guten!*' ('the beautiful for the good') is an entitlement phrase that Beethoven uses to justify special privileges for good artists. It never works for him: Beethoven does not get to sleep with beauty. There is a gritty recording of this piece by Leif Segerstam (2020).

'Tremate', for three voices and orchestra, is an Italian vocal exercise by Salieri; Beethoven messes around with it between 1801 and 1803, finally shoving it into his 27 February 1814 concert between the seventh and eighth symphonies and 'Wellington's Victory'. Segerstam again claims *jus primae noctis* on record.

86

House prices

The Consecration of the House Overture, Op. 124 (1822)

WHEN *THE RUINS OF ATHENS* IS CHOSEN TO OPEN VIENNA'S Theater in der Josefstadt in October 1822, Beethoven is asked for a new overture. In the thick of Missa Solemnis and the ninth symphony he takes a walk in autumnal woods with his nephew Karl and chronicler, Anton Schindler:

> Beethoven told us to go on in advance and join him at an appointed place. It was not long before he overtook us, remarking that he had written down two motifs for an overture . . . He expressed himself also in the manner in which he purposed treating them – one in the free style and one in the strict and, indeed, in Handel's. As well as his voice permitted, he sang the two motifs and then asked us which we liked the better . . . The nephew decided in favour of both.

Beethoven is in full creative flow, inviting others to marvel at the workings of his creative mind. The overture is at once momentous, memorable, augustan, witty, frisky and imperceptibly historic. Beethoven is so pleased with its numinous effect that he reschedules it eighteen months later as a prelude to his ninth symphony.

The inaugural performance is, as so often, a let-down. 'The newly organised orchestra of the Josefstadt theatre did not receive [the score] til the afternoon before the opening, and with innumerable mistakes in every part. The rehearsal which took place in the presence of an almost-filled parterre scarcely sufficed for the correction of the worst of the copyist's errors'. Beethoven conducts the orchestra with one ear bent low to the floor, trying to 'hear' vibrations.

The overture instantly acquires totemic value. In August 1824 Berlin plays it at the opening of the Königstadt Theater. Richard Wagner takes the noun '*Weihe*' ('consecration') and attaches it to *Parsifal*, his *Bühnenweihfestpiel* (festival play for the consecration of the stage). It becomes required listening at the opening or reopening of any German concert and opera house, all the more so after 1945 when many theatres rise again from total ruins. So emblematic is its status, it comes close to standing, *über alles*, as a metaphor for German resilience.

The aged Felix Weingartner at Abbey Road in 1938 welds austerity to drama in a reading that he could trace back to musicians who knew Beethoven. Other imposing performances include Igor Markevitch (1958), Lorin Maazel (2004) and Herbert von Karajan (1970). I am torn between Claudio Abbado's Milanese solemnity with the Berlin Philharmonic (1994) and Riccardo Muti's Neapolitan theatricality in Philadelphia (1988), together representing eternal Italian renewal, north and south.

BEETHOVEN INSPIRED

Like a virgin

Leonore Overtures 1, 2 and 3, Opp. 138, 72, 72a and 72b (1803–1814)

BEETHOVEN'S ONLY OPERA, *FIDELIO*, IS A SERIAL FAILURE. HE revises it four times, renames it, despairs, resumes work on it and never writes another. He is no fan of opera, disparaging its immoral liaisons and slick resolutions. The deafer he gets, the harder it is for him to interact with the multiple actors in an opera, not just the singers and orchestra players, but the librettist, director, designer, stagehands, hair and makeup artists, all of whom have to be kept informed and engaged for the production to reach the stage. This is not Beethoven's idea of a good way to work.

But the offer of free lodgings at the Theater an der Wien in exchange for an opera helps focus his mind. Emanuel Schikaneder, Mozart's *Magic Flute* librettist, gives him a script titled *Vesta's Fire*. It is about a lady in Rome with many virile lovers who, when the time comes to get married, reverts to being a virgin. Beethoven tears up this plot. 'Imagine language and verses such as could come out of the mouths of women apple-sellers in the Vienna markets,' he snorts. But he likes living in Schikaneder's theatre and he agrees instead to compose *Leonore* by Joseph Sonnleithner, a 'triumph of married love'. That seems perfectly attuned to Beethoven's idealised image of holy monogamy. The problem, again, is the plot.

Florestan is jailed by the tyrant Don Pizarro. His wife Leonore needs to get him out. Cross-dressing as a boy called 'Fidelio' ('fidelity' – get it?), Leonore gets a job inside the jail as a warder. She is young and attractive, unforeseeably to both sexes. Another guard's daughter, Marzelline, falls in love with her boyish charms and Leonore finds herself fending off girly lunges. None of this appeals much to Beethoven and one can sense that his heart is absent from this plot twist. Music and drama go their separate

ways, joined here and there by stretches of dreary declamation and recitation. If there is one note of complete conviction it is in Beethoven's identification with the unfortunate Florestan, a man locked through no fault of
his own in a soundless cell from which only a *deus ex machina* can spring
him. Beethoven has no faith in any *deus ex machina*, which accounts for
the lack of conviction in the opera's rescue music.

There are anticipations in *Fidelio* of Puccini's *Tosca*, a situation where a
woman attempts to free her man from jail at all costs. In *Tosca*, the heroine
is offered a deal to have sex with the jailer, whom she fends off and kills in
a scene of monumental and not altogether convincing self-righteousness.
Fidelio fudges the sexual element in Leonore's dilemma and keeps her
technically unmolested, although there is much in her bisexual charac-
terisation that suggests she is prepared to swing either way. *Tosca* is a sex-
for-freedom offer. *Fidelio* is an opera that speaks of freedom and totally
suppresses sex. Tosca is flirt or fight. Fidelio is only flight. The characters,
undeveloped as they are, arouse little sympathy and the audience lacks
enough substance in the plot to form a satisfying moral or intellectual
judgement.

They go home instead humming the overture. Richard Wagner, hearing
the overture at the age of thirteen in 1826, is overcome by an epiphany:
'The direct result of this performance was my intense longing to compose
something that would give me a similar feeling of satisfaction.' All of
Wagner flows, in some sense, from this orchestral overture. But which one?

Beethoven writes four overtures and only experts can tell the difference. Bear with me for a moment while I prise them apart. *Fidelio*, with
the original overture (Leonore 1), is premiered in three acts on 20
November 1805. The score that comes back from the publisher is titled
'Leonore'. If that is not confusing enough, Beethoven sets about a first revision of the opera with a new overture, which he bafflingly titles Leonore 3.
It is demonstrably superior to Leonore 1, but the opera still needs work. A
third overture is added in 1814, catalogued as Leonore 4, opus 72. Leonores
2 and 3 are listed as 72a and 72b. The earliest overture, Leonore 1, is
numbered opus 138, the last item in the Beethoven catalogue. Leonore
overtures are Beethoven's blight on music librarians.

Leonore 1 lasts 9 minutes, Leonore 2 and 3 run 14 minutes. There are
recordings of 1 and 2 by bluff John Eliot Gardiner (1997), bleak Fritz

Busch (1950), lordly Bernard Haitink (2005) and understated Stanisław Skrowaczewski (1994). Claudio Abbado and the Vienna Phil give good value in Leonore 4.

The pick of the overtures is Leonore 3. Thanks to Gustav Mahler, it is also one of the most performed of Beethoven's works. Mahler, impatient during a second-act scene change in a Vienna *Fidelio*, interpolated an orchestral reading of Leonore 3 to stop the audience chatter. He liked the music so much he performed it eighteen times in symphony concerts with the Vienna and New York Philharmonic orchestras. Leonore 3 is a substitute for all the action that is missing in *Fidelio*, yielding a deep emotional resolution. Mahler's performance is reported to have been among his most scintillating.

His apostle Bruno Walter conducted a 1936 recording in Vienna, crackling with ambient tensions. Ferenc Fricsay made two tremulous recordings in 1960–1 Berlin. Furtwängler (1953) is frankly neurotic, torn between nebulous hints of erotic possibilities. Leonard Bernstein is wildly exciting in a 1976 Amnesty benefit concert. Sergiu Celibidache is inhumanly slow. Mariss Jansons (2019) generates a glowing warmth.

88

Shipwreck

Fidelio, Op. 72 (1805–14)

'THIS OPERA WILL WIN ME A MARTYR'S CROWN,' SAYS BEETHOVEN, who elsewhere calls it 'the shipwreck'. Wilhelm Furtwängler says: '*Fidelio* is not an opera in the sense we are used to, nor is Beethoven a musician of the theatre.' An opera needs tension, shock, excitement, great arias. *Fidelio* is short on the first three and, while it has pleasing set pieces, no one sings '*O, komm Hoffnung*' ('oh, come hope') in the shower. German opera houses maintain *Fidelio* in their permanent repertoire. New York's Metropolitan Opera last staged a new production in the year 2000.

It is not so much an opera as a broken jigsaw. Beethoven identifies with Florestan and sinfully desires his wife. He dare not make the music too sexy without guilt creeping in. By suppressing lust he kills the story. Nobody has the hots in *Fidelio*. Florestan and Leonore admit no marital passion. The chorus 'let him who has the love of a noble wife lend his voice to our song of rejoicing' rings false. Leonore will never be a *Hausfrau*. Florestan will always wonder what she had to do to get him out. This marriage can surely not survive for very long.

The opera's gender ambiguities are usefully analysed by the Argentine historian Esteban Buch, who sees Leonore in a guard's uniform as 'both a declaration of queerness – a woman out of place, performing a male's task – and an acknowledgment of straightness – a woman in her place, [beside] her husband'. Neither text nor music can decide. *Fidelio* is performed in 1815 for all the worst despots of Europe – Metternich, Talleyrand, Wellington, Razumovsky – gathered at the Congress of Vienna to restore power to hereditary potentates. By what measure does that make it a liberation opera?

That myth first arises after 1945 when Germanic states, desperate to cleanse themselves of Hitler's crimes, recruit Beethoven as a character witness. The Vienna Opera, as Tom Stoppard reminds us usefully in his *Leopoldstadt* play, reopened with an international gala performance of *Fidelio* under the baton of a conductor, Karl Böhm, who never renounced his former Nazi convictions. Böhm's cast – with Irmgard Seefried, Martha Mödl and Anton Dermota – is among the most impressive on record. Fricsay's is even finer – Seefried, Leonie Rysanek, Fischer-Dieskau and Ernst Haefliger. Erich Kleiber recorded *Fidelio* a few days before he died with Birgit Nilsson, Hans Hopf, Ingeborg Wenglor and Gottlob Frick. Beat that? Bernstein (1978) had Gundula Janowitz as Leonore, René Kollo as Florestan and the irresistible Slovak mezzo Lucia Popp as Marzelline. Abbado in 2010 twinned the Swedish Wagnerian Nina Stemme with the sweet-voiced Bavarian Jonas Kaufmann, both too awed to make meaningful love.

One recording is epic. In January 1961, the elderly Otto Klemperer arrived at Covent Garden to make a belated opera debut in London. Back in 1927, Klemperer's *Fidelio* at Berlin's Kroll-Oper inaugurated a modern era in spartan design, with white walls and no stage clutter. Before very long Hitler shut the Kroll and Klemperer fled into exile. In America, he suffered mental illness and physical decay. The EMI producer Walter Legge brought him to London, where the Philharmonia Orchestra renewed his appetite for music making on a grand scale and Covent Garden offered a dream *Fidelio* cast of the Canadian Jon Vickers as Florestan and Sena Jurinac as Leonore. An opening night tape recording, on the Testament label, combines elements of three Golden Ages – Mahler's Vienna, 1920s Berlin and London on the eve of its Swinging Sixties. An EMI studio version, assembled by Legge, lacks quite the same edge of danger as Klemperer's energy flagged (he died in 1973 aged eighty-eight).

Post-modern approaches to *Fidelio* are led by the Spanish director Calixto Bieito, who allegorises the plot as a medieval maze: 'all the characters, not just the imprisoned Florestan, are lost in this labyrinth, trying to find its centre'. *Fidelio*, says Bieito, 'has a desperation, a hysteria, in its desire to be free'. But from what? And for what? Bieito doesn't say. The philosopher Ernst Bloch assures us that 'every future storming of the Bastille is implicitly expressed in *Fidelio*'. Is it? The Bastille still stands. It is the home of the Paris Opéra, where the middle-classes enjoy tax-funded cheap seats and sip vintage champagne as, above and below, Africans bussed in from outlying suburbs clean toilets and expunge their smells. If this is all that *Fidelio* stands for, Florestan can never be considered free so long as our society makes the oppressed poor pay for the bland bonuses of a business-class existence. It is easier to appreciate *Fidelio* as a travesty of freedom in our times than as its unattained apotheosis. Oh, come hope? Some hope.

89

Lopsided

Piano Sonata No. 30, Op. 109 (1820)

BEETHOVEN KNOWS WHEN TO STOP. HE WRITES HIS TENTH AND last violin sonata in 1812, and never looks back. Eight years on, he reaches thirty-two piano sonatas, and shuts the book. There is symmetry to 32 – two to the power of five – but Beethoven is not bothered, as Arnold Schoenberg will be, by numbers. He goes from score to score, not counting, just knowing when enough is enough.

After the Hammerklavier, when he might have stopped, a publisher bids for three more sonatas and Beethoven, still paying bills from his custody battle, obliges. His closing triptych, opus 109–111, is gentler on the fingers than Hammerklavier but more taxing in mental preparation. Opus 109 hides large ideas behind soft furnishings. Every key he presses leaves an imprint. Every note is existential.

He opens with the right hand at the top of the keyboard and the left chanting Amen down below. Two movements of three or four minutes are followed by a quarter-hour finale. A thanksgiving theme yields six forceful variations, all in E major, his happy key, but drifting down to B and then to a remote D sharp. Impossible to tell where he's going until Missa Solemnis is revealed. Then we know that this is no ordinary finale: it is the gateway to heaven.

He dedicates the thirtieth sonata to Maximiliane, nineteen-year-old daughter of beloved Antonie Brentano and her husband, the Frankfurt businessman Franz. His inscription to Maximiliane is an exhortation from a man in a new domain, almost at peace with himself:

A dedication!!! Well, this is not one of those dedications that are used and abused by thousands of people. It is the spirit which unites the noble and

finer people of this earth and which time can never destroy. It is this spirit
which now speaks to you and which calls you to mind and makes me see
you still as a child, your father imbued with so many truly good and noble
qualities and ever mindful of the welfare of his children ┆ . . The memory
of this noble family can never fade in my heart. May you sometimes think
of me with a feeling of kindness. My most heartfelt wishes. May heaven
bless your life and the lives of all of you forever. (Translated by Martin
Cooper.)

Beethoven begins to leave us with this benediction. Knowing this,
players try to balance aspiration with acquiescence. Friedrich Gulda
(1958) is daringly hushed, Maria João Pires (2001) subtly complex. Rudolf
Serkin (1987) gives a syntactical masterclass. You can almost hear Charles
Rosen (1971) analysing each phrase as he plays it.

The perfect pianist for opus 109 is one who has cogitated the entire
cycle before attempting the pre-penultimate work. On first hearing,
Vladimir Ashkenazy (1983) sounds too reticent. A reluctant exile from
Soviet Russia, Ashkenazy made his home in Iceland and Switzerland, raising his family far from intrusive media. Although he was chief conductor
of historic orchestras in London, Prague, Tokyo and Sydney, he never
spoke above *sotto voce* or was seduced by maestro status. 'Don't go for the
career,' was his motto. 'Just go for the music you are playing.' In opus 109,
he combines modesty with melody, fulfilling Beethoven's instruction,
'*Gesangvoll*' ('full of song'). His performance, filmed by Christopher
Nupen (on YouTube), just grows and grows down the years.

90

Ultima vera

Sonata for Piano No. 32 in C minor, Op. 111 (1821–2)

THE LAST SONATA OF LUDWIG VAN BEETHOVEN DEFEATS ITS first performers. Some complain of 'scientificality' and 'studied eccentricity', deeming it 'harmoniously unpleasant'. A Berlin reviewer detects 'sounds of the grave'. The opening chords are sombre, unyielding – a self-epitaph, perhaps? To our ears it marks the birth of something entirely new – an avant-garde that functions a century or two ahead of its time. Opus 111 belongs to a world of fast cars and wireless connectivities. Listen, for instance, to the Portuguese pianist Maria João Pires and you will hear no hint of morbidity or finality, only the opening of unforeseen horizons. Pires, in her seventies, pioneered a transmission project where senior musicians learn from starters, and vice-versa. She understands in this first movement that Beethoven goes beyond the known world.

The first to grasp this, and in the last year of his short life, is Franz Schubert. Dying, Schubert takes a first-movement theme from opus 111 and, changing key, pastes it onto Heinrich Heine's resigned poem 'Der Atlas':

I, unlucky Atlas, a World,
Bearing an entire world of pain,
I bear what is unbearable
And it will break me.

Schubert, aged thirty-one, accepts that life kills and art cannot save life. He often quotes unconsciously from Beethoven's second and seventh symphonies and there's a Coriolanus snippet in his 'Trout' quintet. In Der Atlas the affinity is heard in a three-note (C-E*b*-B) motif drawn from the opening of opus 111. Schubert is prone to say, 'I shall continue where Beethoven left off'. He is also inclined to complain that Beethoven will 'goad people to madness instead of dissolving them in love.' Schubert, however, is prepared in his Swansong cycle to walk down that same stark path.

Other composers import opus 111 quotes – Chopin in his morose second sonata, Prokofiev in his second symphony. An English electronic prog-rock band which takes the name 'Opus 111' scores its biggest chart hit with a bleak dance track titled, with irony, 'It's a Fine Day'.

Beethoven's last sonata has just two movements, one rough, one smooth. Is there a third? It's an open question. The initial moments – *brio ed appassionato* – are brutal and hard-driven. Three minutes into the second movement, Beethoven starts to rock the melody provocatively from side to side in a kind of syncopation, close to boogie-woogie or ragtime. This is late-night riffing, sociable and seductive, nearly jazz. The Swiss pianist Edwin Fischer, in a titanic 1954 recording, gets huffy with rhythms that are way off his cultural rails. Beethoven calls his sonata 'not very difficult' but his 12/32 mark on Maelzel's metronome is a nightmare for straight-down-the-line pianists. It takes an offbeat artist to get this right, a pianist who has lived a bit, and in more than one civilisation.

Schnabel is alternately clumsy and quick. Arrau is ponderous. Gulda achieves psychedelic serenity. Levit is one-paced. Anatol Ugorski, 11 minutes on first movement and 27 on the second, wins the endurance record. Young pianists are brutally exposed. Ivo Pogorelich, aged twenty-three, was timed at Carnegie Hall at 31 minutes and 31 seconds by the *New York Times* critic Harold Schonberg, a measurement from which his career barely recovered. Angela Hewitt waited until she was sixty, informed social media next morning:

> It's done! I performed Beethoven's Op. 111 in public for the first time last night at a friend's barn in Devon for 65 people. On a Bosendorfer. Very intimate. I got all choked up just talking about it at the beginning of the concert . . . let alone playing it. Now I have the rest of my life to try to play it better.

Daniel Barenboim inflects the finale with tango. Vladimir Ashkenazy finds the wintry darkness of a Siberian night, filled with ghostly exhalations.

Maria Yudina shakes off inhibition and takes to the floor in a dance that must end in death. Mitsuko Uchida, raised in Vienna as a Japanese diplomat's child, later opting for British identity, transcends cultural barriers and achieves ethereal closure. The vision she conjures is of an imaginary act of manumission where Beethoven lays down his weary pen at the close of opus 111 and hands it, full of ink, to the foredoomed Franz Schubert. Great art will always outlast us. Thomas Mann, in his ambivalent novel *Doctor Faustus*, has one character say of Beethoven's opus 111: 'art always throws off the appearance of art'. That is concisely what Uchida does, what every artist longs to do in every performance.

}

Thomas Mann, winner of the 1929 Nobel Prize for Literature, reaches for this sonata at the lowest moment in his life. When Hitler seizes power, he stays abroad while Nazis burn his essays and evict his Munich neighbour, Bruno Walter. Mann's wife Katia is, like Walter, Jewish. Mann takes a chalet on a Swiss mountain and stays *stumm*.

Finally, in January 1936, he is smoked out. Eduard Korrodi, a Zurich newspaper editor and Mann fan, writes a virulent article arguing that Hitler has done a service to German literature by ridding it of Jews. 'Those who have emigrated are above all from the novel industry,' snorts Korrodi, 'not one poet among them.' Mann's journalist son Klaus implores him to do something: 'Earnestly beg you respond . . . This time it really is a matter of life and death for us all.' Katia Mann drafts a response. Mann sweats four days and nights over it in an agony of indecision, substituting adjectives, shortening, lengthening, prevaricating. On a Monday morning he submits a pusillanimous version to the editor, by hand, at the newspaper building: 'May I [he begins] make a few comments, perhaps even raise a few objections?' He points out that many non-Jewish writers had fled Germany – himself, his brother Heinrich, Bertolt Brecht, Annette Kolb – along with dozens of poets. The damage to German literature is incalculable. Mass exile, he warns, 'threatens to bring about a terrible, ominous alienation between the land of Goethe and the rest of the world.' When his letter appears in print the Nazis add Mann's bestselling novels to their bonfire. Mann is shaken, but unsurprised. His ego is big enough to cope.

He is, after all, the most celebrated living writer in the German language. 'Where I am,' he declares, 'there is German culture.'

Migrating to America, he teaches at Princeton before settling in California, where he makes wartime broadcasts to the Germans. In July 1942, at the height of the Wehrmacht advance into Russia, he declares that victory can never be achieved.

> There is no such thing – it is not within the realm of the acceptable, permissible, thinkable. It will be prevented; rather, [Hitler] himself will always prevent it, the sorry scoundrel, because of himself, simply because of his nature, because of his impossible and hopelessly deranged disposition, which does not permit him to think, want, or do anything which is not false, mendacious, condemned beforehand.

Thomas Mann believes he knows Hitler better than anyone because he knows the German mind in all its serpentine perversions, from Goethe's *Faust* to the crafted lies of Joseph Goebbels.

'Not with Faust's soul, the soul of humanity, will this stupid Satan go down to hell,' prophesies Thomas Mann to his people, 'but *alone.*' Hitler, he declares, is a historical aberration. A powerful allegory is germinating in his mind.

Mann's novel *Doctor Faustus* describes the life and crimes of a German artist. Its anti-hero, the composer Adrian Leverkühn, sells his soul to the devil in exchange for a new method of composition that will grant him world fame. Leverkühn is first inspired by a lecture given by the town organist, Wendell Kretschmar, on the subject: 'Why did Beethoven not write a third movement to the Piano Sonata Opus 111?' Beethoven's last sonata, argues Kretschmar (in John E. Woods' translation), 'left the snug regions of tradition, and, as humanity gazed in horror, climbed to spheres of the totally personal, the exclusively personal – an ego painfully isolated in its own absoluteness, and, with the demise of his hearing, isolated from the sensual world as well.' Leverkühn wants to be the one who resolves these disparities.

Beethoven's departure from earthly values becomes a metaphor for Mann's exile, his wife's despair and Germany's inhumanity under Hitler. All, he implies, is foretold in Beethoven's last sonata. Opus 111 represents, in his view, 'an end without any return.'

Mann is instructed in music by a fellow-exile, the Marxist philosopher Theodor W. Adorno, a part-time composer with an itch for making mischief. Adorno teaches Mann how Arnold Schoenberg invented a modernist method of composing with all twelve notes, arranged in variable order of a flexible scale. Schoenberg's twelve-tone row is described in great detail in Chapter Eight of *Doctor Faustus* as Leverkühn's personal gift from the Devil.

The novel appears in 1947 to little attention outside the book pages of the *New York Times* and other self-regarding journals. Among the German exile colony on the Pacific Palisades, however, it lands like an atom bomb. Schoenberg is outraged that Mann has attached his method to a syphilitic, etiolated and altogether unoriginal composer of his supposed imagination. He fires a diatribe at Mann in an American journal. The Nobel Prize winner responds in kind and much chatter is heard among the café klatches, as Adorno has always hoped. The furore dies out. Schoenberg dies in poverty, Mann in wealth, neither ever setting foot again on German soil. Beneath this final eruption of cultural rage, detailed in a book by Larry Schoenberg, the composer's grandson, lies the very frustrations of creation in an imperfect world that Beethoven presents in opus 111.

In 2018, Angela Merkel's federal German government allocates thirteen million dollars to purchase the house where Mann wrote *Doctor Faustus* and convert it into 'a German state residence for intellectuals.' In July 2021 Mann's piano, a Wheelock baby grand (known as 'a poor man's Steinway'), is installed by his grandson, Frido Mann, who knows it as 'the Faustus Grand'. In October 2021 the piano is formally reconsecrated in the living room at 1550 San Remo Drive by the Russian-German-Jewish pianist Igor Levit. He plays the opus 111 sonata, on the very date it is believed to have been composed two hundred years before.

Opus 111 carves a further niche in world literature. In 1975 the Czech novelist Milan Kundera, exiled in France, attempts to recover memories of his lost home in *The Book of Laughter and Forgetting*. Kundera writes about the gathering dementia of his musicologist father Ludvik Kundera in their home in Brno:

Once he called me into his room. The variations from the Opus 111 sonata were open on the piano. 'Look,' he said, pointing to the music (he had lost the ability to play the piano), and again, 'Look,' and then, after a prolonged effort, he managed to say: 'Now I know!' He kept trying to explain something important to me, but the words he used were completely unintelligible and, seeing that I did not understand him, he looked at me in amazement and said: 'That's strange'.

Kundera is racked by guilt: 'I could not forgive myself for asking him so little, for knowing so little about him, for losing him. In fact, it is that very remorse which suddenly made me see what he must have meant to tell me the day he pointed to the Opus 111 sonata.' What that is, Kundera struggles to specify. Within opus 111 there is, for the elder Kundera, a secret that contains all others. His son calls it 'that *second* infinity, the infinity of internal variety concealed in all things'.

Milan Kundera composes his 'novel in the form of variations'. Beethoven, he realises, has created 'another space' for others to explore and where every creative soul is challenged. He is stunned that in a theme 'which often consists of no more than sixteen measures, Beethoven goes as deeply into these sixteen measures as if he had gone down a mine into the bowels of the earth'. Beethoven, in his last sonata, reconnects us, suggests Kundera, with those who have lost hearing, speech, thinking, or being. There is more in Beethoven than we can possibly know, touching us even through the fading stages of a creative life.

9 1

Schubert bears it

String Quintet in C major, WoO62, 'Letzter musikalischer Gedanke' (1827)

AMONG THE WELL-WISHERS AND THRILL-SEEKERS WHO VISIT Beethoven as he lies dying is Vienna's only home-grown musical genius, the fast-rising Franz Schubert. They have never met before. Schubert is too shy to approach Beethoven in a music shop, though he offers him the dedication of a set of Variations on a French Theme for Piano Duet (1822). We don't know if Beethoven acknowledged it.

Schubert is young, in his twenties, raging (says one friend) with 'the passions of an eagerly burning sensuality'. The Beethoven biographer Maynard Solomon calls him out as 'the central figure in a coterie of homosexual and bisexual Viennese artists'. Plump and bespectacled, Schubert is hardly a love god. An introvert with a stubby nose and cleft chin, barely five feet tall and with receding hair, he is prone to crippling mood swings and considers himself 'the most unhappy and miserable person in this world.' He is believed to pay for sex. By 1823 he is syphilitic. Four years on, writing *Winterreise*, a song cycle infused with a death wish, he summons all his courage to pay a visit to the dying Beethoven.

Beethoven is too far gone to recognise anyone, but Schubert has heard that he once praised his songs and declared that the young man will one day 'make a great stir in the world'. He leaves Beethoven's room with head bowed and, days later, is numbered among thirty-six torchbearers at the funeral.

Out of nowhere he writes a C major score for string quartet with extra cello, a work that ranks among his most exalted. Where does he get the idea?

The publisher Antonio Diabelli flourishes a Beethoven manuscript from an unchecked drawer which he declares to be the 'last work of the composer'. The piece is four minutes long, incomplete, a string quartet with an extra cello for added resonance. Schubert writes his C major string quintet in the same format, same key, opening with a low rumble that signifies irreparable loss. It is the acme of its kind, imbued with the unquenchable spirit of Beethoven and the irresistible lyricism of his humblest admirer, Franz Schubert.

In November 1828, on his own deathbed, Schubert asks to hear Beethoven's C sharp minor string quartet, opus 131. Musicians are summoned and he sighs with pleasure. He is buried, at his last request, beside Beethoven.

Of the late Beethoven quintet fragment there is a 2019 DG recording by Daniel Hope and Ikki Opitz (violins), Amihai Grosz (viola), Tatjana Masurenko (viola) and Daniel Müller-Schott (cello). Schubert's is a class apart.

92

Small balls

7 Bagatelles, Op. 33, (1801–3); Bagatelles, Opp. 119 (1822), 126 (1825)

A BAGATELLE IS A TABLE GAME INVOLVING STICKS AND BALLS. It is played indoors by landed gentry on rainy days. The French composer François Couperin attaches the term to a musical work in 1717. Beethoven uses it for 'Kleinigkeiten', trivialities.

His earliest bagatelle is written when he is twelve. Twenty years later he rolls out a set in opus 33, adding odd harmonies. He is not just playing around. He is testing a plinky piano for the forthcoming Eroica Variations. The Scottish pianist Steven Osborne (2012) finds a delicate balance on record between work and play.

Beethoven does not touch bagatelles again until 1822 when, while writing the ninth symphony, he receives a request for a new set from the Leipzig publisher, C. F. Peters. He breaks off to compose the bagatelles and Peters bats them right back. 'I had them played by several people', writes Peters, 'and *not one of them* believes that they are by you. I asked for *Kleinigkeiten*, but these are too small, and also mostly so easy that they are unsuitable for advanced players; as for emerging pianists, many passages are too difficult.' Beethoven protests that they are still pretty good and he's quite proud of them. Peters retorts: 'In order not to be misunderstood, I will say no more except that I will never print these *Kleinigkeiten*, and would rather lose the fee I have already paid.'

Beethoven mails his bagatelles to London, where Clementi issues them as 'trifles for the pianoforte, consisting of eleven pleasing pieces composed in various styles by L. van Beethoven'. Trifles and various are about right. This music reads like a desk clearance. Schnabel interprets them as minor musings. Steven Osborne offers something more coherent. Could be Peters was right, after all.

Beethoven, though, won't leave it at that. Having assured all of his publishers that he is done with writing for piano, Beethoven spontaneously turns out a third set of bagatelles, opus 126, and dedicates them to his brother Johann in memory of their shared childhood. But these bagatelles are far from child's play, whether in content or complexity. Beethoven informs the publisher Schott that 'some of them are . . . probably the best pieces of this kind that I have written.' There are six pieces, one of which crosses an Orphean bridge between all of his works up to this point and the immanent worldliness of his emergent last string quartets.

The philosopher Adorno may be the first to appreciate that these bagatelles 'appear not as themselves but as signs of something else', with the fourth bagatelle as 'the most important'. What's buried in this B minor bagatelle? Two types of death, says Adorno – (a) the death of the individual, and (b) the living death that many people accept, 'inorganic, object-like', as they avoid thinking about their end. According to Adorno, Beethoven is trying to teach us how to live with the reality that all this will come to an end. 'Individuals shrink to the nodal points of conventional reactions and the modes of operations objectively expected of them', he formulates. Those who refuse to think of death drain the vitality from their extant lives. One has to be mindful of death in order to live life to the full. Beethoven's bagatelle combines one's own death in its tune and the denial of it in its form, or something along those lines. Adorno is very pleased with this original analysis, and rightly so.

That a concept of such profundity can arise from a pianistic bon-bon suggests that Beethoven no longer distinguishes between substantive and insubstantial works. All of his music from here is charged with depth. The fourth bagatelle opens fast, angry and heavy with admonition. The left hand growls around the low regions, never satisfied, while the right hand flashes away, seeking a solution to a problem that is never identified. We don't know what's bugging him, but he leaves us with a very soft, unresolved closure in B major. Adorno, elsewhere, puts a name to it. Death, he says, 'is imposed only on created beings, not on works of art.' Every note of Beethoven's from here on is immortal.

Sviatoslav Richter interprets the last three bagatelles as glimpses of eternal life. Schnabel is stumped, furiously so. Piotr Anderszewski is spiritual, Brendel cerebral, Gould unmedicated, Wilhelm Kempff earthbound, Stephen Kovacevich surreal (and my pick of the pack). No two pianists play these Bagatelles alike.

93

Gelato con gelignite

String Quartet No. 12 in E flat major, Op. 127 (1824–5)

BEETHOVEN NOW WRITES ONLY FOR HIMSELF, NOT CARING what others make of his music. Twelve years have elapsed since his last string quartet, the eleventh, which was supposed to be the serious one. The twelfth quartet proclaims, with a heavy unison chord, an introspective impenetrability.

The quartet is in E flat major, ostensibly his happy key. It has four movements and is forty minutes long. But from the start it feels unstable. A lyrical theme is broken up by nervous chatter in the lower strings. Twice Beethoven interjects a half-repeated motif and for no obvious thematic reason. There's a temptation to play harshly at the edge of the note; atonality is not far away and beauty should be the last thing on a player's mind. The second movement is slow, built on six variations of rising unfathomability. The third plucks away at itself like a scab. In the finale, Beethoven flicks in a brief reward, a theme we recognise from the ninth symphony. Is this joy? Where is he going? Does he know?

The impetus to return to string quartets comes from his cello-playing Russian friend, Prince Nikolai Galitzin and the occasion is the prince's wedding. What Beethoven delivers proves, in practice, unplayable. The premiere by Ignaz Schuppanzigh's quartet in March 1825 is unacceptably cacophonous. Beethoven, hearing of its failure, sacks Schuppanzigh and calls in Joseph Michael Böhm, violin professor at the Conservatoire, to attempt a second performance. Böhm is ecstatic. This is a once-in-a-generation opportunity to topple Vienna's top-gun violinist. Böhm writes:

When Beethoven learned of the poor performance – for he was not present – he became furious and let the performers have no peace until the disgrace was wiped away. He sent for me first thing in the morning, and in his usual curt way said to me, 'You must play my quartet,' and the thing was settled. Neither objections nor doubts could prevail; what Beethoven wanted had to take place, so I undertook the difficult task. It was studied and rehearsed frequently under Beethoven's own eyes. I said 'eyes' intentionally, for the unhappy man was so deaf he could no longer hear the heavenly sound of his compositions . . .

With close attention his eyes followed the bows and therefore he was able to judge the slightest fluctuations in tempo and rhythm and correct them immediately. At the close of the last movement of the quartet there occurred a 'meno vivace' which seemed to me to weaken the general effect. At the rehearsal, therefore, I advised that the original tempo be maintained . . . Beethoven, crouched in a corner, heard nothing, but watched with strained attention. After the last stroke of the bows he said, laconically, 'let it remain so,' went to the desks and crossed out the 'meno vivace' in the four parts.

Imagine, for a moment, how hard, how desperately hard, Böhm and his three players must have worked at this utterly unyielding score. Hour after hour, night after night, and all to no avail. Opus 127 is beyond their capabilities. After a single performance, Beethoven sacks them and calls back Schuppanzigh, without so much as an apology to either set of players. Poor Böhm is remembered not as the brilliant interpreter he would have liked to be but merely as a capable teacher, one whose prized pupil was Joseph Joachim. Once again, as in the violin concerto, it is Joachim who will rescue an intractable work of Beethoven's from oblivion.

Joachim, as part of his responsibilities as director of performance at Berlin's Royal Academy of Music, forms a string quartet in 1869 with Ernst Schiever, Heinrich de Ahna and Wilhelm Müller, all members of the royal orchestra and respected teachers. Schiever is a part-time conductor; De Ahna is a concertmaster. Rather than giving ad hoc concerts, Joachim reimagines the presentation of string quartets in concert.

A Felix Possart painting shows the Joachim Quartet sitting on a dais, two by two and facing each other, while the audience sits around them on all four sides, creating domestic intimacy in a thousand-packed hall. Their recitals of the Beethoven quartets are 'ritual in-gatherings of the faithful who came to experience elevation and renewal', according to one eyewitness, an account amply evidenced in the rapt Possart painting. No pin would be allowed to drop in such a trance-like setting. The Belgian virtuoso Eugène Ysaÿe credits Joachim with fostering 'a sort of Bayreuth on a reduced scale' at his Beethoven string quartet cycles in Berlin.

As his orchestral partners grow older, Joachim replaces them with outstanding soloists. The cellist Robert Hausmann gives the world premiere of Bruch's Kol Nidrei and, with Joachim, the Brahms double concerto. The violinist Carl Halir is the first to perform the Sibelius violin concerto. Each of Joachim's players raises a dynasty of apostles. Halir's student David Mannes goes on to found the Mannes School of Music in New York, bringing the late Beethoven quartets to a new world. The works owe their public acceptance to the abundant personality of Joseph Joachim, who lives just long enough to see Arnold Schoenberg's string quartets breach the tonal wall, opening the floodgates to twentieth-century modernism.

This may be no more than coincidence, but Joachim's origin appears to give Hungarian quartets bragging rights on record in opus 127. Like Böhm, to whom Beethoven entrusted the quartet's second performance, Joachim is Budapest-Jewish. The first to record this quartet in 1926 is a Hungarian, Jenö Lener, who invokes hints of klezmer bands and gypsy dancing. Compare his *paprika* tempi to the *echt*-German solidity of EMI's Adolf Busch quartet, and there is not much contest for vernacular command. The Hungarians have it, they just do.

Further down the line on record you will find Sándor Végh's quartet (1952), Zoltán Székely's Hungarian String Quartet (1955) and the iridescent Budapest String Quartet who lasted from 1917 to 1967 and whose members were mostly Russian Jews who learned to speak Hungarian, and then English. The most celebrated were the violinist Alexander Schneider and violist Boris Kroyt. The Budapest wound up as house quartet for Columbia Records. Among other legacies, they legislated that wives and partners were never to be allowed into the rehearsal room and that players were to receive equal pay, with no bonus for the leader. The Budapest gave many Americans their first experience of a Beethoven quartet; no group plays the opus 127 adagio with darker foreboding.

The Magyar line continues through the Kodály Quartet (1998), Bartók Quartet (2014) and the Takács Quartet (2005). The latter's current leader, the Englishman Edward Dusinberre, wrote an immersive book about playing Beethoven quartets. Tackling opus 127, he writes, is 'a polarising experience. Along with sleepless nights and long recording sessions came an increase in physical ailments.' There are also 'times of liberation such as when we recorded the slow movement of opus 127 – an evening when nothing else mattered except to be in the midst of this sublime interweaving of musical lines.' This is Beethoven saying: feel *my* pain.

Viennese style, descended from Schuppanzigh, starts with Vienna Philharmonic concertmaster Walter Barylli (1956). His heirs, the Alban Berg Quartet led by concertmaster Günter Pichler, balance sepulchral solemnity with a serenity so fierce it cuts paper. The Alban Berg nurture among their students the Cuarteto Casals, the Belcea and the Artemis quartets, all of whom have made compelling video recordings of opus 127. (In another quirk of lineage, America's Emerson Quartet is led by Eugene Drucker, son of a member of the Busch Quartet). As a matter of personal taste, I turn first to the Takács, followed by the Emerson, the Alban Berg and the Cincinnati-based LaSalle Quartet. All are exemplary. For sheer pleasure, I choose the stiletto-sharp Quartetto Italiano, irresistible as gelato.

There is no one-sound-fits-all solution. One often suspects the players are in it for themselves, not the audience. The violist Rebecca Clarke puts it this way:

> The Beethoven quartets more than any others are pre-eminently for the player rather than the listener . . . Most other chamber music – that by Mozart, for instance – speaks more for itself; it is luminous, lighting its own way. In Beethoven, on the other hand, the player must himself illumine the hidden obscurities and unless he well understands them he cannot hope to make others do so.

94

Relativity

**String Quartet No. 13 in B flat major, Op. 130;
Grosse Fuge for String Quartet in B flat major,
Op. 133 (1825–6); piano version Op. 134**

THE THIRTEENTH QUARTET HAS SIX MOVEMENTS AND LASTS
fifty minutes. It runs so long that the composer is persuaded to replace the
finale, known as the '*Grosse Fuge*', with a shorter ending. The composer
Louis Spohr dismisses this quartet, along with the next two, as 'indeci-
pherable, uncorrected horrors'. On first reception one critic calls the work
'incomprehensible as Chinese'.

The first movement flips from adagio to allegro; the second lasts just
two minutes; the third is a spectral anticipation of Maurice Ravel's *La
Valse*; the fourth accelerates without warning, like a getaway car. The cavatina fifth movement comes from some deep place of psychic healing;
nothing, says Beethoven, 'has so moved him'. A Schuppanzigh player, Karl
Holz, remembers him composing 'the Cavatina amid sorrow and tears;
never did his music breathe so heartfelt an inspiration and even the
memory of this movement brought tears to his eyes.' It may be either a
prayer or a consolation. Is he asking for an end to his pain? Vienna on 21
March 1826 applauds the second and fourth movements. Beethoven is
furious. 'Why these trifles?' he shouts. 'Why not the fugue?'

A fugue is a work of music in which two or more themes interact and
contradict each other. In psychiatry, dissociative fugue is a rare disorder in
which a person cannot remember who they are or where they live. Sufferers
disappear from home for hours, days or weeks; often they return completely
cured, unaware of what has happened to them. The causes of dissociative
fugue have yet to be understood. The Latin word *fugare* means to chase, or to
flee. Psychiatrists cannot be certain if the fugue sufferer is hunter or hunted.

In music, the art of the fugue descends from Johann Sebastian Bach and is likewise not fully understood. Beethoven describes his Grosse Fuge as '*tantôt libre, tantôt recherchée*': a bit free, a bit remote – intentionally vague? Igor Stravinsky rates it as 'an absolutely contemporary piece of music that will be contemporary forever'. Beethoven publishes it as opus 133, separate from the full quartet, but gives no clue to its meaning. Some read it as an acceptance that life ends in failure. The Guarneri Quartet's Arnold Steinhardt argues, to the contrary, that 'it is the chaos out of which life itself evolved'. The poet Sylvia Plath writes in 'Little Fugue' about the death of her father:

> He could hear Beethoven:
> Black yew, white cloud,
> The horrific complications.
> Finger-traps – a tumult of keys.

Plath is mourning her father, envying his understanding of late Beethoven when all she can hear is chaos. He is all-hearing; she is deaf. Beethoven, in the poem, is a metaphor for all she cannot grasp in an unhappy, truncated life.

Beethoven, in opus 130 and its fugal spin-offs, is no longer concerned with answers. He leaves interpreters and listeners to do the work, giving just enough clues to make the search a sensory and intellectual pleasure, a device that connects great minds and relieves them under intolerable stress.

⸘

There is a 1913 Berlin recording of the opus 130 fourth movement led by Karl Klingler, Joseph Joachim's very last quartet member. The other players on this record are a Russian Jew, Josef Rywkind, a Welshman, Arthur Williams, and Klingler's brother, Fridolin. On 1 August 1914, Rywkind and Williams are arrested and interned as enemy aliens in Ruhleben camp, a hub of artistic activity. They emerge four years later, none the worse for the experience. Back home, Williams forms a string quartet in Oxford and recruits, to his eternal delight, the visiting Albert Einstein. It is not unusual for scientists to bond with musicians. Klingler forms a friendship with the Nobel-winning physicist Max Planck, the first German to uphold Einstein's theory of relativity. There is a jolly picture of Klingler and Planck taken at Klingler's country home in the summer of 1944, a pair of distinguished gentlemen sharing their love of music and the unknown.

The image is deceptive. Klingler is terrified for his wife, who is half-Jewish, and for his own safety after his university smashed a bust of Joachim. He is interrogated by the Gestapo, not about Joachim but intensely about Planck, whose son Erwin, a cellist, is suspected of complicity in the July assassination attempt on Hitler. Erwin Planck is hanged in a Berlin prison in January 1945; his brilliant father loses the will to live.

Klingler, late in life, is lionised in Japan. One of his students, Shinichi Suzuki, invents a method for teaching children to play the violin by rote, without having to read music. Suzuki applies for an endorsement from his elderly teacher, who is connected via Joachim to Beethoven himself. The world-circling Suzuki method thus owes its authority to the first recording of a movement of opus 130.

The most satisfying modern recordings of opus 130 are by the Takács, Ébène, Casals, Guarneri, Alban Berg and Emerson quartets. In the Grosse Fuge the Quartetto Italiano rage against what the Welsh poet Dylan Thomas calls 'the dying of the light'. I know of no more absorbing performance.

{

Beethoven himself made the piano version of the fugue referred to by Sylvia Plath. The conductor Felix Weingartner arranged the fugue for string orchestra. Wilhelm Furtwängler, in his Berlin (1952) and Vienna (1954) recordings, seems to be asking, how do we carry on living after the horrors we have seen? In *West Side Story*, Leonard Bernstein takes a bite of the *Fugue* as a trigger for the 'Cool' scene, a gang ritual in which the music runs serially through all twelve notes of the scale. The effect projects the alienation of disaffected, working-class youths in New York. Like Anthony Burgess in *A Clockwork Orange*, Bernstein taps into latent violence in one of Beethoven's most ethereal themes. Beethoven's music speaks for outcasts as much as for privileged insiders.

95

Ghetto blaster

String Quartet No. 14 in C sharp minor, Op. 131 (1825–6)

THE SEVEN MOVEMENTS OF THE SO-CALLED 'EVEREST OF STRING quartets' test emotions, intellect and endurance to an extreme. When the publisher Schott asks what the quartet is about, Beethoven glibly answers that it is '*zusammen gestohlen aus Verschiedenem, diesem und Jenem*' ('put together from stolen odds and ends'). Elsewhere, he tells the violinist Karl Holz that it is his greatest string quartet – and there may be still greater to come. 'Art demands of us that we must not stand still,' he says. 'Thank God there is less lack of imagination than ever before.' Schubert, hearing this work five days before his death, sighs: 'After this, what is left for us to write?'

Misperceptions persist. Richard Wagner, in 1870, considers the opening movement 'the most melancholy sentiment in music' and the finale 'the dance of the whole world itself: wild joy, the wail of pain, love's transport, utmost bliss, grief, frenzy, riot, suffering, the lightning flickers, thunders growl: and above it the stupendous fiddler who bears and bounds it all, who leads it haughtily from whirlwind into whirlwind, to the brink of the abyss – he smiles at himself, for to him this sorcery was the merest play – and night beckons him. His day is done.' It's *The Flying Dutchman* in embryo.

Virginia Woolf quotes opus 131 in her novel *The Waves*. T. S. Eliot alludes to it in his *Four Quartets*: 'Time present and time past / Are both perhaps present in time future, /And time future contained in time past./ If all time is eternally present /All time is unredeemable.' As much as the philosopher Hegel and the physicist Einstein, Beethoven splits the fluidity of time against the finitude of being. His quartet presents an existential conundrum. In Yaron Zilberman's Manhattan movie *A Late Quartet*, a middle-aged string player cries out in opus 131: 'What are we supposed to do: stop – or struggle?' As life enters its later stages, each of us is confronted with that question, rooted in opus 131.

A morose opening gives way to two dance tracks, both macabre. The fourth movement is the heart of the work, a close-knit set of variations. The fifth movement is a high-speed intercity train; it is followed by a two-minute of signal self-contemplation before the finale rocks off the rails. At no point can player or listener pause for breath. It is conceivably the most sustained act of concentration in the whole of Western music. The ending is abrupt as a death rattle.

Some biographers link the quartet to nephew Karl's botched suicide. It's a good theory, but the dates don't tally and nor does the content. The quartet has neither the rage of his fifth symphony, nor the resignation of a late sonata. His mind is on a higher plane, viewing the world from above, watching as 'the grasshopper loses its spring and desire fails, because man goes to his eternal home' (Eccl. 12:5). Opus 131, spanning life and death, imports a tune from an improbable source.

In 1898, a Berlin synagogue choirmaster, Emil Breslaur, recognises that the sixth movement of this quartet begins with the Kol Nidrei melody of the Jewish Day of Atonement, the holiest of the year. What is it doing here? Beethoven had been approached in 1824 to write music for the first synagogue permitted to be built in Vienna's inner city. The Seitenstettengasse Tempel is designed to resemble an opera house, and its founders are fond of arias. They commission Schubert to compose two Hebrew psalms for the Sabbath Eve service. Beethoven is less tractable. He requests Jewish scores as source material but does not fulfil the commission. While rifling through Jewish tunes his eye may have been caught by Kol Nidrei. More likely he heard it while growing up in Bonn, where there was a tiny synagogue with seats for forty-four men and twenty-nine women. On High Holy days, when the weather was hot, the windows would be flung open. It is easy to imagine the boy Beethoven hearing Kol Nidrei as he passes by. Now, that memory returns, thanks to a late connection. In 1825 he meets the attractive and celebrated writer Rahel Varnhagen ('he was dating a Jewish woman . . .' claims an American Beethoven website) and may have wanted to impress her with his quotation of a cornerstone of Jewish liturgy. (The Kol Nidrei prayer originates in eighth-century Iraq, the tune about a millennium later; the non-Jewish Max Bruch reimagines it as a cello concerto in 1880 after hearing it sung by a Berlin cantor.)

On record, the Juilliard Quartet and the Budapest String Quartet give the sixth movement a distinctly Hebraic spin. The Schneiderhan Quartet in 1944 Vienna cleanse their playing of anything un-Aryan. Between these polarities, non-Jewish Quartetto Italiano pluck the tune from a Mediterranean melting-pot.

My opus 131 reference recordings are Busch (1936), Guarneri (1989) and Takács (2005). The one I cherish most is the LaSalle Quartet (1977). Based in Cincinnati, four Hitler refugees – Henry Meyer, Walter Levin (violins), Peter Kamnitzer (viola), Jack Kirstein (cello) – enter late Beethoven in reverse, through the prism of Schoenbergian serialism, informing the past with evidence from the future. Each time I listen I learn something new. Each time I want to seclude myself for a week with this work, and no other.

⁊

Who plays these quartets after Beethoven dies? In Vienna, late Beethoven is shelved. In Paris, even early works go unheard. Berlin has to wait four decades before Joachim forms his quartet. Unaccountably (and largely unaccounted) it is in unmusical London that Beethoven's last thoughts find an audience. The instigator is Thomas Massa Alsager, part-owner of *The Times* newspaper, a self-made man whose career will end in disgrace and his life in suicide.

Son of a clothworker, Alsager starts writing articles for *The Times*, buys a stake in the company, promotes music and puts its first music critic on the payroll. As City Correspondent he profits from inside information. In 1821, aged forty-one, he marries an uneducated girl of seventeen and raises thirteen children. He buys a house in Bloomsbury at 26 Queen Square, where on Christmas Eve 1832 he gives the English premiere of Beethoven's Missa Solemnis, directed by Ignaz Moscheles. It is a time of optimism and enlightenment. Alsager befriends the poets Keats and Wordsworth, the essayist Charles Lamb and the novelist Fanny Burney, as well as the musicians Mendelssohn, Spohr and Joachim. His driving passion, however, is Beethoven's body of string quartets.

In the spring of 1845 Alsager founds a 'Beethoven Quartett Society' to perform all sixteen works (except the Grosse Fuge) over ten weeks. He seats an audience of 250 in a Harley Street mansion and presents each person with a printed score. Guests are requested to arrive at eight p.m. in order to acquaint themselves with the music before an eight-thirty start. Joachim forms a quartet with the violinist Prosper Sainton, violist Henry Hill and cellist Scipion Rousselot. Alsager is so pleased with the first cycle that he declares the quartet festival an annual event, an exclusive ticket in the hubbub of the London matrimonial season.

His hubris does not last long. Like other smart operators, Alsager invests heavily in railways, notably the London to Exeter line. 'Railway Mania' is swiftly followed by corporate crash. Investors see their savings wiped out. *The Times* thunders at speculators. Alsager is accused of using the paper to boost his shares. In October 1845, his wife Elizabeth dies. Eleven months later, Alsager is fired by *The Times* over an error in the paper's accounts, for which he is not responsible. A year after Elizabeth's funeral, he cuts his throat. The clothworkers mourn a brother of 'the strictest integrity'; Wordsworth laments 'a man of sober and sound judgement'. The Quartett Society continues annually until the Great Exhibition in 1851, where all the world's inventions are displayed in Hyde Park and Beethoven is set aside as a thing of the past.

Alsager left a single legacy. He arranged his quartet cycles so that each concert was composed of one early, one middle and one late work, a model still used to this day. Beethoven, Alsager understood, is best perceived in the round.

96

Nuclear chorus

Symphony No. 9 in D minor, Op. 125 (1824)

IN THE BEGINNING, THERE IS THE NINTH SYMPHONY. IN 1793, aged twenty-two, Beethoven talks of composing Friedrich Schiller's 'Freude', published in 1786. In 1811, he writes down its opening line with a reminder to 'work out the overture'. Further mentions of 'the Schiller overture' float through his conversation books. The ninth symphony's opening bars appear in 1817. A year on, he toys with two symphonies. In 1819 he gives up all other work to compose three piano sonatas and Missa Solemnis. Finally in December 1822, ten years after the eighth symphony, he accepts a commission from the Philharmonic Society in London for a ninth symphony. He does not tell them that the symphony will be the largest ever conceived, requiring four soloists and a massed chorus, and sung in German. That may be because he does not yet know.

He allocates 1823 to writing the Ninth. By the end of August he has only fifteen minutes of music. The adagio takes another two months. He stalls once more and takes a cure in Baden. That does the trick. He returns home with a sketchbook in hand, shouting, 'I have it! I have it!'

At the start of 1824, in an unprovoked attack of human brotherhood, he sends new year's greetings to his brother's hated widow, the battling Johanna. Is the Ninth making him a nicer man? He is not naturally prone to reconciliation. He finishes the symphony in February. Friends book the Theater an der Wien orchestra, the best in Vienna. Beethoven, deafness be damned, insists on conducting. Maybe just the overture? say friends. No, says Beethoven: the lot. The theatre declines the booking. They move the concert to the Kärntnertor. Its placard says that 'Herr Ludwig van Beethoven will himself participate in the direction'.

Somebody looks at the date and hast a fit: 7 May 1824 is a Friday. Nobody stages a new work on a Friday when all the rich folk are out of town, hunting boar on their estates. No princes or dukes will be present. Beethoven seems quite pleased. At last he can present a symphony to the real, hard-working people of Vienna.

At seven p.m. on Friday 7 May, Beethoven arrives at the Kärntnertor. He is wearing a green coat because he does not own a black one. A less formal audience, he reckons, won't mind. The house is packed. Some music lovers are carried in on stretchers from, it is said, their deathbeds. The programme is relatively short. The symphony is preceded by the Consecration of the House overture and Missa Solemnis selections. Then a short break, and the great work.

The violinist Joseph Michael Böhm furnished this record from the orchestra:

> Beethoven himself conducted – that is, he stood in front of a conductor's stand and threw himself back and forth like a madman. One moment he stretched to his full height, at the next he crouched down to the floor, he flailed about with his hands and feet as though he wanted to play all the instruments and sing all the chorus parts.

The symphony opens with a tremor of strings, twenty seconds of white noise. It gives way to a pastoral landscape, pleasant and familiar. The second movement, twice as long as any other scherzo, is interrupted by wild applause. The Police Commissioner shouts, 'Silence!' The Kapellmeister, or deputy conductor, a man named Michael Umlauf, grows concerned that the musicians are unable to follow Beethoven's wavery beat. Between movements he tells them to ignore the baton but never to take their eyes off Beethoven, his face, his eyes.

The adagio is not slow as adagios are meant to be, with a metronome mark of 60, a fair clip. For six minutes of the finale, the orchestra meanders and soloists remain seated. Suddenly, with a spurt of pace and a bass shout, 'Oh, friends, not these tones', the world changes. 'Let's sing more cheerful songs,' the bass proposes. 'Joy!' he cries, and 'Joy' again, followed by 'all men shall be brothers'. For the first time, a symphony claims to speak for the whole of humanity.

Beethoven handles the exhortation with moderation. Brotherhood could be mistaken for equality, a dangerous expression of political dissidence. On the other hand, Jesus said: 'be devoted to one another in brotherly love.' Beethoven walks on water, treading a line between official faith and sedition. Where Schiller's line is wistful, Beethoven's music declares human unity to be practically possible.

After over an hour of intense performance, the house erupts in the greatest ovation Vienna has ever heard. The mezzo-soprano Caroline Unger plucks Beethoven's sleeve to show him the clapping, cheering, footstamping audience. 'My triumph is attained,' says Beethoven, 'I can now speak from the heart.'

He has a table booked for dinner at the aptly named 'Zum wilden Mann' on the Prater. On the way, he stops at the box office and learns that after fees, tips and expenses, all he has earned is pennies. Entering the restaurant, he accuses Schindler of swindling him. His three guests get up and walk out, leaving Beethoven alone on his night of triumph. A repeat concert leaves an 800 florin deficit. Only a Philharmonic Society cheque from London for fifty pounds keeps him solvent. His health declines and his pains return. He has put his life on the line in the ninth symphony and there is not much for him to enjoy. He retreats into silence, not realising the magnitude of his achievement. Fifty years will pass before another symphony receives such a reception. When Johannes Brahms presents his first symphony it is instantly dubbed Beethoven's Tenth.

The British premiere of Beethoven's ninth is conducted by Sir George Smart in March 1825, taxing 'the patience of the audience' with 'obstreperous roarings of modern frenzy'. In March 1831, François-Antoine Habeneck conducts the Ninth at the Société des Concerts du Conservatoire de Paris. 'What was Beethoven thinking in this piece?' asks musician François-Joseph Fétis. 'That I cannot understand, notwithstanding my study of it.' The North American premiere is given on 20 May 1846 by the New York Philharmonic Orchestra and British conductor George Loder, with the finale sung in demotic English. John Sullivan Dwight, America's most knowledgeable commentator, writes: 'We went away physically exhausted by the excitement of listening to so great a work, but unspeakably confirmed in all our highest faith.' Seven years pass before anyone attempts a repeat performance.

Over time, the symphony occupies a central, ceremonial place in musical life. Richard Wagner calls it 'the mystical goal of all my strange thoughts and desires' and performs it as his Bayreuth Festival curtain-raiser. 'Everything significant about this symphony comes from Richard Wagner,' says Richard Strauss. Gustav Mahler conducts the Ninth in 1900 with a record 100 musicians and 500 singers – 'carrying out Beethoven's wishes,' he claims, 'and ensuring that nothing the master intended should be sacrificed or drowned in a general confusion of sound.' Believe that if you like; in retrospect it looks like a dry run for Mahler's eighth symphony, involving one thousand performers.

There are, inevitably, haters. The Frenchman Claude Debussy writes in 1901: 'The Ninth Symphony has been shrouded in a fog of noble words and decorative statements. It's the masterpiece about which more nonsense has been spread than any other. One can be amazed that it hasn't long since been buried under the mountain of writings issued forth by it.' Debussy's friend Igor Stravinsky tells the writer Marcel Proust that Beethoven's ninth symphony finale is 'a hopelessly banal tune affixed to Schiller's mighty ode.' He is not alone in this perception. The influential Boston critic Philip Hale writes of 'the unspeakable cheapness of the chief tune'. The English novelist Ian McEwan dismisses it as 'a nursery tune.'

Modernism is caught in two minds. While Pierre Boulez defers to Beethoven, Karlheinz Stockhausen in a 1972 Oxford lecture suggests that the Ninth would be much improved by being compressed into one second's listening. A techno-freak takes him literally and, using computers, does just that.

The most radical literary realisation of the Ninth belongs to Anthony Burgess in *A Clockwork Orange*, where the finale excites fantasies of rape and violence. Alex, the delinquent hero, is subjected to aversion therapy, forcing him to watch vile tortures while the 'Ode to Joy' is playing. Burgess said he thought he was writing 'an allegory of Christian free will'. In a stage version, Alex sings, to the tune of 'Joy': 'Do not be a clockwork orange / Freedom has a lovely voice. / Here is good, and there is evil– / Look on both, then take your choice.'

The therapy wears off and the story ends with Alex having sex with a woman in front of a large crowd with Beethoven booming in the background (Stanley Kubrick's film has a soft-core ending). Both novel and

film are maimed by authorial identity confusion. Burgess, an ambitious
amateur composer, dreamed of becoming Beethoven. But there is no end
to the fantastical conclusions that can be drawn from this symphony.

The ninth was targeted in the first wave of the women's liberation
movement when a musicologist, Susan McClary, decided it represented
all the worst things men have ever done to women. 'The point of recapitulation in the first movement of the Ninth,' she wrote, 'is one of the most
horrifying moments in music, as the carefully prepared cadence is frus-
trated, damming up energy which finally explodes in the throttling
murderous rage of a rapist incapable of attaining release.' While this
quickly became one of the most quotable slogans of the women's movement, its lack of foundation in any recognised musical reality prompted
McClary to modify her statement to 'one of the most horrifyingly violent
episodes in the history of music' and 'our most compelling articulation in
music of the contradictory impulses that have organized patriarchal
culture.'

True or false, wild words have consequences. McClary's contention
prompts the poet and essayist Adrienne Rich to write a poem titled 'The
Ninth Symphony of Beethoven Understood at Last as a Sexual Message'. It
begins:

> A man in terror of impotence
> or infertility, not knowing the difference
> a man trying to tell something
> howling from the climacteric
> music of the entirely
> isolated soul
> yelling at Joy from the tunnel of the ego . . .

She is referring to the ninth symphony. The pianist Charles Rosen,
never lost for words, responds with unusual restraint:

> The phrase about the murderous rage of the rapist has since been with-
> drawn, which indicates that McClary realized it posed a problem, but it
> has the great merit of recognizing that something extraordinary is taking
> place here, and McClary's metaphor of sexual violence is not a bad way to

describe it . . . I cannot think that the rapist incapable of attaining release is an adequate analogue, but I hear the passage as if Beethoven had found a way of making an orgasm last for sixteen bars. What causes the passage to be so shocking, indeed, is the power of sustaining over such a long phrase what we expect as a brief explosion.

Come again? Rosen credits McClary with recognising virility in the symphony, and then reconfigures Beethoven as a sexual superman who can just go on and on and on, which is surely not what the feminists have in mind. And nor does Beethoven who, as he writes the ninth symphony, is immune to the desires which he, even as a young man, chastely refused to consummate. The core of McClary's argument is without foundation in historical or musical fact. None of which dislodges it as a foundation statement in feminist musicology.

The ninth symphony has been abused by multiple ideologies. Hitler and Stalin use it for mass persuasion. The European Union adopts it as a divisive anthem, signifying both the privileged unity of its citizens and the forced exclusion of unwanted immigrants. Schiller's words 'But he who cannot rejoice, let him steal weeping away' can be witnessed on a daily basis on Greek shores, Hungarian barbed-wire fences, Italian prison camps and a Calais jungle where the French government coops up Africans and Asians who plot to reach Britain in sinking plastic inflatables. What price Beethoven's human brotherhood in 2023? When Leonard Bernstein conducted the symphony at the breach of the Berlin Wall in 1989, replacing the word 'joy' with 'freedom', his gesture was ovated in the West and deplored by many on the disadvantaged side who felt neither joyous nor free. The ninth symphony is not infinitely open to interpretation.

On a brighter note, one of the symphony's most uplifting manifestations is the event known in Japan as 'Daiku' or 'Number Nine'. At the end of each year the symphony is performed to ever-increasing demand – fifty-five performances in Tokyo alone at the latest count, with thousands of people rehearsing and singing in the chorus. The tradition dates from 1914 when the Japanese army, on the Allied side, captured a German garrison at Tsingtao in eastern China. The German prisoners formed their own orchestra and chorus and each Christmas they played the ninth symphony, to the delight of their Japanese guards. After the war, those guards brought the symphony back home. Someone said that there was a Leipzig Gewandhaus tradition to sound the ninth symphony's final chord one second before midnight. This legend became national folklore. On Japan's 2,600th anniversary in December 1940, a Polish-Jewish refugee, Joseph Rosenstock, conducted the Ninth on national radio. The reverber-ations continue to this day. The Tokyo earthquake of 2011 was commemo-rated in a New Year's performance with a record chorus of ten thousand. On YouTube, it has been watched by ten million viewers. More intense, less declamatory, is Vladimir Ashkenazy's rapt Tokyo reading in December 2005, achieving ascendant meditation.

⸘

Just how difficult it is to conduct the symphony can be seen from diver-gences in shape and style among major conductors. Take the opening movement. The first known recording, in 1929, conducted by Mahler disciple Oskar Fried, lasts 14 minutes. Klemperer takes 17, Furtwängler 19. As they grow older conductors tend to slow down. Karl Böhm covers the symphony in 1941 in 65 minutes; by 1979 he takes 79 minutes. But symphonic music is not bubblegum there to be distended into any globu-lar shape. There has to be a median range of acceptability that rules out such absurdities as a Brazilian conductor, Maximianno Cobra, who takes one hour forty-five minutes and the Boston iconoclast Benjamin Zander who thinks it should be over in less than forty minutes. They cannot both be right.

In surveying two hundred recordings, I am influenced by remem-brances of live performance. Klemperer, Solti, Abbado and Haitink rush to the fore. Tennstedt, with deconstructionist drive, comes closest to Beethoven's first-movement demolition of sonata form. Solti and Klemperer were always more exciting live than on record.

Three exiles stand out from the discography. Could it be because they are the voices of the have-nots in an art that is monetarily sustained by the haves? The Hungarian Ferenc Fricsay, conducting in a Berlin college hall on New Year's Eve 1957, arouses a 'terrifying', 'barbaric' intensity, according to a perceptive critic present. This recording, which soundtracks Kubrick's film of *A Clockwork Orange*, has lost none of its barbarism. Fricsay stood out in Berlin as a counterpoint to Karajan's ultra-smoothness.

Rafael Kubelík, at Bavarian Radio in 1975, is less angry. A Czech exile, Kubelík always predicted that Communism would crumble and he would return home some day to Prague. When I saw him there in June 1990 after the Václav Havel revolution, I finally understood the optimism that infuses this recording. Kubelík, in person, could be touchy and cheerless, unforgiving to those who collaborated with enemies of freedom. In this performance he is simply inspirational, an instinctive musician with an outstanding orchestra and chorus.

The Polish refugee René Leibowitz recorded a 1961 Ninth with the Royal Philharmonic Orchestra. The performance is starkly modern, informed by the radicalism of his pupils Pierre Boulez and Hans Werner Henze. Stripped of superfluous gesture and garments, like a patient awaiting surgery, it is plainly a matter of life and death.

Period-instrument performances and massive label signings generally leave me cold. Pushed for a shortlist, I would offer a long one:

Furtwängler, Berlin 1942; Toscanini, Milan 1946; Klemperer, Amsterdam 1956; Erich Kleiber, Vienna 1952; Fricsay, Berlin 1957; Szell, Cleveland 1961; Leibowitz, London 1961; Karajan, Berlin 1962; Schmidt-Isserstedt, Vienna 1965; Solti, Chicago 1972; Carlo Maria Giulini, London 1972; Kubelík, Munich 1975; Tennstedt, London 1992; David Zinman, Zurich 1999; Abbado, Berlin 2001; Jansons, Munich 2007; Chailly, Leipzig 2011; Thielemann, Vienna 2011; Andris Nelsons, Vienna 2019.

And one more.

The death of Bernard Haitink, in October 2021, closed out a breed of conductors who beat out symphonic cycles to meet label schedules. Karajan got steadily more mannered, Solti more rumbustious, Bernstein more wayward, Abbado more introspective, Muti more brash.

The exception was Haitink who, sacked by Philips in the late 1990s, returned to live recordings. In February 2019, weeks short of his ninetieth birthday, Haitink conducted the ninth symphony with Bavarian Radio in Munich. Everything is right about this concert. The orchestra and chorus are world class, the soloists impeccable. Haitink allows the army to surge forward, to give of their best without fear of failure. The whole is infused with compassion and comprehension: the finale lifts off into space with a promise of safe return. In a locked cabinet of eternal Beethoven Ninths, this is one of the lasting greats.

{

So, after that: is there a tenth symphony?

The possibility is raised in a letter Beethoven dictates eight days before his death and sends to Ignaz Moscheles in London. He mentions 'a new symphony which lies already sketched in my desk' and asks if the Philharmonic Society might be interested. He is dead before a reply arrives and nothing is found in his desk that resembles a workable symphony. The violinist Karl Holz claims he heard Beethoven play part of one movement. A sketch sheet bears an authentication by Schindler: 'These notes are the last ones Beethoven wrote roughly ten to twelve days before his death. He wrote them in my presence.' We know that, in the early stages of the Ninth, he was writing another symphony in tandem. Could this be it?

Not much happens until 1988 when a British musicologist, Barry Cooper, collates 250 bars of sketches and turns them into a fifteen-minute symphonic movement with three sub-sections: andante – allegro – andante. Cooper's 'tenth symphony' is premiered in London in October 1988 by the Royal Liverpool Philharmonic, conducted by the ex-Vienna Philharmonic concertmaster Walter Weller. Critics are sniffy. One leading reviewer who writes that the 'music sounded half formed' turns out to be the composer Anthony Payne who, not long after, will go on to make a performing version of Edward Elgar's third symphony from sketches that the composer ordered to be burned. Criticism is not an art that requires consistency.

Cooper's 'tenth' gets a second performance a week later at Carnegie Hall, conducted by José Serebrier. Recordings are made by Weller and Wyn Morris. Neither is convincing. The opening is tentative and hints of previous symphonies are clearly contrived by completing hands. The more I listen, the more the music sounds (as car-dealers say) pre-loved. At 8:45, it's the Ninth, at 14 minutes the Pastoral. There's a big theme at 08:30 and, at 11:10, a premonition of atonality, but neither is developed. Unlike Mahler's tenth symphony which is fully conceived in skeletal form, or Mozart's *Requiem* and Bruckner's Ninth, which were completed by others but are still performable as the composer left them, Beethoven's tenth symphony is a torso of scant interest.

Until computers enter the mainframe. First, Pierre Henry, a *musique concrète* composer, feeds all nine symphonies into a Paris desktop and runs the collage on radio as a Beethoven tenth 'remix' (you can find it on YouTube). Then, in 2019, data scientists endorsed by the Beethoven-Haus in Bonn apply algorithms to sketches of the supposed Tenth, augmenting them with themes taken mostly from the string quartets. The result? A mess of pottage. Performed by the Beethoven Orchester of Bonn, it fails at every level. Anything that sounds like Beethoven is cribbed from another score, the rest is just dull. There is not one Eureka moment, no spark of genius or ingenuity, no sense of Beethoven pushing out boundaries as he always does. The whole is not worth a nanosecond of anyone's time. It's a media gimmick. What would Beethoven make of Artificial Intelligence? In a crusty mood he once tells a critic: 'What I shit is better than anything you write.'

97

Gone for baroque

String Quartet No. 15 in A minor, Op. 132 (1823–5)

THE TRIGGER IS A MEDICAL EMERGENCY. IN MAY 1825 Beethoven suffers severe intestinal pain. The doctor tells him to avoid spirits, eat a light diet and, most important, stop composing at night. Beethoven, grumbling, obeys. Convalescing in an out-of-season spa, he is refused alcohol and liver dumplings, supposedly on doctor's orders. Enraged, he composes a quartet deep into the night.

Its five movements frame a central section titled *Heiliger Dankgesang eines Genesenen an der Gottheit, in der Lydischen Tonart*, 'a holy song of thanks to Godliness from a convalescent, in the Lydian mode'. The Lydian is a seven-tone scale used by the sixteenth-century composer Giovanni Pierluigi da Palestrina to persuade the Pope not to reimpose grey, Gregorian chant at the expense of fresh melody. Palestrina is celebrated as a saviour of church music. Beethoven may see himself as saving the string quartet from triviality.

He opens with a nod-to-Bach fugue. Two themes clash in a Tristan-like love duet. The third movement will inspire Arnold Schoenberg's 1946 string trio, written after a near-fatal heart attack. Another quote is heard in Bela Bartók's third piano concerto. Beethoven, on his score, jots the words '*Neue Kraft fühlend*' ('feeling new strength'). He repeats that in Italian and posts a copy to his physician, with a prescription: 'Doctor, shut the door against death, / Notes [of music] will help anyone in need. The work is another step up a Jacob's ladder where no man has climbed before.' He knows what awaits Jacob at the top of the ladder.

The 15th, written before the 14th, is premiered on 14 November 1825. Beethoven is in his mid-50s, fifteen years beyond average male life expectancy. Every day, every score, is a gift.

He continues to challenge musicians to perform the impossible. In the middle movement he indicates to end in unison with all four players bowing half-notes together *sforzando*, with abrupt emphasis. How is that doable? America's Emerson Quartet develop a technique they call 'park and go' – half-stopping the bow after the *sfz*, and then speeding up. It works, sometimes, just about.

On record, the Emersons stand out for brilliance of technique. The Soviet-era Borodin Quartet are all struggle and strife, redolent of Shostakovich. The LaSalle Quartet bring depth and dignity to the thanksgiving movement, the Quartetto Italiano proffer lyricism. The French Quatuor Ébène (2020) are provocatively slow, echoing the hushed unfolding of a Palestrina chorale. Their concluding allegro is supple and kindly, a kiss on Beethoven's brow, or his on ours.

98

Diabolical

Variations in C major on a Waltz by Anton Diabelli for Piano, 'Diabelli Variations', Op. 120 (1823)

BEETHOVEN HAS DECLARED THAT THE PIANO IS 'AND ALWAYS will be, an unsatisfactory instrument'. That statement acts as an incitement to publishers to tempt him back. Nothing sells like piano scores and no more Beethoven is bad for business. Several try, and an unusual character succeeds. Anton Diabelli is a monk who left his Salzburg cloister after composing six masses and made a living in Vienna as a piano and guitar teacher. With an ear trained in the confessional for the lowest human weaknesses, he tries his hand at publishing piano versions of brothel songs and works his way up to signing Franz Schubert to compose the Erl-king ballad, a dramatic departure in Lieder repertoire, requiring one singer to act out four roles. It is logged as Schubert's opus 1 and is toured by Franz Liszt in a piano reduction, later expanded to full orchestra.

Diabelli does not sit back and cash in. He writes to every composer he can think of, fifty-one in all, asking them to write variations on a new waltz of his own. Franz Xaver Mozart, son of, submits two variations. Schubert, Hummel, Moscheles, Czerny, Liszt and Archduke Rudolph all respond. Beethoven takes his time, at first dismissing Diabelli's theme as 'a cobbler's patch'. Diabelli ups his offer. Beethoven tells him the new amount will buy at most five or six variations.

He winds up writing twenty-five, then thirty-three. Once started, he is unable to stop. Every Beethoven variation is a jewelled object, each one echoing Diabelli's original tune without repeating it. Despising variations as he does, he turns them upside down and inside out. Variations 16 and 17 are flipsides of each other. The 22nd is a potted history of popular opera arias. The 23rd mocks Mozart's *Don Giovanni*. Another takes off from

Bach. The fadeout finale is based on Beethoven's 32nd piano sonata. Arnold Schoenberg, who writes the textbook of modern tone relations, says: 'In respect of its harmony [the Diabelli Variations] deserves to be called Beethoven's most adventurous work.' Alfred Brendel considers it 'the greatest of all piano works'. It appeals unfailingly to high minds, not the mass market that Diabelli has envisaged.

Diabelli's sales pitch is hyper-hyped:

> We present here to the world Variations of no ordinary type, but a great and important masterpiece worthy to be ranked with the imperishable creations of the old Classics – such a work as only Beethoven, the greatest living representative of true art – only Beethoven, and no other, can produce. The most original structures and ideas, the boldest musical idioms and harmonies are here exhausted; every pianoforte effect based on a solid technique is employed, and this work is the more interesting from the fact that it is elicited from a theme which no one would otherwise have supposed capable of a working-out of that character in which our exalted Master stands alone among his contemporaries. The splendid Fugues, Nos. 24 and 32, will astonish all friends and connoisseurs of serious style, as will Nos. 2, 6, 16, 17, 23, &c. the brilliant pianists; indeed all these variations, through the novelty of their ideas, care in working-out, and beauty in the most artful of their transitions, will entitle the work to a place beside Sebastian Bach's famous masterpiece in the same form. We are proud to have given occasion for this composition, and have, moreover, taken all possible pains with regard to the printing to combine elegance with the utmost accuracy.

Pianists are terrified, reviewers confused. The London *Harmonicon* concludes that Beethoven has 'from deafness, lost some of that discriminating judgement which he possessed in so striking a degree'. A Beethoven biographer, Wilhelm von Lenz, deprecates the variations as 'an aberration of genius'. The Wagner conductor Hans von Bülow calls the Diabellis 'a Gothic cathedral', to be marvelled at but never scaled by a sane musician.

Artur Schnabel plays it in recital to annoy the rich: 'I am the only person here who is enjoying this, and I get the money,' he chortles; 'they pay and have to suffer.' He finds only two people left at the end (one is the

young Rudolf Serkin). Schnabel's 1937 Abbey Road recording is monumental in structure, magisterial in its teachings and magnificent in his
flip-switch from frolics to solemnity.

Serkin's Diabelli set in 1958 can move stones to tears. Brendel's 1977
recording is fifty minutes of exemplary serenity. The Polish-Hungarian
Piotr Anderszewski walked out of the 1990 Leeds piano competition
because he felt he was not playing the Diabellis as well as he should. His
2018 recording trumps all others. Anderszewski finds symphonic development in the work. His second variation whispers a secret that the third
can barely contain. Daringly quiet, he takes the 30th variation like a mara-
thon competitor entering the Olympic stadium, running on long-depleted
energy. The shock of his final note takes several seconds to absorb. Piotr
Anderszewski deserves a gold medal for his Diabellis.

99

The end?

String Quartet No. 16 in F, Op. 135 (1826)

BEETHOVEN GIVES A TITLE TO THE FINALE OF OPUS 135. HE calls it '*Der schwer gefasste Entschluss*' – 'the very difficult decision'. Under the opening chords, marked slow, he inserts the phrase '*Muss es sein?*' – 'must it be?' As the next theme rises he writes, '*Es muss sein!*' ('It must be!'). Musical authorities interpret these inscriptions as an anticipation of death by the composer and its calm acceptance.

But is it? Beethoven talks of this work elsewhere as the first of a triptych of quartets, a new beginning. The viola opens with a six-note question: shall we? What follows is an early-morning country walk, a skip down a lane, none too steep. The scherzo is all winks and chuckles. The third movement is sober, not sombre, with a huge, all-embracing melody. Only the finale is clouded as the composer injects that juddering existential question.

He composes the quartet in the two months after his nephew's suicide attempt, though you would never guess it. Everything in the quartet is benign, up to the nagging question, and even that is not Beethoven at his gloomiest. The three notes of '*es muss sein*' are firm and settled, not defeated. An alarm jangles in the upper strings near the end. What does it all mean?

The publisher Moritz Schlesinger offers this account:

Regarding the enigmatic phrase Muss es sein? that arises in the last quartet, I think I can explain its significance better than most people, as I possess the original manuscript with the words written in his own hand, and when he sent them he wrote as follows; 'You can translate the Muss es sein as showing that I have been unlucky, not only because it has been extremely difficult to write this when I had something much bigger in my mind, and because I have only written this in accordance with my promise to you, and because I am in dire need of money, which is hard to come by; it has also happened that I was anxious to send the work to you in parts, to facilitate engraving, and in all Mödlingen [he was living there then] I could not find a single copyist, and so have had to copy it out myself, and you can imagine what a business it has been!'

Beethoven, in his familiar chaos, is making a joke of his impracticality. The 'something much bigger in mind' is Karl shooting himself, the rest is daily noise. He does not even bother with his regular complaint of aches and pains. The scribbled inscriptions in this score, like Gustav Mahler's in his ninth and tenth symphonies, are emanations of a transient despair, a low moment in his morning from which he will soon recover. He is not dying in this quartet, not yet.

The Busch Quartet set the gold standard on record in 1933. The Cuarteto Casals (2017) frame '*muss es sein?*' impartially, following it with youthful rebuttal. I find much to cherish in the Brodsky Quartet's whispering caress in the third movement (2017), the faintest repetition of that earlier Kol Nidrei mood.

100

All things being equal

Drei Equale, WoO30 (1812)

ON THE LAST DAY OF NOVEMBER 1826, 'OPPRESSED BY THE SAD prospect of . . . being helpless in the case of sickness in the country', Beethoven leaves his brother Johann's estate and returns to Vienna. After two days of rattling around on wintry roads in an open-topped milk cart, he has a hacking cough, high fever and pain in both sides. His personal doctor refuses to come out. An emergency physician, summoned from the general hospital, fails to attend. A second request to the hospital produces Professor Andreas Wawruch, an ex-priest who, since marrying the hospital director's daughter, has become a distinguished pathologist. Wawruch, an enthusiastic cellist, leaves detailed notes of his care for Beethoven, a patient who is his own age and equally aware of his mortal limitations. Wawruch finds Beethoven jaundiced and choleric, unable to empty his bladder. He manages an interim remedy and visits daily. Beethoven's brother is summoned. Nephew Karl organises his diet. The housekeeper, Sali, struggles to protect his privacy.

Five days before Christmas, Wawruch summons a surgeon to empty the bladder with the aid of a catheter inserted in the penis. It is an uncomfortable procedure, a stab in the dark. Urine floods onto the floor and Beethoven jokes: 'Professor, you remind me of Moses striking the rock with his staff.' Weak, exposed and in fierce pain, he manages to show good humour and an appetite for distraction.

A forty-volume Handel edition arrives from London. 'I can still learn from him!' he cries. The pains reach his chest. A worried Wawruch calls a case conference of leading specialists, among them Dr Malfatti, uncle of the lovely Therese. At Malfatti's suggestion, Beethoven is subjected to a sweat bath, which brings no relief. A singer fresh from a Munich performance of

Fidelio brews him juniper berry tea. The Philharmonic Society in London sends a hundred pounds to help with medical bills.

On the second morning of the year 1827, nephew Karl leaves for his barracks in the Czech town of Iglau. Beethoven calls a lawyer to declare Karl his sole heir.

The apartment door squeaks with comings and goings – the devoted Count Moritz Lichnowsky, the sombre Schuppanzigh and his second violinist Karl Holz, Therese Malfatti's sister Anna (whom Beethoven fails to recognise), the Hummels, the Streichers, the composers Hüttenbrenner, Hiller, Schubert and more from all corners of his conversation books.

After a fourth encounter with the surgeon on 27 February, Beethoven succumbs to despair. 'No words of comfort could brace him,' writes Dr Wawruch, 'and when I promised alleviation of his sufferings with the coming of the vitalising weather of spring, he answered with a smile, 'My day's work is finished. If there were a physician who could help me, "his name shall be called Wonderful!"'. His calm acceptance, with the quote from Handel's *Messiah*, bring the doctor close to tears. There is nothing more he can do.

On 16 March, Wawruch tells him that the time has come to 'do his duty as a citizen and to religion'. Beethoven understands. 'Have the priest called,' he declares. According to Hüttenbrenner, he thanks the priest after receiving final rites and tells him, 'You have brought me comfort.' Hüttenbrenner also claims to have seen Beethoven's sister-in-law Johanna, Karl's mother, in the room, a claim refuted by Karl, who says Johanna was not informed (the legend of her deathbed presence persists on Wikipedia). Schubert's friend, the lithographer Josef Eduard Teltscher, sits in a corner sketching the dying man.

On 20 March, Beethoven tells Hummel, 'I shall soon, no doubt, be going above'. He thanks Elisabeth Hummel for freshening his face with her handkerchief; she, unnoticed, takes a lock of his hair, along with other objects. The lawyers arrive, quibbling over his will. On 23 March, Beethoven cuts their text to five crisp lines. In a hand curving down to the right he inscribes: 'My nephew Karl shall be the sole heir [and] my estate should fall to his natural or testamentary heirs. Vienna, March 23, 1827. Ludwig van Beethoven.' Karl will become a model civil servant, husband and father of five. He dies in 1858 at the age of fifty-three.

Beethoven loses consciousness on 24 March. On 26 March, Schindler and Gerhard von Breuning head to the Währing cemetery to choose a grave. Just after five, as night draws in, the heavens open in an electrical storm. Hastening back to the Schwarzspanierhaus where Beethoven lies, they are greeted with the words 'it's over'. Brother Johann, the composer Hüttenbrenner and the faithful housekeeper Sali are the only ones present. Hüttenbrenner, who snatches a lock of hair, will embellish Beethoven's last moments for a biographer: 'The dying man suddenly raised his head from Hüttenbrenner's arm, stretched out his own right arm majestically – like a general giving orders to an army. This was but for an instant; the arm sunk back; he fell back; Beethoven was dead.'

An autopsy is performed, revealing cirrhosis in the liver, kidney damage, severe pancreatitis, gallstones, distention to the stomach and excess fluid in the skull, none of which is the single, direct cause of death. A plaster death mask is taken and many copies are made and sold; the artist Josef Danhauser makes a sketch of the corpse, which he falsely claims is the last living image. A row breaks out over share certificates that have gone missing. Johann van Beethoven has a panic attack. Breuning breaks the lock of a drawer and produces the shares, together with the Immortal Beloved letter and a portrait of one of the Brunsvik girls.

At three in the afternoon of 29 March, the body of Ludwig van Beethoven begins its final journey. Breuning has ordered troops from the Alser barracks for crowd control. Eight Kapellmeisters carry the coffin. Thirty-six musicians light the way with candles. A carriage bears the coffin to the small Holy Trinity Church, while a brass band plays the funeral march from the opus 26 piano sonata and four trombones intone two of the three Equale.

Nine priests conduct the service. The church is dangerously crowded, with soldiers barring many relatives and friends. Wax drips in dollops from walls and chandeliers. The priests sing an Ignaz von Seyfried setting of *Libera me*.

In the distress surrounding Beethoven's death, no thought has been given to music. On the morning of 26 March, the publisher Tobias Haslinger remembers he has an unedited Equale for four trombones that Beethoven wrote for All Souls' Day while visiting his brother Johann. Haslinger takes the score to the conductor Seyfried, the fastest orchestrator in Vienna. Seyfried, in twelve hours, sets the music of an Equale to words of the *Miserere* (Psalm 51) for a male chorus to sing, alternating verse by verse with trombones. The modern Dutch trombonist Sebastiaan Kemner writes:

> The work has a transcendental weirdness, pointing both at a baroque, Monteverdian austerity and at the unsettling sounds that Beethoven imagines in his eighth symphony. Beethoven is up to his usual deceptions. Upon hearing the opening statement of the first Equale, one is immediately thrown off guard by the lack of confirmation of the main key of D minor. The first three bars sound almost like a plagal cadence in A, as if the composition begins in the middle, without a clear beginning.

The trombone, in church lore, is linked with heavenly trumpets, reminding all present of the fragility of life on earth. The Equale continues to be heard in Vienna cemeteries on 2 November, All Souls' Day, when citizens visit the tombs of their dear departed.

An actor delivers a eulogy by the playwright Franz Grillparzer: 'Thus he was, thus he died, thus he will live to the end of time.' This is the largest non-political funeral Vienna has ever seen. One eyewitness estimates ten thousand people, others claim twenty thousand. A visitor approaches an old lady in the crowd to ask who they are mourning. 'Don't you know?' she exclaims. 'The general of the musicians has died.'

{

Eighteen months later, Schubert is laid beside him. In the absence of descendants, both graves fall into disrepair, so much so that, in October 1863, the Gesellschaft der Musikfreunde has the two composers dug up and reburied. During the exhumation, parts of Beethoven's remains are mislaid, including a fragment of skull. In June 1888, his bones are transferred with Schubert's to Vienna's central cemetery. There they are buried, once and for all time, in a grove of honour for immortal composers, alongside Mozart, whose corpse cannot be found.

Why Beethoven?

A DOZEN YEARS AGO, I WAS PACING UP AND DOWN THE LIBRARY at Random House with my US editor trying to agree a title for a manuscript I had just delivered. The book was transgeneric, neither a formal composer biography nor a study of the music, but both of these and then some. As we switched one bookstack for the next, one of us said, 'Why Mahler?' and all was resolved.

Why Mahler? The unasked question was staring me in the face. Never had a composer, reviled in his lifetime and silenced for half a century after, risen again to dominate symphonic debate. Why Mahler? What was it about this self-styled 'three times homeless' composer that provoked such extremes of rejection and adulation? Somewhere, between the man and the music, there had to be an answer. 'Seeking Gustav Mahler,' I wrote, 'is a route to the few things that are worth fighting for in the short time we spend on this good earth.'

So, why Beethoven? Because the opposite applies. Never in the history of music has there been a composer whose genius was instantly recognised and lastingly acknowledged in its totality. Others received, at best, partial acclaim. Johann Sebastian Bach's oratorios lay untouched for a hundred years. The operas of Handel were hardly seen for two centuries. Mozart, popular as his operas may have been, had his symphonies and concertos used as kindling. Peter Diamand, secretary to Artur Schnabel, told me that, after he revived the 27th piano concerto in 1927, its first public hearing since Mozart's time, he received a call the next morning from Claudio Arrau, asking on behalf of Arturo Toscanini if it was any good. No one thought that all works of a great composer were necessarily great.

Schubert's piano sonatas gathered dust for generations. Schumann's symphonies were discarded, as were several Verdi operas. Beethoven, alone among classical and romantic composers, was embraced first to last, his time to ours. Why is that? Clearly, it is not a matter of charisma since his personality deterred more than it attracted. Nor is it down to marketing, given that he did everything possible to ensure that his concerts would fail, cramming them with far too much music. Beethoven was not so much disorganised as a wilful organiser of musical chaos. Little that he did penetrated on first hearing, yet musicians and public understood that it was somehow exalted, existing on a plane higher than anyone else's.

He had the good luck, it is true, to lack competition. Apart from Rossini's operas and the last words of the aged Haydn, his rivals consisted of Cherubini, Salieri, Paganini, Clementi, Hummel and Hüttenbrenner. If it was easy to stand out in such company, it was nonetheless remarkable to stand so tall that lovers of music from St Petersburg to Philadelphia bowed unquestioningly before his genius. That line in Grillparzer's eulogy – 'thus he will live to the end of time' – resonates with contemporary certainty that Beethoven is eternal, immutable and entire, a rock of ages.

The charisma in Beethoven lies in his music, each work exerting a distinct pull, each promising the unexpected. No composer is so demanding, so consistent and so serious in his demands of himself and his listeners. A string quartet preparing to play Beethoven, amateur or professional, does so in a different frame of mind from playing Haydn, Schubert, Brahms, Bartók or Shostakovich. Beethoven requires more. There may be joy in the music, but beneath it lies an awe of the kind we feel when standing before the cathedral at Chartres, the *Mona Lisa* or the Taj Mahal. To experience Beethoven requires a higher degree of attention.

The way he sets himself apart is demonstrated by the immutability of his music. He is practically unquotable, yielding few spinoffs. Those who drew variations on a Beethoven theme – Robert Schumann, Max Reger, Franz Schmidt – largely failed. 'There's a place for us' in *West Side Story* is drawn from the opening of the Emperor concerto's second movement, a Leonard Bernstein lecture to his Broadway audience that he is cut from superior cloth. John Lennon's song 'Because' samples the Moonlight Sonata backwards. Alicia Keys uses Moonlight as backdrop in 'Harlem's Night'. Billy Joel's 'This Night' references the Pathétique Sonata. The Jacques Loussier Trio play jazz variations on the allegretto of the seventh symphony. But that's about it – pretty slim pickings from an output as substantial and original as the works of Ludwig van Beethoven.

He is empirically inimitable. Nobody has emulated the ninth symphony, the Hammerklavier, the Archduke trio or the late quartets. The last works of Dmitri Shostakovich, sometimes cited in comparison, are a tribute act, a telegram to Beethoven that a Soviet composer feels his pain.

Music without him is unimaginable. Beethoven dragged music from background to foreground. He stopped people talking while music was played and made them listen. They went home not just humming the tunes but thinking the thoughts. He took music beyond entertainment. German music was deemed inferior to Italian when he arrived, never again. In our time, seven million minutes of Beethoven are consumed each month online.

Beethoven stands – with Shakespeare, Leonardo and Michelangelo – as a pillar of Western civilisation. He towers above the rest of his art, unsurpassed. The steely look in his portraits that follows you around the room can feel discomfiting yet few great creators are more empathetic. The philosopher Ludwig Wittgenstein, sharing the same first name, identified strongly with Beethoven, the more so as he struggled to define aspects of his own identity. In a manuscript jotting, dated 1 March 1931, Wittgenstein wrote:

Beethoven is a realist through & through; I mean his music is totally true, I want to say: he sees life totally as it is & then he exalts it. It is totally religion & not at all religious poetry. That's why he can console in real pain while the others fail & make one say to oneself: but this is not how it is. He doesn't lull one into a beautiful dream but redeems the world by viewing it like a hero, as it is.

Beethoven's conduct, often disagreeable, still arouses admiration. Wittgenstein, describing him throwing a tantrum after a day and a half of composing without food, said: 'that's the sort of man to be.' Beethoven is a hero to great thinkers.

No composer offers so exemplary a life lesson in overcoming adversity. Even Mahler, who suffered racial mockery, marital infidelity and agonising maladies, lacked general remedies to war and peace, life and death. Beethoven, in his deaf domain, points a way through flood and fire, bombs and famine, sickness and pestilence. In Covid-19 isolation, I could not have wished for a better companion.

Without the Eroica amid the daily death toll, without the late sonatas when funerals were zoom-only, without the middle sonatas on days when it seemed pointless to start writing while the world was shut down, without lesser-known works of Beethoven on record and online I don't know how I could have got through the pandemic with body intact and spirits high. Why Beethoven? Because, like Mont Blanc, he's there. Immovable, indomitable, impervious but always reachable, he is the composer who never fails to express human needs and distress. In every thinking life, there needs to be some Beethoven.

In lockdown, I saw a different version of the man. For all that I knew that Beethoven was unruly, a bad friend, meddlesome brother, foul in habits and hopeless around the house, I grew to like him more and more, respecting his determination to improve the world with every score he wrote. He was put on earth to do this work. He, the creator, owed it to the Creator of all things. We owe him the gratitude we reserve for the greatest of our species.

That recognition cannot be overestimated. We live now in a twenty-first century when historical values are being rewritten and cultural icons toppled. One culture can no longer be considered more advanced or accomplished than any other. Children are taught in state schools that beating a dustbin lid in time is no different from playing a violin in tune. The US national symphony orchestra can only perform a Beethoven cycle in conjunction with the works of two African-American composers, George Walker and William Grant Still, neither of whom would presume to be considered his equal. Today's leading culture is cancel culture.

There have been calls for Beethoven to be banned on account of his whiteness and maleness, that he should be silenced to make space for suppressed voices. It will not be long before some tenure-seeking academic with a cousin in PR will come up with proof that Beethoven held shares in a slave-trading company, made teenaged singers in his ninth symphony kiss him on the mouth, hurled abuse at minorities and exposed himself in a public place to pass water in broad daylight. Actually, all but one of these claims is certifiably true, as verified in the book you have just read. A ban on Beethoven is, in the present climate, no further away than a woke headline in the *New York Times*.

Ban Beethoven? Consider what we'd lose. The lack of Beethoven would leave a black hole in the heart of music. Without Beethoven, there could be no Wagner, Verdi or Mahler; no Nina Simone, Michael Jackson or John

Williams; no Alana, Lizzo or Justin Bieber. His music launched careers from the violinist Jascha Heifetz to the cello-playing Ed Sheeran. 'See if you can tell where Beethoven ends and Kanye [West] begins!' demands LA's Yeethoven project. Beethoven is the rock; the rest is dust. Cancel him, and the house collapses.

And more than just the house of music. Humans have an urge to reach for the exceptional. Even societies that vaunt equality need idols they look up to, be it the politician Lenin, the scientist Einstein, the astronaut Neil Armstrong, the industrialist Elon Musk, the actor George Clooney or the billionaire basketball player LeBron James. Musk, it so happens, wires his cars with the Moonlight Sonata. Armstrong played the fifth symphony on the Moon. James is known as 'the Beethoven of basketball' for the way he 'composes' a game. Each has been shaped in some fashion by Beethoven's benefaction.

The battle to save Beethoven will rage for years to come and the outcome cannot be predicted. His case has been weakened before trial, the terms of argument have been altered and freedom of expression is constricted. Many would like to punish the likes of Beethoven for outrages that elites, past and present, have inflicted on less privileged peoples. Beethoven is at risk, let there be no doubt of that. All we can do is demonstrate the life-improving capacity of his music in any social situation where music can make a difference.

Which music best makes his case? When asked 'what Beethoven should I listen to?' I reply, 'depends who you are.' Not all art is suited to each person. We relate to music as we do to colour; your favourite is not mine. This one moves me as others don't. Some people don't get Beethoven. I understand, even empathise, with that disconnect. At times in my life I felt alienated, even threatened, by the forcefulness of his sound. He represented a culture to which I only partly belonged and a discipline that I totally rejected. My generation sang 'roll over, Beethoven.' Over time, I learned to approach Beethoven work by work, finding something to relate to in each score. At my present stage in life, I connect most intimately with the violin concerto, that struggle of an abused child against the adult world, of innocence against cynicism, of vulnerability against power. The concerto proffers justice for the weak and attention for the excluded – above all, thankfulness for a wayward genius who walks on unpaved paths and brings dirt into the house. Beethoven's footprint is present in every bar of this awkward and astonishing work.

His violin concerto takes conflict to the max. No prisoners are taken. Up to the closing bars, you cannot tell which way the fight will go. The conductor is a dodgy referee, not to be trusted, never in control. The protagonists snarl or smile. The music sways them back and forth for fifty minutes until resources are exhausted. Moments before the end, the orchestra beats a retreat, conceding to the soloist what must surely be the last cry. The violin plays an ascending scale, gleaming with triumph. Just as it crests the stave, and entirely unforeseen, the orchestra roars back with a crashing wave on the final two notes.

It's a last-ditch score-draw, a concession of equality and a salute to a good thing done well – done, indeed, as well as anything we might ever see or hear so long as there is life on earth. There are no losers, no winners, no victims or avengers, no greed or grudges in this concerto: only an eruptive, collective delight in being alive and human at this climactic moment in music, experiencing together the best of all possible worlds. That is Beethoven's signature, his inexhaustible ode to joy at the unending glories of creation.

Bibliography

ALEXANDER THAYER'S *LIFE OF BEETHOVEN*, FIRST PUBLISHED in German between 1866 and 1879, remains the primary source work, based as it is on testimonies of those who knew the composer and on original documents pertaining to his life. This vital work has been revised by several other hands and was last republished in 2015.

Barry Cooper's *Beethoven Compendium* of 1991 is a remarkably useful guide to some of the byways and minor characters in the composer's life.

Maynard Solomon's much-celebrated psychobiography of 1977, too contentious to go unchallenged, and still demands to be read.

Martin Cooper's 1970 study of Beethoven's last decade stands the test of time in its musical analysis.

Laura Tunbridge's 2020 study of nine selected works is highly readable.

Esteban Buch's 1999 political history of Beethoven's ninth symphony is both groundbreaking and thought-provoking.

Edward Dusinberre's *Beethoven for a Later Age* (2016) takes us intimately between the lines of the string quartets.

Charles Rosen (2002) is indispensable on the piano sonatas.

A 2020 *Life of Beethoven* by Jan Cayers encapsulates recent research.

Some other works cited:

Theodor W. Adorno, *Quasi una fantasia* (1963)
Rukun Advani, *Beethoven Among the Cows* (1994)
Charles Barber, *Corresponding with Carlos* (2011)
Kurt Blaukopf, *Mahler* (1969)
Anthony Burgess, *A Clockwork Orange* (1962)
Jindong Cai and Sheila Melvin, *Beethoven in China* (2015)
Jonathan Carr, *The Wagner Clan* (2007)
E. M. Forster, *Aspects of the Novel* (1927)
Fred Gaisberg, *Music on Record* (1946)

Peter Gay, *Reading Freud* (1990)
Nadine Gordimer, *Beethoven Was One-Sixteenth Black* (2007)
Ronald Harwood, *Taking Sides* (1995)
Oliver Hilmes, *Franz Liszt* (2016)
John L. Holmes, *Conductors on Record* (1982)
Allan Janik, *Wittgenstein's Vienna* (1973)
Stephen Johnson, *How Shostakovich Changed My Mind* (2018)
Bruno Monsaingeon (ed.), *Sviatoslav Richter: Notebooks and Conversations* (2001)
Theodor Reik, *The Haunting Melody* (1953)
Artur Schnabel, *My Life and Music* (1961)
E. Randol Schoenberg (ed.), *The Doctor Faustus Dossier* (2018)
Tom Stoppard, *Leopoldstadt* (2020)
John Tyrrell (ed.), *Intimate Letters: Leoš Janáček to Kamila Stösslová* (1994)
Bruno Walter, *Theme and Variations* (1946)
Elizabeth Wilson, *Mstislav Rostropovich* (2007)
—, *Playing with Fire: The Story of Maria Yudina, Pianist in Stalin's Russia* (2022)

≀

Among biographical websites consulted I would strongly recommend:

Robert Eshbach's Joseph Joachim website: https://josephjoachim.com/2014/10/20/about-this-site-3/
The Emil Gilels Foundation: http://archiv.emilgilelsfoundation.net/en/
The David Oistrakh website: http://oistrakh.ru/en/david_oistrakh/biography/
The Association for Adorno Studies: https://www.adornostudies.org/

Acknowledgements

ANY BOOK THAT ENGAGES WITH A SUBJECT OF THIS MAGNITUDE is founded on a lifetime's conversations, long walks, endless listening and restless research. My deepest debt is to my nearest and dearest, who prefer on the whole, to be nameless. Two I must name, nonetheless. My first thoughts were formed while being walked to infant school by my late sister, Myriam, who seemed to know everything and whom I never thanked enough for her care. Myriam taught me how to receive information, to test it, cross-reference, retrieve it and remember. Everything I have done in life stems in some way from her.

My sister Beatrice died suddenly as I was working against deadline to submit the final draft of this book. In the following days I realised that we had never once, in the course of two long lives, exchanged a cross word. Although both strongly opinionated, we exempted each other from criticism and gave nothing but encouragement. Beatrice's unqualified support was the key factor that first gave me the confidence to become a full-time writer. I only wish I had told her.

On the life and times of Beethoven, I owe a great debt to the forensic skills of Dr Michael Lorenz of the University of Vienna, a scholar who tracks down birth, marriage, death and testamentary documents of musicians with the persistence of Inspector Maigret and the intuition of a Hercule Poirot. He has pointed me down paths I never knew existed and saved me from errors that appear in many other Beethoven texts.

At a very late stage, my Israeli publisher Shmuel Rosner came up with two ideas of staggering originality without which this book would not be the same.

Others along my research trail gave vastly of their time, expertise, friendship and moral sustenance.

In Vienna: Dr Sylvia Kargl, Albin Fries, Dr Renata Stark-Voit, Dr Wolfgang Herles, Peter Poltun, Gerhard Strassgschwandtner, Karin Höfler, Oskar Hinteregger, Claudia Kapsammer, André Comploi, Annina and the late Felix Mikl; the late Dr Kurt and Dr Herta Blaukopf.

In Bonn/Cologne: Ilona Schmiel, Gabriele Schiller; the late Jonathan Carr.

In Berlin: Till Janczukowicz, Douglas Kennedy, Clemens Trautmann, Kirill Gerstein; the late Hellmut Stern.

In New York: Sir Clive Gillinson, Deborah Borda, Adam Crane, Manuela Hoelterhoff, Steve Rubin, Tim Page, Allan Kozinn, Jane Gelfman, Marty Asher, Rafi and Daniella Grunfeld, Lena Kaplan; the late Gilbert E. Kaplan. In Los Angeles, the late Betty Freeman and Ernest Fleischmann.

In Israel: Dr Amir Mandel, Oded Zehavi, Yehoshua Engelmann, Moshe Kahn, Jonathan Kahn, Bruria Ben-Baruch, Dan Yakir, Shmuel Rosner, Yehezkel Beinisch, Gili Haushner; the late Noam Sheriff; and the sadly missed Aviva Astrakhan, whose tact and good taste helped reconcile a much-younger me to the long-reviled Pastoral Symphony.

And elsewhere: Peter Alward, Vladimir Ashkenazy, Lin Bender, Ivan Binstock, the late Harrison Birtwistle, Tom Bower, Declan Cahill, Peter Donohoe, Joseph Dweck, Israel Elia, Tom Feltham, Ann Foden, John Gilhooly, François Girard, the late Berthold Goldschmidt, Gili Hauschner, the late Seppo Heikinheimo, Gavin Henderson, the late Tatiana Hoffman, Stephen Hough, Steven Isserlis, the late Mariss Jansons, Wasfi Kani, Douglas Kennedy, the late Michael Kennedy, Esther Klag, Gidon Kremer, Anthea Kreston, Michael Lamey, Robert Lantos, Yair Lapid, Shlomo Levin, Eli Levin, Robert Low, Juan Lucas, Joanna Mackle, Fiona Maddocks, the late Sir Neville Marriner, Neil MacGregor, Libor Pešek, Costa Pilavachi, Dr Irene Polinskaya, Daniel Poulin, the late Zsuzsi Roboz, the late Albi Rosenthal, Claudia Rubenstein, the late Dr Michael Schachter, Vesa Siren, Leonard Slatkin, Ed Smith, Dr Ayethan Sohrabe, Dickon Stainer, Graham Stewart, Luis Suñén, Jamie Taylor, Ariane Todes, Valerio Tura, Veronica Wadley (Baroness Fleet), Elizabeth Wilson, Roger Wright, Simone Young, Sheng Yun, Nikolaj Znaider.

My agent Bill Hamilton has the subtlest of minds and the discreetest of nudges. My editor at Oneworld, Sam Carter, is an Olympian enthusiast: if he likes what I write, his approval lights up a room. I could not have written this book without their support, or without the careful line editing and gentle challenging of Rida Vaquas at Oneworld. I am grateful to each and every person mentioned above. Anyone I have forgotten will be remembered in the paperback edition.

Index

All musical works referenced are by Beethoven unless otherwise indicated.

and Choral Fantasy 218
and Diabelli variations 311
and piano concerto No. 5: 233
and piano sonatas 171, 219
and Schnabel 74
and Vox recordings 55
Brentano, Antonie 40, 88
Brentano, Bettina 119
Brentano, Maximiliane 275–6
Breslaur, Emil 295
Breuning, Eleonora von 87
Breuning, Gerhard von 317
Breuning, Helene von 87
Breuning, Stephane von 87
Bridgetower, George Augustus Polgreen
159–61, 162–3
British Federation of Recorded Music Societies
18
Britten, Benjamin 146, 201
Broadwood, John 119
Broadwood, Thomas 63
Brodsky Quartet 314
Bronfman, Yefim 149, 194
Brontë, Emily 243
Browne, Countess Anna Margarete von
(Annette) 64, 67
Browne-Camus, Count Johann Georg von 64
Bruch, Max 152, 236, 289, 296
Bruckner, Anton 42, 88, 306
Brüggen, Frans 42, 142, 143
Brunsvik, Countess Josefine von 40, 74, 87,
88–9
Brunsvik, Thérèse von 87–8, 89, 97
Buch, Esteban 272
Buchbinder, Rudolf 75, 233
Budapest Quartet 177, 289, 296
Bull, Anna 161
Bülow, Hans von 311
Burgess, Anthony: *A Clockwork Orange* 301–2
Burns, Robert 256
Busch, Adolf 36, 289, 296
Busch, Fritz 270–1
Busch Quartet 314
Bushakevitz, Ammiel 5
Busoni, Ferruccio 97

Caeyers, Jan 91
Callas, Maria 215–16
Cantatas on the death of Emperor Joseph II
(WoO88) and on the accession of Leopold
II, WoO89: 200
Capuçon, Gautier 255
Capuçon, Renauld 190
Caramia, Giacinto 34
Cardus, Neville 66–7, 75
Carnegie Hall 238–9

Casals, Pablo 24, 44, 48, 199, 246
Castagna, Bruna 205
Caussé, Gérard 32
CDs (compact discs) 19
Celibidache, Sergiu 271
cello sonatas:
Nos. 1 and 2, Op. 5: 44–5
No. 3 in A major, Op. 69: 57
Cetti's Warbler 37–8
Chailly, Riccardo 77, 123, 131, 218, 305
and Symphony No. 4: 144
and Symphony No. 6: 225
and Symphony No. 7: 240
Chamayou, Bertrand 218
Chaplin, Charlie 149
Cherubini, Luigi 208, 320
China 5, 10, 11, 105–6, 107–9, 110–11
and 'Für Elise' 101
Chopin, Frédéric 70, 88, 111, 134, 278
Choral Fantasy, Op. 80: 22, 217–18
Christ on the Mount of Olives, Op. 85: 81, 186–7
Christie, William 142
Chung family 197
Churchill, Winston 7, 149, 161
Ciani, Dino 133, 219
Clarke, Rebecca 35, 290
Classic FM Hall of Fame 236
Clayderman, Richard 105
Clement, Franz 151
Clementi, Muzio 50, 132, 157, 320
Cliburn, Van 20, 137, 140
Clockwork Orange, A (film) 301–2, 304–5
Clooney, George 323
Coletti, Paul 32
Collin, Heinrich von 207
Concentus Musicus Wien 142
Concerto for Pianoforte and Orchestra in D,
Op. 61a 157
Consecration of the House Overture, The, Op.
124: 264–5
Contredanses, WoO14: 123
Cooper, Barry 306
Cooper, Martin 254–5
Copland, Aaron 65
Corea, Chick 101
Corigliano, John 194
Coriolan Overture, Op. 62: 207
Cortot, Alfred 24, 166, 199
Couperin, François 285
Covid-19 pandemic 5–6, 7, 321–2
Cramer, Johann Baptist 135
Cranz, August 139
Creatures of Prometheus, The, Op. 43: 123, 127
cricket 176
Cuarteto Casals 36, 176, 290, 293, 314
Currentzis, Teodor 143